GLOBAL HISTORY OF THE PRESENT
Series editor | Nicholas Guyatt

In the Global History of the Present series, historians address the upheavals in world history since 1989, as we have lurched from the Cold War to the War on Terror. Each book considers the unique story of an individual country or region, refuting grandiose claims of "the end of history," and linking local narratives to international developments.

Lively and accessible, these books are ideal introductions to the contemporary politics and history of a diverse range of countries. By bringing a historical perspective to recent debates and events, from democracy and terrorism to nationalism and globalization, the series challenges assumptions about the past and the present.

Published

Thabit A. J. Abdullah, *Dictatorship, Imperialism and Chaos: Iraq since 1989*

Timothy Cheek, *Living with Reform: China since 1989*

Alexander Dawson, *First World Dreams: Mexico since 1989*

Padraic Kenney, *The Burdens of Freedom: Eastern Europe since 1989*

Stephen Lovell, *Destination in Doubt: Russia since 1989*

Alejandra Bronfman, *On the Move: The Caribbean since 1989*

Nivedita Menon and Aditya Nigam, *Power and Contestation: India since 1989*

Hyung Gu Lynn, *Bipolar Orders: The Two Koreas since 1989*

Bryan McCann, *The Throes of Democracy: Brazil since 1989*

Mark LeVine, *Impossible Peace: Israel/Palestine since 1989*

Forthcoming

James D. Le Sueur, *Between Terror and Democracy: Algeria since 1989*

Kerem Oktem, *Angry Nation: Turkey since 1989*

Nicholas Guyatt is lecturer in American history at the University of York.

About the author

Mark LeVine is Associate Professor of modern Middle Eastern history, culture and Islamic Studies at the University of California, Irvine. He is a contributing editor for *Tikkun* magazine, and has written for the *Los Angeles Times*, *Le Monde* and the *Christian Science Monitor*. He is the author and editor of half a dozen books, including: *Heavy Metal Israel* (2008), *Why They Don't Hate Us* (2005), *Overthrowing Geography* (2005), *Religion, Social Practices and Contested Hegemonies* (2004) and *Twilight of Empire* (2003).

Impossible Peace: Israel/Palestine since 1989

Mark LeVine

Fernwood Publishing
HALIFAX | WINNIPEG

Zed Books
LONDON | NEW YORK

Impossible Peace: Israel/Palestine since 1989 was first published in 2009

Published in Canada by Fernwood Publishing Ltd, 32 Oceanvista Lane, Site 2A, Box 5, Black Point, Nova Scotia BOJ 1BO

<www.fernwoodpublishing.ca>

Published in the rest of the world by Zed Books Ltd, 7 Cynthia Street, London N1 9JF, UK and Room 400, 175 Fifth Avenue, New York, NY 10010, USA

<www.zedbooks.co.uk>

Set in OurTypeArnhem and Futura Bold by Ewan Smith, London
Cover designed by Andrew Corbett
Printed and bound in Malta by Gutenberg Press Ltd

Distributed in the USA exclusively by Palgrave Macmillan, a division of St Martin's Press LLC, 175 Fifth Avenue, New York, NY 10010.

A catalogue record for this book is available from the British Library
US CIP data are available from the Library of Congress

Library and Archives Canada Cataloguing in Publication:
LeVine, Mark, 1966–
    Impossible Peace: Israel/Palestine since 1989 / Mark LeVine.
Includes bibliographical references and index.
ISBN 978-1-55266-257-1
    1. Arab–Israeli conflict–1993- – Peace. 2. Israel–History–1993-
3. Palestinian Arabs–History–20th century. 4. Israel–Politics and govern-
ment–1993- 5. Palestinian Arabs–Politics and government–1993-
I. Title.
DS119.76.L48 2007   956.9405'4   C2007-905191-X

ISBN 978 1 84277 768 8 hb (Zed Books)
ISBN 978 1 84277 769 5 pb (Zed Books)
ISBN 978 1 55266 257 1 pb (Fernwood Publishing)

Contents

Acknowledgments

I would like to thank numerous colleagues who gave helpful comments during research for the book and on various drafts, including: Daniel Schroeter, Salim Tamari, Rema Hammami, and the anonymous referees who commented on the first completed draft. A very special thanks is owed to Nicholas Guyatt and Ellen McKinlay, my editors, for the steadfast support and detailed comments that helped shape this book into its final form and without whom this project would never have come to fruition.

This book is dedicated to Sara Alexander, a wonderful composer, musician, and peace activist, who taught me that it is never too late to forge new connections between people who aren't supposed to be in dialog.

Chronology

1830s–1860s   Zionism first imagined by Jewish writers as a potential solution to the 'Jewish problem' in Europe.

1850s–1880s   Economic and political reforms initiated by the Ottoman state lead to solidification of a new non-Jewish elite in Palestine, who are the nucleus of Palestinian nationalism.

1878   Foundation of Petah Tikva, first Zionist settlement in Palestine.

1894–1906   The Dreyfus Affair, in France, convinces a young Austrian Jewish journalist, Theodor Herzl, that the only solution to Europe's continued anti-Semitism is the creation of a Jewish state. In 1896 he authors the book *The Jewish State*, and forms the World Zionist Organization one year later.

1909   First kibbutz, Degania, and first Jewish town, Tel Aviv, established.

1911   *Falastin*, the most important Arabic-language newspaper in Palestine during the pre-1948 period, is established.

1917   British conquer Palestine.

1921   First widespread Palestinian violence against Zionism erupts on May 1.

1922   Mandate for Palestine awarded by the League of Nations to the British.

1929   Second major eruption of violence against Zionism by Palestinians.

1936–39   'Great Revolt' by Palestinians against both Zionism and British rule.

November 1947   UN approves Partition Plan for Palestine, leading to eruption of civil war between Palestinian Arabs and Jews which lasts until May 1948.

May 15, 1948–July 1949   Establishment of State of Israel and beginning of full-scale war for control of Palestine, which continues for the next year despite three truces, until the present internationally recognized borders are established.

1956   Suez War, also known as 'tripartite' aggression, in which Israel, the UK and France invade Egypt.

1967   Six Day War results in occupation of remainder of Palestine by Israel.

1973   October ('Yom Kippur' or 'Ramadan') War leads to Egyptian–Israeli negotiations.

1979   Camp David Agreement between Israel and Egypt.

1982   Israeli invasion of Lebanon, beginning nineteen-year occupation.

December 1987   Eruption of intifada

1991   First US–Iraqi Gulf War results in Iraqi missiles being fired on Israeli territory.

October 1991   Madrid pace conference marks first direct and public negotiations between Israel, surrounding Arab states, and a delegation of Palestinians.

December 1992–August 1993   Secret negotiations between Israeli and Palestinian delegations in Oslo.

September 13, 1993   Signing of first Oslo Agreement, the 'Declaration of Principles,' at White House.

April 29, 1994   Signing of Paris Agreement on economic relations between Israel and the Palestinian Authority.

May 4, 1994   'Gaza–Jericho Agreement' signed.

September 24, 1995   Signing of 'Taba' Agreement, otherwise known as 'Oslo II,' becomes reference point for future negotiations towards comprehensive agreement.

November 4, 1995   Israeli prime minister Yitzhak Rabin assassinated at peace rally in Tel Aviv.

January 16, 1996   Palestinian elections, likely the freest in the Arab world, elect Yasser Arafat president of the PA along with eighty-eight members of the first Palestinian Legislative Assembly.

May 29, 1996   Benjamin Netanyahu elected prime minister of Israel in first direct elections for that post.

September 1996   Mini-intifada erupts in response to opening of excavations by Israel along Western Wall.

January 15, 1997   'Hebron Agreement' is signed by Netanyahu and Arafat calling for transfer for 80 percent of Hebron to Palestinian rule.

October 23, 1998   Wye River Memorandum signed by Netanyahu and Arafat, calling for further Israeli redeployments from various areas of the West Bank and Gaza in line with terms of Oslo II Agreement.

May 17, 1999   Ehud Barak elected prime minister of Israel.

September 4, 1999   Sharm El-Sheikh memorandum signed by Barak and Arafat, with goal of jumpstarting the negotiations and implementing the terms of Oslo II.

July 2000   Failure of 'Camp David' negotiations leads to collapse of the peace process.

September 2000   Outbreak of al-Aqsa intifada after provocative visit by Ariel Sharon to the Temple Mount.

April–September 2002   Sieges of Jenin and Nablus by Israeli forces.

November 11, 2004   Yasser Arafat dies.

December 2005   Hamas victory in municipal elections reflects unprecedented rise in political power of the movement.

January 25, 2006   Hamas wins majority in second legislative elections in Palestine.

Summer 2006   Israel–Hezbollah war.

Abbreviations and acronyms

AIPAC	American Israel Public Affairs Committee
CNN	Cable News Network
FTA	free trade agreement
GDP	gross domestic product
GNP	gross national product
HDI	human development index
IDF	Israel Defense Forces
IMF	International Monetary Fund
MEFTA	Middle East Free Trade Area
MENA	Middle East and North Africa
NAFTA	North American Free Trade Agreement
NATO	North Atlantic Treaty Organization
NRP	National Religious Party
OCHA	(UN) Office for the Coordination of Humanitarian Affairs
PA	Palestinian Authority
PFLP	Popular Front for the Liberation of Palestine
PLC	Palestine Legislative Council
PLO	Palestine Liberation Organization
PNC	Palestinian National Council
QIZ	qualifying industrial zone
UNESCO	United Nations Educational, Scientific and Cultural Organization
UNRWA	United Nations Relief Works Agency
USAID	United States Agency for International Development
USIP	United States Institute of Peace

Introduction: an impossible peace

As I began writing this book, the Israel Defense Forces had just removed the last Jewish settlers from the Gaza Strip. The headline in *Ha'aretz*, Israel's *New York Times*, proclaimed that 'Gaza Settlement Era Ends with Netzarim Evacuation,' while Prime Minister Sharon and PA Chairman Abbas were scheduled 'to meet soon to discuss a "new page" in relations' between their two peoples. As I finished editing it, Hamas had blown up a small section of the border between the Gaza Strip and the Egyptian town of Rafah. It did this so that besieged Gazans could escape the lockdown imposed upon them by Israel in response to renewed Hamas rocket attacks on the nearby Israeli town of Sderot. Less than two weeks after President George W. Bush made his first (and only) visit to the Holy Land to 'press the case for peace,' Prime Minister Ehud Olmert declared that Israel was 'at war' in Gaza.[1]

In 1994, Gaza figured prominently in the 'first redeployment' of Israeli soldiers (but, crucially, not settlers) in fulfillment of the 'Declaration of Principles on Interim Self-Government Arrangements' – better known as the Oslo accords. The first Oslo agreement had been signed publicly by Israeli foreign minister Shimon Peres and PLO negotiator Mahmoud Abbas on the White House lawn on September 13 of the previous year with President Clinton, Yitzhak Rabin, Yasser Arafat, Warren Christopher and Russian foreign minister Andrei Kozyrev looking on. The agreement declared that during the ensuing five-year 'interim period' Palestinians would achieve an ever-increasing measure of self-rule, while negotiations on 'permanent status issues' would lead within three years to the establishment of what everyone assumed – but could not declare openly at the time – would be a Palestinian state in the vast majority of the territories conquered by Israel in 1967. As we now know, things didn't turn out quite as planned – or at least, according to what most people have assumed the plan was.

Navigating a tortured landscape

Israel and Palestine – or Israel/Palestine, or Palestine/Israel, or Palestine, or Eretz Yisrael, or just Palestine. It's nearly impossible to name the country's tiny landscape, whose total area of roughly 26,300 square kilometers (8,000 square miles) is about the same size as the American state of New Jersey, without also making a political claim at the same time. The country is home to about eleven million inhabitants, 5,300,000 of them Jews living in Israel (half a million of them in the settlements, including those surrounding East Jerusalem), with about 1,400,000 Palestinian citizens of the state, along with 2,500,000 Palestinians in the West Bank and upwards of 1,500,000 people in Gaza. For the purposes of this book, I will use 'Palestine' to refer to the country from the Roman through Mandate periods, 'Israel' to refer to the State of Israel inside its 1967 borders, 'Palestine/Israel' and 'Israel/Palestine' to refer to the territory of Mandate Palestine during the late Ottoman and Mandate periods, and since 1948 respectively,[2] and the 'West Bank' and 'Gaza' to refer to the constituent Palestinian territories since 1948. Whatever name you choose, however, the facts of demography and geography remain: the country as a whole is today roughly evenly split between Israeli Jews and Palestinian Arabs, a situation that will have profound consequences for its future if a viable two-state solution is not reached in the next few years.

When you traverse this beautiful, incredibly diverse yet much-conflicted land, the contradictions that have driven the post-1989 history of Israel/Palestine are impossible to miss. If you drive south or west along the roads on the borders between Israel and the West Bank you'll see on your right modern-looking cities with First World living standards (Israel ranks twenty-third on the Human Development Index – HDI – far above almost every country in the Arab/Muslim world), interspersed with cookie-cutter settlements on either side of the Green Line – the internationally recognized border between Israel and the Occupied Territories. If you head into the interior regions of Israel you will run into development towns (cities established beginning in the 1950s to house Jewish immigrants from Muslim countries) and the occasional 'unrecognized Arab village,' for which the government in the main refuses to provide infrastructure or services. If you move farther away to the north, you'll arrive in Galilee, the only region in Israel that still has a significant Palestinian population.

On your left, to the east and south, the much poorer and spatially compressed Palestinian towns of the West Bank will come into view, where the HDI ranking sinks further below 100 with each passing year. There space is at such a premium that much of the new building is on top of existing structures – which often makes it 'illegal,' according to Israeli occupation laws, and thus subject to demolition. Farther in the distance is the biblical heartland of the West Bank, 'Judea and Samaria,' and then the desert and the Jordan River. Farther south still, once again inside Israel, is the Negev Desert.

Another day you can start your morning in Tel Aviv, recently declared a World Heritage Site by UNESCO because of its unparalleled collection of 1930s- and 1940s-era buildings built in the high modern/international styles of architecture. After breakfast at a café along the Mediterranean, perhaps in the once proud Palestinian city of Jaffa (today merely a hip neighborhood of Tel Aviv, although leaders of the 20,000-strong Palestinian community do their best to remind their community of the town's past glory), you can drive towards Jerusalem, which has been completely encircled by 'red roofs' (red being the usual color of the Mediterranean-style roofs of most Jewish settlements). After a delicious mezza in one of the restaurants along Salah-ad-Din Street in the Palestinian part of town (or if you prefer, the noisy Hummus Pinati on King George Street, a Jewish Israeli institution), you can make your way to Ramallah, the de facto capital of what remains of the Palestinian dream, at the entrance of which you'll pass the ostentatious McMansions of the Palestinian elite.

The drive used to take under half an hour; today it can take hours thanks to the innumerable checkpoints and the 'separation,' 'security' or 'apartheid' – depending on your view – wall built by Israel deep into the territory of the West Bank. Israel's goal in building this heavily contested structure has been twofold: to create a de facto border with the West Bank that is more favorable to Israel than the *de jure* 1967 border, and at the same time to lower the incidence of terrorist attacks inside the country. Most Israelis, joined by Israel's supporters in the United States and Europe, point to the reduction in the number of terrorist attacks to support the wall's construction; far fewer are willing to acknowledge the implications of its being built deep inside the West Bank, a policy that has been declared illegal by the International Court of Justice.[3]

If, as often occurs, the Occupied Territories have been declared a closed military zone for the day, you have to turn around and head back to Israel proper, unless you're a settler, in which case you can head over to one of the wide bypass roads that criss-cross the West Bank, cutting off most of the major Palestinian towns from each other. But regardless of the political order of the day, the landscape offers some of the most biblically striking scenery imaginable. If you do make it to Ramallah for lunch, you can drive south to Hebron, or north to Nablus, Jenin or Tulkarm, the core bases of the resistance against the occupation, and get an even better feeling of the intensity of the anger and violence that it daily generates. For a better view – since Israeli Jews have colonized most of the high places in the West Bank – you can visit one of the dozens of settlements along the way, and perhaps stop for a swim in the community pool or a *café hafukh* (cappuccino) in the local coffee house, where you can have a chat with a barista who may or may not be part of the strange subculture of ultra-religious hippy settlers who continue to erect outposts on the hilltops of the West Bank, even as their government declares its continued willingness to trade land in return for peace.

Writing a history of the present

The wall, the settlements, the hilltop outposts and the violence that surrounds them – all reflect the continued salience of more than a century of conflict between Zionist Jews and Palestinian Arabs in Palestine and Israel. They are literally landscape upon which the architecture of the Oslo peace process was designed, and then constructed. The goal of this book is to provide a comprehensive analysis of that Oslo process, one grounded in the longer-term historical processes that unfolded in the space of Palestine/Israel during the last two centuries while remaining focused primarily on the country's post-1989 history.

This book will argue that the Oslo accords collapsed not merely because of a failure to live up to the agreements signed by the leaders of the two peoples. Instead, they failed because the terms of, ideologies underlying, and history behind the agreements made it impossible to fulfill the stated goal of a comprehensive peace between the two peoples. Put simply, Oslo was never going to bring peace or justice to Palestinians or Israelis. To understand why, we need not only to explore the history of Israel/Palestine but to examine the increasingly globalized world order of the last quarter-century.

To write a proper history of Israel and Palestine since 1989 from this perspective is to write a 'history of the present.' By this I do not mean merely a history that covers the present day; but rather one that is grounded in a comprehensive reading of the country's history during the last century, which allows us to see the 'very conditions of possibility' of contemporary Israeli and Palestinian experience.[4] The problem is that most histories of Israel/Palestine are not just histories of the present, but histories *in* the present; that is, they are inseparable from the power relations and political struggles surrounding the country and its history, including those surrounding the representation of the conflict within academia and the media.

To borrow a phrase from Nietzsche, like other actors in the Israeli–Palestinian conflict historians 'bear visibly the traces of those sufferings which … result [from] an excess of history.'[5] These scars include not only the physical and psychic suffering of Palestinians and Israelis produced by over a century of conflict. Historiography has also been a victim, as it has too often been reduced to an essentialistic, teleological, and (for Israelis and the West more broadly) triumphalist view of the country's history, and of global history more broadly, both in its post-1989 narrative and in the long *durée* of Palestine's modern history.

Such a view characterizes Zionism as an ideology, which from the start centered on the return, not just of Palestine's 'original' inhabitants, but of a people that was imagined to be far more politically, socially and economically 'advanced' than the current population.[6] This supposed 'backwardness' of Palestine's non-Jewish inhabitants gave Jews alone the ability to develop it productively (that is, 'make the desert bloom'), and thus granted Jews alone, and not Palestinian Arabs, 'the right to rule the country' (as Israel's first prime minister,

David Ben-Gurion, argued.)[7] The similarities between such claims and those deployed to support European imperialism and colonialism – including the settler colonial projects in the Americas, southern Africa and Australia – have been well documented by scholars.[8]

The seminal post-war French philosopher Michel Foucault well understood how easily history falls prey to ideological and political agendas (he first diagnosed the dynamics of this process systematically after teaching in Tunisia during the student uprisings of 1967 and 1968).[9] He believed that to overcome such a tendency, history must 'uncover the past to rupture the present into a future that will leave the very function of history behind it.'[10] Specifically, through his archaeological and later genealogical methodologies Foucault attempted to establish a more critical relation between the past and the present, which was the *sine qua non* for imagining scenarios for the future that transcended the uncritical and teleological narratives offered by states and oppositional ideologies alike.

There are several complicating factors in constructing the kind of history of Israel/Palestine that would open up the present realities in the way Foucault's writings did for the prison or health systems. Chief among them is the problematic role of modernity, and to-day globalization, in the Israeli–Palestinian conflict during the last two centuries. From the start, Zionism defined itself as a 'modern' nationalist movement whose goal was to be a 'beacon' of freedom and progress to a somnolent and backward Middle East (the city of Tel Aviv, established in 1909, epitomized this ideology, as the first sentence of its bye-laws defined it as a 'modern' town and the first town logo was a lighthouse).[11] Eighty-five years later, as we'll explore below, Shimon Peres would justify Israel's place in the Middle East through its role as the main conduit for the spread of modernity's post-cold-war incarnation, globalization, through the region.

The problem was, and remains, that modernity is inextricably tied to a matrix of forces that makes peace and coexistence very hard to achieve in Palestine and other formerly colonized parts of the world. The 'coefficients' of this matrix include exclusivist nationalism, as exemplified by Zionism, Palestinian nationalism, and most every other nationalist ideology; capitalism, whose success similarly depends on the production of hierarchies and divisions within and between societies; and colonialism, which in many ways was the 'generative order' that fueled all three, not just in Palestine/Israel, but around the world.[12]

The powerful contemporary role of colonial discourse (as generated by the policies of the Israeli government in the Occupied Territories) and imperialism (as epitomized by the economic and strategic policies of the United States, major European countries, and international institutions such as the World Bank in the Middle East more broadly) has meant that today, as a century ago, the 'West's' promises of freedom, prosperity and modernity remain an impossible dream, one that recedes farther into the distance the closer people think they are getting to it. Understood this way, that glorious early fall afternoon of September 30, 1993, when Yitzhak Rabin reluctantly shook Yasser Arafat's hand, marked the birth of an illusion that would aggravate rather than improve the prospects for a just and lasting peace between Israelis and Palestinians.

The illusion remains hard to spot. An inordinate amount of scholarly, political, and media detritus prevents us from seeing Israel/Palestine clearly, and a reader has to move beyond this to arrive at an accurate recounting of the country's history. During the Oslo years, the 'peace process' was all over the papers and the TV news, making it hard for people to accept a history that doesn't conform to the coverage on CNN or the editorial page of the *New York Times*.

To correct the distortions produced by such narratives, we need to provide a full enough discussion of the century of history leading up to 1989 so that the analysis of the main period under review will be on a sure footing. Only such a foundation will allow us, in Foucault's worlds, to 'follow lines of fragility in the present – [...] to grasp why and how that-which-is might no longer be that-which-is ... [and to] open up the space of freedom understood as a space of concrete freedom, i.e. of possible transformation.'[13]

This transformation can't be grounded merely in the appropriate temporal-historical perspective. As important is finding the right geographical framework. As I have already argued, the history of Palestine/Israel and the two competing national movements that emerged there has from the start been powerfully impacted by the unfolding of various stages of globalization during the late nineteenth, twentieth and now twenty-first centuries. This necessitates a sufficiently 'global,' or, better, transnational, perspective; one that is both grounded in the space of Israel/Palestine yet moves beyond the nation-state as the primary arena of identification and investigation, and which rejects the triumphalist and uncritical narratives associated with globalization. Instead, we need to focus on the movements, flows, circulation and interpenetrations of peoples, commodities, and ideas, both between the two communities and into and out of the space of Israel/Palestine.

Doing so is crucial to overcoming the essentialisms and ethnocentrisms that for so long characterized the writing of Palestine/Israel's history – and for many continue to do so today – as they have historiography in the West more broadly.[14] Widely held notions about the conflict, such as that it is essentially religious and/or 'driven by ancient hatreds,' that it's disconnected from and unrelated to larger political and strategic issues in the region, that a democratic and essentially peace-loving Israel is facing an intransigent and increasingly fanatical opponent – all owe their continued popularity to the kind of historical and geographical myopia described above.

The need for a new Oslo narrative

Once the failure of Oslo became apparent in the fall of 2000 a discourse of blame quickly emerged in the political and media spheres. For their part, some Israeli leaders, joined by most of their diaspora Jewish colleagues, argued continuously that Arafat was not 'doing everything he could to fight terrorism.' Others claimed that the Palestinian Authority (PA), the interim government of the Palestinians, was incredibly corrupt and not living up to its obligations under the various Oslo agreements.

There was enough truth to these accusations to cause many 'liberal' supporters of the peace process to despair over time of the possibility of Palestinians ever making the 'hard choices and concessions' necessary to achieve a lasting peace with Israel. This rhetoric would come to a head with the collapse of the Camp David talks in July 2000, when President Clinton joined Israeli prime minister Ehud Barak to blame Yasser Arafat for torpedoing the peace process.

As most Palestinians will tell you, this accusation flew in the face of Clinton's assurances to the Palestinian leader before the summit that he would not be blamed if the talks failed. For their part, Palestinian leaders argued that Israel was failing to live up to the core idea of the Oslo accords: trading land for peace. In the Oslo years, Israel had massively expanded the settlements and their population.[15] Israel also constructed an extensive road network for the exclusive use of settlers, destroying Palestinian agriculture and encircling Palestinian villages in the process. Meanwhile, successive Israeli governments imposed devastating closures on the Territories. Settlement expansion and closures severely harmed a Palestinian economy that was supposed to assume the prerogatives and powers of sovereignty during the Oslo years. This was the backdrop to Oslo's failure, and the wave of violence that followed it.

The facts at hand reflect the validity of most of these claims: according to Amnesty International, during the 'peace process' years from September 30, 1993, till the outbreak of the al-Aqsa intifada almost seven years later to the day, the number of Israeli settlers 'increased from about 240,000 to about 380,000 – an increase of more than 50 percent. In the same period Israel built an extensive network of [bypass] roads ... seizing and destroying large tracts of Palestinian agricultural and pasture land for this purpose.'[16]

Over 35,000 acres of Palestinian land were confiscated for this purpose and roughly 20,000 new housing units were built (with the largest number being constructed during the last year of the peace process, under the premiership of Ehud Barak), while 740 Palestinian homes were demolished, with an additional five thousand more since the start of the al-Aqsa intifada. Similarly, the closures in the Occupied Territories and the continued Israeli dominance of the Palestinian economy caused billions of dollars in damage through destroyed or spoiled goods, lost tax revenues, and lost income from jobs inside the 1967 borders of Israel, which were now closed to Palestinian workers.

While close to 1,100 Israeli civilians were killed from the outbreak of the al-Aqsa intifada in 2000 through mid-2007, most of them by terrorist attacks (predominantly suicide bombings), close to five thousand Palestinians lost their lives at the hands of Israeli forces, who destroyed well over $1 billion in infrastructure during the same period. It is this context which led most astute observers to conclude that the Oslo process as envisioned by its Palestinian and Israeli architects was 'history,' even as politicians and pundits celebrated the Israeli withdrawal from Gaza.[17]

Oslo through the prism of globalization

The confusing and schizophrenic landscape of Israel/Palestine reflects the contradictions that are at the heart of globalization. The term is one of the most ubiquitous yet misunderstood and misapplied terms in contemporary political and scholarly discourse.

Lying at the crossroads of Europe, Africa and Asia, Palestine has long been a nexus of some of the most important economic and cultural networks connecting the three continents. In the modern era, particularly during the nineteenth century (from Napoleon's invasion in 1799 through World War I), Palestine's experience of globalization reflected the ambivalent nature of the first era of fully fledged global integration, that of the European High Imperialism that began with the so-called 'scramble for Africa' in the 1870s and the outbreak of World War I in 1914. During this period the Ottoman state became increasingly weak in the face not just of Europe's growing military prowess, but as important (as epitomized by the 1838 Anglo-Turkish Commercial Convention), increasing European dominance of the global economy and, concomitantly, economic penetration of and influence throughout the lands of the empire.

This process did not prevent – in fact, in some ways it enabled – a fairly rapid level of economic growth across much of Palestine (apart from the period of the Crimean War and its aftermath). Indeed, the development of the country during this late Ottoman period helped make Zionism on the soil of Palestine a viable proposition, as well as the rise of a local Palestinian commercial and intellectual elite.[18] Once Palestine was conquered by the British in 1917, and Zionist colonization rapidly intensified, it became increasingly difficult for most Palestinian Arabs to determine the shape and scope of their participation in the local, regional and global economies.

Because of these dynamics, it is not surprising that the question of precisely how globalization has impacted Palestine/Israel should be central to understanding the larger history of the country, particularly since 1989, when a combination of the intifada, the end of the cold war, the beginning of the large-scale immigration of Soviet Jews, and the full integration of Israel (and through it, although in a highly distorted and disadvantageous fashion, the Occupied Territories), together laid the groundwork for a transformation of the basic parameters of the Israeli–Palestinian conflict. But to understand globalization's role in the evolution of the conflict, and the peace process, we first need to understand how the term 'globalization' has been used – and as often misused – in discussing the evolution of the world, and Middle Eastern, economies.

The term 'globalization' was coined in the 1980s as a verbal noun to refer to the 'globalization of markets' – that is, the expansion of multinational corporations into new markets in untapped regions of the world, where they could sell their products 'as if the entire world were a single entity.'[19] The definition has broadened significantly in the two decades since to include various political and cultural processes, but the focus on globalization's economic – and corporate – dimension has remained. Indeed, what most mainstream analyses and commentary describe as globalization today in fact represents the dominant ideology of the major industrial powers and international financial institutions (both 'public' institutions such as the World Bank and the IMF, and 'private' institutions such as international banks and multi- and transnational corporations) that govern the international economy.

This ideology – often referred to as the 'Washington Consensus'[20] model, given the role of the US Treasury and the World Bank/IMF in its promotion around the world – promotes global economic integration based on principles of supposedly 'free' trade, low tariffs and taxes, free exchange rates, and the privatization and liberalization of national economies. In the developing world, such policies are usually accomplished by the use of structural adjustment programs (often centered on the extension of large-scale loans) administered by the World Bank and the IMF, whose goal is to 'open' countries to private, Western, and increasingly East Asian and Gulf Arab, corporate and elite economic interests.

There are numerous problems with this understanding of globalization, not least of which is that in practice the growth in the trade, investment, and overall economic integration that define globalization has been surprisingly concentrated among the advanced industrial economies, a relatively small number of 'advanced transitional economies,' and now the relatively small petro-sheikhdoms of the Persian Gulf. As important, neoliberal globalization has on the whole led not to greater global integration, distribution of wealth and resources, or more open migration policies. Instead, it has led to greater concentration of wealth, inequality and conflict, within as well as between countries, in addition to the marginalization of significant sections of the globe from the much-lauded process of integration.[21] Until oil prices spiked again in the mid-2000s, the Middle Eastern countries that avoided a precipitous rise in poverty and inequality were those, unlike Israel and the Occupied Territories, that by and large did not 'globalize' according to the dominant Washington Consensus model.[22]

In the space of Israel/Palestine this dynamic began in the late 1970s and was intensified during the 1980s and 1990s. Indeed, as we'll see in Chapter 4, since the Israeli economy began its process of liberalization in the late 1970s, the majority of Israelis (while certainly better off than Palestinians) have seen their incomes and living standards deteriorate while the economy serves the narrow needs of private Israeli and global capital.

In many ways, the Palestinian Arab experience of globalization mirrors that of the region and much of the developing world: exclusion from the management and direction of globalization within their territory and marginalization from most of the core processes – the growth in the world economy, integration of financial markets, increasing foreign investment, and the enhanced informatization and increasing efficiency and speed of production and communications – that are taken to define globalization.[23]

The reason for this dynamic lies in the roots of globalization in the evolution of European imperialism and colonialism, and through them capitalism. As I explained above, nationalism, capitalism and even modernity itself are inextricably linked to the processes of European imperialism and colonialism.[24] Without the exploitation of peoples and resources made possible by imperialism and colonialism, the development of capitalism, the nation-state, and the modern discourses of Western progress and advancement vis-à-vis the rest of the world would have been unimaginable.

These dynamics have led the eminent geographer David Harvey to argue that contemporary globalization 'represents the "new imperialism,"' in which corporations and governments have found it as easy (if not easier) to 'accumulate by dispossession' (that is, by controlling a country's resources, land and labor) as through expanded but sustainable production.[25] As demonstrated most fully in the writings of Israeli economists Jonathan Nitzan and Shimshon Bichler,[26] in the Middle East and North Africa (MENA) globalization has also been inseparable from the globalization of warfare in the late twentieth century. That is, defense establishments, and in some cases an 'arms–petrodollar complex,' have earned unparalleled profits and achieved increasing power within the national economies of many states, making it impossible to establish truly liberal and free systems of international trade, capital flows and migration.

This dynamic intensified in the wake of September 11, with the transformation from what could be termed 'globalization lite' to a 'heavier' and more militarized globalization. Even before then, boosters of globalization occasionally let the cat out of the bag: as *New York Times* columnist Thomas Friedman admitted, economic globalization 'will never work without a hidden fist. McDonald's cannot flourish without McDonnell Douglas ... the hidden fist that keeps the world safe for Silicon Valley's technologies to flourish is called the US Army, Air Force, Navy and Marine Corps.' It is ultimately violence – and a lot of it, as we see in Iraq, Afghanistan, Palestine, and numerous other places – which is necessary to make the 'free' market system function as intended by those who designed and manage it.

For two generations Israel has acted as one of the enforcers of the system in the Middle East. As we'll see, in the case of Palestine, designing and enforcing the 'new,' Oslo-inspired system would entail a significant amount of violence too. Specifically, a combination of what I term 'sponsored' or 'managed' chaos, in which Israel has deliberately sought to weaken Palestinian political institutions and the bonds of society at large, has been coupled with the 'shock doctrine' of neoliberal structural reforms demanded by the United States and international financial institutions such as the World Bank, the IMF, and European donor countries, to cause significant damage to the Palestinian economy, social and political institutions.

I first noticed the creeping chaos inside the Occupied Territories around year two of the al-Aqsa intifada while traveling around the particularly troubled areas of Nablus and Gaza: the violence was more random, the actors were younger and acting without any supervision, there was less control or strategic purpose to the violence around me. As I watched more and more of Palestine sink into disarray, I came to understand that the slow disintegration of Palestinian political life was being generated and managed by Israel for a specific purpose: to weaken Palestinian society enough to impose a final settlement unilaterally, something Israel was unable to do in the Oslo years when the two sides were negotiating directly. The chaos could also be hidden inside larger trends, as when neoliberal economic policies became part of the Israeli landscape in the late 1970s through mid-1980s. And sometimes it would assume the role of forerunner of trends to come, as when the growing chaos generated by Israel inside the Territories anticipated the strategies and results related to the United States' deployment of a similar policy in Iraq.

Cultural globalization has also played an important role in how the Oslo process and the Israeli–Palestinian conflict have unfolded in the last two decades, as will become clear in Chapter 5, when I discuss the development of groups such as Hamas and Shas. British sociologist John Tomlinson offers a definition of globalization that better accounts for the interplay of economic and cultural dynamics, when he describes it as a 'complex connectivity' among states, societies, corporations and ecosystems.[27] This view is in marked contrast to the mainstream understanding of the role of culture in the Middle East, which is almost always as an impediment to modernization and globalization. Indeed, nearly every major analysis of the country – and the Arab world at large – by a mainstream scholar, or by institutions like the World Bank, the IMF, or UNDP, argues that the 'failure' of Palestinians and other Middle Eastern peoples to successfully globalize is attributable largely if not exclusively to internal factors such as political and economic backwardness and, as important, a host of 'cultural impediments to development.'[28] Even in reports written by mainstream Arab scholars, such as the famed Arab Human Development Report, the impact of European imperialism and colonialism is left almost entirely out of the discussion.[29]

As for political globalization, a decade and more ago many scholars were predicting that as globalization progressed the nation-state 'would fade away.'[30] This notion has been largely discredited by the persistence of state structures and institutions even under globalization. (Witness the recent failure of the European Union's member states to agree on a common constitution.) But many weaker states, particularly in the developing world, have been forced to adopt Washington Consensus policies or else their governing elites have found it in their economic and political interests to do so. Because of this, governments have had less leeway to design and implement policies that don't follow the Washington Consensus, even when they are in the best interests of the majority of their peoples. This has led to what from a social scientific perspective is the relatively new phenomenon of weak states *and* weak societies, a dynamic that makes it exceedingly difficult for citizens to develop, pursue and achieve policies that contradict or challenge the aims and policies of more powerful political and economic actors.[31]

The underlying rationale for the 'fading away' of the state vis-à-vis Oslo was best expressed by Shimon Peres not long after he authored the most important exponent of the neoliberal agenda in Israel/Palestine and the region more broadly: *The New Middle East*.[32] As he argued, 'We live in a world where markets are more important than countries,' and if the peace process continued on track, the day would soon come when Israelis' and Palestinians' 'self-awareness and personal identity will be based on a new ultra-regional reality [that is] outside the national arena.'[33]

Peres was arguing that as the latest phase of globalization arrived in the Middle East, Israel was naturally positioned to play the role of economic and cultural engine for the rest of the region. It should be no surprise that most Arabs, including Palestinians, did not latch onto Peres's vision. Sixty years earlier, US Supreme Court Justice Felix Frankfurter put it more honestly, when he explained that 'Palestine is inexorably part of the modern world. No cordon sanitaire can protect her against the penetration of the forces behind Western ideas and technology.'[34]

Indeed, economic and political elites across the developing world have increasingly used liberalization and privatization programs to strengthen their control over or stake in their countries' economies (Egypt and China are two good examples of this process). Opponents have been ridiculed or even criminalized for rejecting these policies, and local elites have had enormous leeway to implement policies that satisfy the IMF and the US Treasury Department at the expense of the indigenous working and middle classes. New architectures of control have been developed, such as prisons, enterprise zones, and industrial estates, which in Israel/Palestine are deeply connected with the ongoing architecture and spatialization of occupation.

In the last analysis, however, these dynamics have been unable even to create a sustainable, if corrupt, national elite in the Occupied Territories, because Oslo never could – and, I argue, was never intended to – lead to the the creation of a viable Palestinian state. Instead, Palestine has joined other post-9/11 para-states such as those 'governing' Iraq, Afghanistan and other countries along the 'arc of instability' stretching from Central Africa to Central Asia, as embodiments of the 'managed' or 'sponsored' chaos described above, in which higher levels of violence and chaos have become important tools in the management and exploitation of these strategically important countries or regions. If a 'state' is established in the West Bank and Gaza in the future, it will likely remain a ward of the international community, existing somewhere between Haiti and Kosovo, for the foreseeable future.

Structure of this book

In the following chapters we'll explore how the Oslo dream was born, its serpentine trajectory, and its tragic denouement. Chapter 1 explores the role played by the larger developments in the world and regional economies, political and social systems in shaping the conflict between the Zionist movement and the indigenous Palestinian Arab population of Palestine during the late Ottoman, Mandate and post-1948 periods, ending with the 1967 war. I explore why both Zionist and Palestinian nationalisms became increasingly militant over time, even as Palestinian Arabs and Jews continuously interacted and even worked together as 'comrades.' At the same time, I explore the post-1948 history of Israel and the now dispersed Palestinian national movement and its various populations, during the period of the cold war. Here the emphasis is on understanding the transformation in Israel from the historically dominant Labor Party to the Likud in 1977, at the very moment that neoliberalism was transforming the economies of the West (in particular the US and the UK). I also explore how this transformation set the stage both for the intifada and the perception by leaders on both sides of the need to reach a 'historic compromise' as the cold war wound down.

Chapter 2 reviews the main events and processes surrounding the Oslo peace process. Here the focus is on the rebirth of the Israeli Labor Party as a party of urban professionals whose ideological goals, while firmly ethno-nationalist, also sought to situate Israel as a Middle Eastern epicenter of globalization. This process went hand in hand with a gradual retrenchment of the Israeli welfare state that began under the Likud, and also the increasing disengagement or 'divorce' of Israel and its economy from Palestinian workers, as enacted through the policy of economic closure of the Occupied Territories and the replacement of Palestinian workers by migrant labor from the global south (eastern Europe, Africa and southeast Asia in particular).

In each case I weave the discussion of contemporary issues into a more detailed historical narrative going back to the beginning of the conflict, in order to explain why, if peace was never a viable outcome of the Oslo process, an ongoing and politically and economically useful 'peace process' was quite desirable for most of the major actors. These included Palestinian leaders who had been coopted into, and in some cases corrupted by, a process they knew could not deliver on the promise of full independence and justice for their people.

Chapter 3 charts the ever-expanding map of settlement in the Occupied Territories since 1967, and especially since the start of the Oslo process. The settlement system – that is, the settlements, the bypass roads, and the system of laws and military regulations that has created a 'matrix of control' over Palestinian movement and the possibilities of controlling or utilizing their lands – was already well entrenched by 1989. Paradoxically, the system was strengthened during the Oslo years, and is one of the primary reasons for the failure of the peace process.

Chapter 4 focuses on the all-important but often neglected economic dimension of Oslo. Among the most powerful motivations behind the peace process was the desire of Israel's emerging liberal economic elite to make Israel the hub of globalization in the Middle East, and thereby to increase their own political-economic power within Israel. The very terms of neoliberalism would prevent Oslo from bringing either independence or economic development to the majority of Palestinians. As part of this analysis, the relationship between the economic and territorial forms of control will be clarified.

Chapter 5 explores the rise of these three movements in the context of the resurgence of so-called 'fundamentalism' in the global era. I examine how the rise of socio-religious movements in both societies has been fueled by, while helping to solidify, a maximalist view of territory coupled with a minimalist view of the importance of peace and reconciliation with the 'Other.'

The concluding chapter looks at the phenomenon of violence that is at the heart of the conflict and asks why it has been so hard for the two peoples to move beyond violence and towards peace; or at the least to use other than violent means to achieve their ends. How could a 'peace process' produce an Israeli state that is more militarized than ever before? Why did the Peres/Labor vision for a 'New Middle East' wind up producing something very close to the old one? What is the relationship between the outbreak of the al-Aqsa intifada and the post-9/11 militarization of globalization? The answers to these questions force us to move beyond the conventional wisdom. The history that made Oslo an impossible dream demands that we reimagine Israeli and Palestinian identities if the two communities are to build a common future.

1 | From modernity to the Messiah on the Mediterranean

The Israeli–Palestinian conflict has always been a dispute over territory – which community had the stronger historical claim to the land between the Jordan river and the Mediterranean Sea; who between them was better equipped physically, ideologically, politically and financially to bring Palestine into the 'modern world'; who, in Ben-Gurion's words, had the greater right to 'rule the country.' Exploring this period of Oslo's 'prehistory' is crucial to understanding why Oslo was from the start an 'inherently flawed' process;[1] as we proceed to the chapters dealing specifically with the peace process, we will see that the failure of negotiations rested partly upon the inability (or unwillingness) of Israelis and Palestinians to learn from their shared and disputed history.

Jews retained a strong religious attachment to the Land of Israel throughout the more than 1,800 years, beginning with the destruction of the Second Temple by Rome in 70 CE, that the majority of the community lived in the diasporic exile. As a territorially focused nationalist identity, however, Zionism emerged in the mid-nineteenth century. This was a moment when two discourses were reaching maturity in Europe – the nation-state and 'High Imperialism' – which would each profoundly shape the Zionist enterprise.

It was the Russian pogroms and the Dreyfus Affair of the 1880s which sparked an organized political movement to return to the ancient homeland of the Jews. Indeed, until, at the earliest, the middle of the twentieth century's first decade, there was no consensus about whether the proposed 'Jewish National Home' (described with the German word *heimstatt* in most of the Zionist literature of the day) would be an autonomous territory under the sovereignty of the Ottoman Empire or a fully independent state.

Not until the British conquered Palestine in 1917 did the idea of creating an independent state become a feasible goal. Even then, it took the Holocaust to sway the majority of Ashkenazi – that is, European – Jews worldwide, and much of non-Jewish opinion as well, towards actively supporting a Jewish state. Jews from Muslim countries retained a more ambivalent attitude towards Zionism, even as the vast majority of them emigrated to Israel during the 1950s.

The idea of a modern Palestinian identity – that is, one in which Palestinian Arabs understood themselves to be part of a unique people whose national territory comprised the rough borders of Mandate Palestine – emerged soon after the first stirrings of political Zionism, in the last quarter of the nineteenth century. While strongly rooted in local traditions (particularly religious festivals that brought people together from all over the country each year), Palestinian identity was also encouraged by the wider spread of nationalist ideologies across Eurasia, the growing challenge of European imperialism and soon after Zionism, and the weakness of the Ottoman state.

From the start, the Zionist and Palestinian movements argued over who had the ability to develop the country and thus the right to rule it. Adopting the dominant European colonial discourses of development, Zionists argued that Jewish-Zionist and Palestinian Arab societies were essentially separate and autonomous societies at very different stages of historical development.[2] If Mark Twain anticipated the Zionist view of Palestine as 'sit[ting] in sackcloth and ashes [with] withered [...] fields and fettered [...] energies,' Zionists were firm in the conviction that they could 'make the desert bloom' and breathe new life into an old land (thus the title of Herzl's novel about Zionist colonization in Palestine was *Altneuland, Old-New Land*).[3, 4]

Palestinian leaders saw things quite differently. They admitted the advanced nature of European and Zionist technologies and even political ideologies; but they understood, first, that Palestine had also undergone significant development during the late Ottoman period, and second, that many of the reforms or advances in agriculture, town planning or other areas discussed by Zionist leaders or the British were not going to benefit them, but rather would further Zionist efforts to 'conquer' Palestine's territory and economy.[5]

The exclusivist ideology underlying Zionism, and Palestinian nationalism as well, was reflected in the burgeoning economic and territorial conflicts between the two communities. Together, they made a long-term, zero-sum conflict between Zionists and Palestinians inevitable by the time the British entered Palestine in 1917.[6] The transformation from Ottoman to British imperial control nevertheless produced a 'shock' to Palestinian Arab society,[7] one that was exacerbated by the fact that the British government was unbounded by even the minimum obligations of the country's former Ottoman rulers to Palestine's indigenous population. Instead, the British government threw its support behind the Zionist colonization enterprise, as exemplified by the Balfour Declaration of November 1917.

The Balfour Declaration stated that 'His Majesty's Government view with favour the establishment in Palestine of a national home for the Jewish people, and will use their best endeavours to facilitate the achievement of this object, it being clearly understood that nothing shall be done which may prejudice the civil and religious rights of existing non-Jewish communities in Palestine, or the rights and political status enjoyed by Jews in any other country.' The most crucial part of the Declaration was its advancement of political rights for Jews in Palestine, compared with a commitment merely to safeguard – rather than advance – 'civil' and 'religious' (and not political) rights of Palestinian Arabs. This imbalance would characterize British rule through most of the Mandate period, with disastrous consequences for the political and economic development of Palestinian society.[8]

Out of the myriad changes that impacted the development of Palestine in the late Ottoman and Mandate periods, four are most relevant for understanding the country's post-1989 history:

1. *Modernization and the development of the two nationalisms* The nineteenth century was a period of large-scale transformation in the political economy of the Ottoman Empire. A series of reforms, known as the 'Tanzimat' (but which in fact began well before the Tanzimat decree of 1839), codified the capitalization of land, encouraged commercial treaties with European powers, granted equal rights to Jews and Christians, and reformed land and tax laws, and the legal and political system more broadly. All these changes increased

the power of Europeans vis-à-vis the Ottoman state, and in Palestine in particular.

At the same time, however, the greater openness of the Palestinian economy to the world economy facilitated the emergence of a modern merchant and capitalist class (with a focus on oranges, soap and olive oil) that spearheaded a significant development of the Palestinian economy in the last century of Ottoman rule, as trade increased both with Europe and within the empire. The liberalization of land tenure laws and the growing capitalization of land did not impact all classes equally, however; they also encouraged the dispossession of tens of thousands of Palestinians when Zionists started engaging in widespread land purchases. The realignment – but by no means transformation – of Palestinian class structure weakened the poorer segments of the Palestinian peasantry in favor of the 'notable' or upper classes (a dynamic that would be repeated a century later under the Palestinian Authority).[9]

At the same time, the emergence of a Turkish-centered identity among the Ottoman elite lessened the willingness of the Ottoman state to protect Palestinians just when their position in the country began to be threatened. As the Ottoman elite moved from a cosmopolitan to a more exclusive nationalist – Turkish – identity, Palestinians responded by shifting their allegiance away from the empire and towards a similarly more local, nationalist focus.[10]

At first, pan-Arab ideologies were popular among some segments of the elite, but a Palestine-focused nationalism had become the dominant form of nationalist expression before World War I. One dynamic that influenced this development was the rise of a Palestinian public sphere, as half a dozen or more newspapers were operating by the end of the Ottoman era. They were joined by an increasing number of local civic organizations, which supported an emerging national identity among the burgeoning Palestinian intellectual class.[11]

At the end of World War I, the Wilsonian discourse of self-determination that seized the imagination of the world public and influenced the birth of the League of Nations demanded that the territories conquered by the British and French during the war be treated as 'mandates' rather than colonies. Britain and France were not granted sovereign power over Palestine, Lebanon, Syria and Iraq; instead, under Article 22 of the League of Nations Covenant, they were authorized, or mandated, to govern these territories only until such time as they would be deemed capable of self-government.[12]

In practice, however, Palestine and the other British (and French) mandates were treated as colonies acquired as the spoils of war. As the British explained to the League of Nations, 'A mandate was a self-imposed limitation by the conquerors on the sovereignty which they exercised over the conquered territory.'[13] And the British government was not about to impose any limitation on its position in Palestine that would interfere with its larger strategic interests. Because of this, the country faced most of the same unfavorable trade and revenue conditions as existed in Egypt or India, most important among them the unwillingness of the British government to spend funds on the development of the country and the productive potential of its people.[14]

In this situation, while the League of Nations recognized Palestine's 'provisional independence' in its Charter, it was Jewish rather than Arab Palestine which became the focus of British attention. Indeed, the huge influx of Jewish capital became a substitute for government revenue, giving Zionist leaders disproportionate influence in how and where the money was allocated.[15] So great at times was this influx of capital, and so skewed was the expenditure of funds for development towards the self-evidently 'modern' Jewish sector, that Palestinians had the impression that 'the Jews can buy everything,' including their patrimony.[16]

Despite the disproportionate economic power of the Zionist movement, and the 'economic warfare' between the two communities, there was significant growth in the Palestinian Arab agricultural sector, and even more the industrial sectors, during the Mandate.[17] But many of the most profitable Palestinian enterprises, such as the Jaffan citrus trade, were controlled by Jews by the 1930s. This imbalance was aggravated by the 'Great Revolt' of 1936–39, as the combination of violent resistance and strikes by Palestinians was used by the Zionist leadership to strengthen their cooperation with the British government, and their position in the economy.

In truth, Zionism had become part of Palestine's economic

landscape much earlier, at the beginning of the 1880s. In 1891, the writer and moralist Ahad Ha-Am wrote a stinging critique of the then still embryonic Zionist settlement project in Palestine. Entitled 'The truth from Eretz Yisrael' (Eretz Yisrael is the Hebrew name for the Land of Israel), it argued that '[The Jewish settlers] treat the Arabs with hostility and cruelty, trespass unjustly, beat them shamelessly for no sufficient reason, and even take pride in doing so.'[18]

The common chauvinism of colonists towards the colonized was not the only reason why Zionism had by the first decade of the twentieth century become, in the words of Israeli sociologist Gershon Shafir, a 'militant nationalist movement.'[19] Equally important was the economic competition faced by Jewish immigrants from cheaper and often better-skilled Palestinian Arab workers. In response socialist Zionist leaders developed the strategy of the 'Conquest of Labor' to facilitate the creation of jobs for Jewish immigrants by creating Jewish-only employment. When this proved ineffective, the 'Conquest of Land' became the focus, involving the purchase of land for exclusive Jewish settlement and, through it, employment for Jewish immigrants.[20] While this was unique in its particulars, replacing rather than merely exploiting the indigenous population was a strategy common to most settler colonial movements, including the United States, South Africa, and Australia.

2. *Increased immigration and land purchases* During the late Ottoman period, from the 1880s till the outbreak of World War I, the non-Jewish Arab population increased from around 500,000 to something over 700,000, while the Jewish population rose from some 25,000 to upwards of 85,000. During the Mandate period the number of Jews in Palestine increased more than ninefold, from approximately 57,000 to 555,000 between 1917 and 1945. The country's Palestinian Arab population did not quite double during this period, increasing from 660,000 to 1.2 million people. Proportionately, Jews increased their percentage of the population during this period from about 9 to 31 percent.[21]

Jewish land purchases did not increase nearly as significantly as the Jewish percentage of the population; even at the end of the Mandate, Jews owned only about 7 percent of the land of Mandate Palestine. Nevertheless, it is impossible to overestimate the importance of the land purchases made during the Mandate period. Indeed, the increasing intensity of the policies of 'conquering' labor and land were proportional to the increase in the country's Jewish population; the latter encompassed enough territory to enable Jews to create a socially, politically and ultimately militarily viable presence along the coast, Galilee and Negev region of the country. The number of Jewish settlements grew from about 29 in 1920 to over 270 at the end of the Mandate.

By the 1930s, a decade after the 'land question' had become a central dynamic within the Zionist–Palestinian Arab conflict, Palestinian peasants (rather than just the large local or absentee landowners) were being forced by deteriorating economic conditions to sell land to Jews. Even as the British imposed increasing restrictions on land sales to Jews, more land was purchased between the 'Great Revolt' – the period during 1936–39 when various segments of Palestinian society offered coordinated and often violent resistance against the rapidly growing Zionist presence in the country – and the end of the Mandate than during the sixteen years previous to it; more than half of that was purchased during the last two years of British rule. Land was also settled without government permission by the construction of small and easily defensible 'tower and stockade' (*Homa Umigdal*) settlements by Jews. The same model was adopted by settlers after 1967, and even during and after the Oslo years, when Israeli governments threatened to withdraw from more sparsely settled regions of the West Bank.

3. *Doomed politics* The modern history of Palestine has been defined by episodes of resistance by the indigenous population against foreign interference of all sorts. This 'spirit of resistance' was nurtured by centuries of on-and-off-again warfare between Bedouins and towns, coupled with periodic invasions by foreign forces (Crusaders, Egyptians, Syrians or Europeans), and communal revolts that gripped the country, beginning with the 1834 revolt against Ibrahim Pasha, and continuing to the present day with the al-Aqsa intifada.[22]

Bedouins, peasants, or city-dwellers, the non-Jewish Arab populations of Palestine did not react passively to changes imposed from above, whether by the Ottomans, Egyptians, Zionists or the British. As in many countries, however, the incorporation of Palestinian elites (however unevenly) into the economic and political structures of the late Ottoman Empire and then the British Mandate marginalized the poorer segments of Palestinian society. They responded with the standard forms of subaltern resistance – slacking off work, petty thefts, and violence when necessary (against the growing European presence on their lands, later against Zionists, the British and even their own elites).[23]

What made this dynamic particularly damaging in Palestine was that in the context of the growing competition with a better-organized and financed national movement that had the institutional support of the occupying power, the 'notable' class failed to put the broader nationalist interest ahead of their narrower economic interests. A major problem faced by Palestinian society was that a factional political culture based (in principle if not reality) on kinship and patronage relations, which had gradually evolved during the late Ottoman period, suddenly had to function horizontally, across class lines, in order to establish a cohesive level of political solidarity. 'Notables' would have had to mobilize the working class with whom they had no direct or indirect relations of patronage or reciprocity in order to confront the threat of Zionism; but the entry of the peasants and working class into Palestinian Arab politics generally was, on the face of it, as much a threat to the power of Palestinian elites as was the growing power of Zionism.

To cite just one example of how this dynamic played out on the ground, when pressed by Jewish labor negotiators to better wages and conditions for Palestinian Arab workers, the vice-mayor of Jaffa responded: 'Why do you bother us and meddle every day in the interests of the workers? ... We don't have democracy, we scorn democracy ... We only understand one thing: the worker that puts forth demands to us is a worker that wants to be lord over us and this we will not suffer.'[24] It wasn't just that advancing the interests of the Palestinian working class challenged their hegemony; also important was the price of true nationalist activities, as the British would jail or even exile leaders who endorsed the kind of activism that might counter the growing threat from Zionist colonization.[25]

More serious than the internal problems was the lack of any reference, and because of this, commitment to supporting a Palestinian Arab as well as a Jewish national home in Palestine. This meant that Palestinians were denied many of the attributes of statehood afforded to the Zionist movement. Moreover, the government saw independent and democratic institutions as a threat to British rule and stability, since such bodies would necessarily reflect the almost universal desire to curtail if not prohibit outright the Zionist enterprise in Palestine. When institutions such as the Arab Executive were established, they had far less power than their Jewish counterparts, were not representative of the larger population, and were either coopted or weakened by a combination of British repression and Zionist influence.

This dynamic helps us understand why such a large portion of the Palestinian elite fled the country in late 1947, and why national institutions failed to function to properly organize and maintain the Palestinian population in place during the war. It would have a profound impact in the war of 1948 and after,[26] and would be repeated with the Oslo-era Palestinian leadership, which was never given adequate authority over Palestinian territory and economic life to function as a proper government.

4. *Violence and war* Palestine's Mandate-era history was not solely determined by intercommunal conflict. Palestinian Arab and Jewish workers cooperated periodically on labor issues, and elites did business together, right up till the end of the Mandate.[27] Yet violence was crucial to the construction of nationalist geographies in Palestine. Small intercommunal clashes during the late Ottoman period gave impetus to the desire of many Jews to establish separate quarters in mixed towns such as Jaffa or Haifa and Jerusalem. The 'revolt' of May Day 1921, the 1929 violence, and the 'revolution' of 1936–39 were all results of increasing spatial and economic proximity and competition between the two communities. Most of the time, the Zionist movement was the main beneficiary of the fighting, which by and large failed to advance core Palestinian political or economic interests, while each of the various outbreaks of violence during the Mandate period led to major 'national victories' for the Zionist movement.

While ostensibly Jews were vastly outnumbered by Palestinians and the surrounding Arab states at the start of hostilities in 1948, in terms of men on the ground in Palestine, the Yishuv (Palestine's Jewish community) was able to field upwards of 40,000 men. The combined number of Arab forces was about 25,000 troops from Egypt, Transjordan, Iraq, Syria, Lebanon and Saudi Arabia, while Palestinians could field at most about five thousand men (the majority of Palestinian fighters had been sidelined by a combination of harsh British repression and internal Palestinian struggles). The two periods of truce also helped shape the final outcome of the war, as the Palestinian leadership, in disarray, was unable to use them to improve the situation of its people in the least, while the new Israeli leadership took advantage of the lulls in fighting to acquire more arms and, when possible, territory.

This reality negated the possibility of successful Palestinian resistance to the Zionist, and after May 15, 1948, Israeli conquest of 78 percent of Palestine (in the 1947 Partition Plan, Jews were allocated 56 percent of Palestine, versus 43 percent for the Palestinian state, while the area of Jerusalem and Bethlehem was to become an international zone). The surrounding Arab states, as well as much of the Palestinian notable class, were likely aware of this reality, which is one reason the former did not send sufficient forces to succeed in their stated objective of repelling the 'Zionist aggression,' 'exterminating' the nascent Jewish state, and clearing the way for a unitary 'democratic' state in all of Palestine, while the latter fled in the hope that their Arab brethren, or the international community, would prevent the very outcome that did occur. Indeed, while Arab leaders declared their intention to 'fight for every inch of their country,'[28] their primary interest was preventing the emergence of a Palestinian state led by Grand Mufti Jamal Husseini and a large influx of Palestinian refugees.

The advantage in the number and quality of men under arms and the limited strategic (as opposed to ideological) goals of the Arab countries helped ensure that the Zionist movement and nascent Israeli state would emerge victorious from the bloody conflict in 1948. But these were not the only reasons for the Zionist/Israeli victory. Also important was the strategic use of targeted attacks on civilians to win control of key territory without large Jewish casualties. This strategy was epitomized by the Dir Yassin massacre and more broadly by 'Plan Dalet' (Plan D), whose goal was to create 'defensible' borders by, when possible, emptying and often destroying Palestinian towns and villages located near Jewish settlements or in strategically important locations. Arab/Palestinian forces also engaged in massacres of Jewish civilians, including during their capture of the Gush Etzion bloc of settlements in late 1947 and 1948.

Scholars continue to debate whether or not most Palestinians 'fled' or were forcibly evicted from their homes during the 1948 war. The preponderance of evidence, including the early and continued support by Zionist leaders for the idea of transferring a large share of the indigenous Palestinian Arab population outside the country, supports the latter view. But regardless of the motivations of Zionist leaders or the deliberateness of the actions that led to their flight, Palestinians had and continue to have a right to return to their homes once the fighting was over. This right was denied to them by the new Israeli state, even though the terms of the agreement that admitted Israel to the United Nations included an acceptance of General Assembly Resolution 194, Article 11 of which states that 'refugees wishing to return to their homes and live at peace with their neighbours should be permitted to do so at the earliest practicable date' (Ben-Gurion summed up the Zionist/Israeli view after watching the Palestinian population of Jaffa flee the city en masse, when he declared simply that 'war was war').[29]

Finally, if Palestinians had the option of leaving Palestine during the fighting, the Jewish population had no option of waiting out the war in Alexandria, Beirut or Amman. In the wake of the Holocaust and with nowhere to go, the war was, in the words of Benny Morris, 'a fight for survival or death' – a perception that has persisted in Israel's national psychology to this day. Ultimately, however, a combination of superior Zionist/Israeli military capability, the hostility of nearly every Arab government or great power to Palestinian nationalism, the refusal of Arab leaders to send adequate troops and supplies to Palestine, and even the collusion of some of them with Great Britain and Israel to frustrate its objectives, determined the course and outcome of the 1948 war.

Statehood and exile: Israel/Palestine 1948–67

It is impossible to exaggerate the consequences of the 1948 war in Palestine. For the Palestinian people, utter disaster: the loss of well over 70 percent of the territory of Mandate Palestine (although, it is rarely pointed out, this was only 22 percent more than they were to lose under the terms of the Partition Plan), well over five hundred villages destroyed, upwards of three-quarters of a million refugees scattered across at least six countries (in fact, the world), and the decimation of their political life. For the newly established State of Israel, a miracle: out of the ashes of the Holocaust, against the invading armies of five countries and a Palestinian population that outnumbered them roughly two to one, political sovereignty was achieved over a territory that was over a dozen times larger than that controlled by Jews before the war, and well over 20 percent greater than what was allotted to the Jewish state in the 1947 UN Partition Resolution.

As important for the new State of Israel, the Palestinian population of the areas encompassed by the state was reduced from its pre-war level of between 750,000 and 874,000 (depending on the source) to only about 160,000, some 14 percent of Israel's population of 1.73 million after the war. The percentage would be reduced further in the next decade as approximately 600,000 Middle Eastern and North African Jews immigrated to Israel, tipping the demographic balance towards the country's Jewish population.[30]

Despite the radically transformed realities on the ground, the post-1948 relationship between Israelis and Palestinians was rooted in the dynamics established over the previous five decades. Five processes played particularly important roles in shaping the environment in which Oslo emerged.

1. *The refugee problem* At the end of 1948 roughly 350,000 Palestinian refugees were in the West Bank, 200,000 in Gaza, 100,000 in Lebanon and more than 60,000 in Syria. As I indicated above, at the heart of the debate over the refugee 'problem' is whether the Zionist and then Israeli leadership had a long-term plan to expel the majority of the country's Palestinian population, or whether their flight was, in the words of Benny Morris, 'an incidental if

favourably regarded side-effect of [Zionist/Israeli military] operations, not their aim.'[31]

Whether planned or just (from the Zionist/Israeli perspective) an extraordinarily fortuitous development, once the majority of the Palestinians were outside the borders of the new Jewish state 'they [were] not coming back' (as Israeli foreign minister Moshe Sharrett put it).[32] This attitude was hardly unprecedented; only the year before, the war that accompanied the establishment of India and Pakistan produced tens of millions of refugees in one of the largest permanent population transfers in world history. And as with the conflict on the subcontinent, Israel immediately articulated a policy of rejecting the repatriation of any significant number of refugees. With this decision, Palestinian refugees became one of the largest and longest-standing displaced populations in the world.

The refugee problem was a core reason why no peace treaty was possible between Israel and the surrounding states in the aftermath of the 1948 war, despite the willingness of some Arab and Israeli leaders to negotiate a compromise. As Benny Morris explains it: 'Israeli and Western documentation indicates that windows of opportunity for peacemaking between Israel and several of its neighbors certainly existed during late 1948–July 1962. However, the opportunities were not exploited ... because Israel was unwilling to make concessions for peace, and Arab leaders felt too weak and threatened by their own people and their neighbors to embark on, or even contemplate, peace unless it included substantial Israeli concessions.'[33]

2. *The ethno-class society* Approximately 900,000 Jews lived in Arab/Muslim countries in 1947; by the 1960s upwards of 99 percent of them were compelled to leave their homelands, with two-thirds coming to Israel. The (often unwilling) departure of these long-standing communities was the result of secret negotiations between the Israeli government and their home countries, although increased discrimination against Jews in the wake of the creation of the state of Israel also contributed to their leaving.[34]

The large-scale immigration of Jews from elsewhere in the Middle East and North Africa (hereafter MENA Jews) ensured a sizable Jewish majority in the new state until the next wave of large-scale immigration, from the (former) Soviet Union, in the late 1980s. Of equal significance from the standpoint of the conflict was the manner in which these communities were incorporated into Israeli society; from the start MENA Jews faced political, economic and cultural discrimination and marginalization at the hands of the European/Ashkenazi leaders of the new state.[35]

The policies of the Israeli government towards the new state's Palestinian citizens were carried over, if in a less intense form, in its treatment of the hundreds of thousands of Jewish immigrants who began arriving from Arab and other Muslim countries soon after the establishment of the state. These immigrants were sent to 'development towns' established in frontier regions of the new state, with the goals of isolating them from the European majority while asserting a strong Jewish presence in formerly Palestinian Arab regions of the country (to this day, senior government ministers, including former prime minister Ariel Sharon, have used the word 'judaization' – *yehud* in Hebrew – to describe such settlement policies).[36] A similar strategy would be used to settle 'frontier' regions of the Occupied Territories after 1967.

The Israeli state's patronizing attitude towards their Middle Eastern or North African heritage ensured that most MENA Jews would distance themselves from Palestinians, with whom many shared a common culture, language, and, at least in theory, a common class perspective vis-à-vis the country's Ashkenazi elite. Instead, as I discuss in more detail in Chapter 5, these dynamics led to the creation of an 'ethno-class' system, and through it an 'ethnocratic' state, which was structurally dominated (politically, economically, and culturally/civically) by one ethno-religious group, Ashkenazim, despite the official policy of political equality and democracy.[37]

As the MENA Jewish community became established in Israel, a three-tiered socio-economic system emerged, in which European/Ashkenazi Jews remained the country's political, economic and cultural elite, while MENA Jews, and farther down still Palestinian citizens of Israel, filled the rungs below. Indeed, Palestinian citizens of the Jewish state, who until 1966 lived under military government, naturally faced a qualitatively greater level of discrimination and segregation than MENA Jews. The primary goal of such policies was to prevent the emergence of the kind of cohesive nationalist identity that would constitute a serious threat to the stability and security of Israel as a self-defined Jewish yet democratic state. Once the government felt secure in its spatial and political control over the remaining internal Palestinian population, Palestinian citizens were afforded a significant enough level of social development, economic growth and political liberalization to ensure their continued pacification without systematic violence.

After 1967 another group would appear at the bottom of the social scale, as Palestinians from the West Bank and Gaza entered the labor force in Israel. In the 1980s Ethiopia's small Jewish community would be moved, en masse, to Israel. These arrivals were followed by Jewish immigrants from the former Soviet Union, and increasingly by non-Jewish guest workers from as far afield as Thailand and the Philippines. All these new populations again remade the political and economic landscape of Israel/Palestine, with two dynamics most important. First, they added to and thereby ensured the demographic superiority of Jews in the country for the coming decades. Second, they enabled the replacement of Palestinians in the Israeli workforce with a new, less politically dangerous and (especially for 'foreign' workers) cheaper and more exploitable pool of employees, which was mandated by Oslo's politics of 'separation' or 'divorce,' and its economic discourse of privatization, liberalization, and neoliberalism more broadly. As we'll see in Chapter 4, these processes produced disastrous consequences for the West Bank and Gaza economy, and thus the chances for peace, during the Oslo period.

3. *Economic disparity: the Israeli economy* At the conclusion of the 1948 war Israel was an internationally recognized state with a viable, if struggling economy, while Arab Palestine ceased to exist. In its stead were two now separate economic and political units, the West Bank and Gaza Strip, which until their reintegration in 1967 were governed by two entirely separate regimes.[38]

The economic dimensions of Israeli state-building also saw a sometimes wide gulf between political rhetoric and reality. While officially Israel was governed by the socialist ideology of the Zionist

Labor movement, from its establishment leading Israeli capital-ists would establish a powerful if largely unappreciated (at least by commentators) position in the economy, through which they would lead the drive towards privatization once Israel entered a period of neoliberal adjustment in the 1980s (sponsored by the same econo-mists who designed the British, American and Chilean neoliberal transformations).

Until 1965, Israel sustained a very high rate of economic growth. Buttressed by strong protectionist measures, German war repara-tions, subsidies, and import-substitution strategies, real GNP grew by an average annual rate of over 11 percent, and per capita GNP by greater than 6 percent.[39] The 1967 war had a timely positive impact on the Israeli economy. First, the newly conquered territories became a captive market for Israeli products, and thus a huge boon to its econ-omy. Second, tens and eventually hundreds of thousands of Pales-tinians came to work inside Israel. Third, the growing role of Israel as a major arms purchaser and supplier, and the rapidly developing relationship with the United States, led to soaring defense spending, much of it paid for through US military and other economic aid. The massive levels of US aid allowed successive governments to subsidize investment in industrial expansion for military purposes, which later helped give birth to the country's high-tech economy.

By the mid-1970s, however, the Israeli economy began experienc-ing a sharp downturn as it entered a period of structural adjustment that laid the groundwork for the neoliberal period that helped drive Oslo.[40] A considerable degree of trade liberalization began during this period, which continued during the ensuing two decades, par-ticularly with respect to monetary policy, domestic capital markets, and the government's role in the economy. As occurred elsewhere, these policies led to a rapid increase in inequality, as Israel went from being among the developed countries with the least income inequality to one of those with the most. As I detail in Chapter 4, it was in the midst of this dynamic that the neoliberal dream of a 'New Middle East' was born, and died.

In contrast, the Palestinian economy faced what economic histor-ians Roger Owen and Sevket Pamuk describe as a 'host of crippling conditions' from which it has never recovered.[41] The economy of the

West Bank stagnated, as Palestinians with capital chose to invest either in Jordan proper or outside the region.[42] The Gaza Strip fared even worse under Egyptian rule; there was little incentive for Egypt to invest scarce capital there – not just because it was never considered Egyptian territory but also because, compared with the West Bank, the population was poorer, more heavily concentrated with refugees, and dependent on foreign aid and relief (distributed primarily by the United Nations Relief Works Agency, UNRWA).

Once the West Bank and Gaza were reunited under Israeli rule, Israel restricted Palestinian access to land, water and industrial development, thereby precluding the development of the Occupied Territories.[43] Yet the Palestinian economy did grow significantly during this period,[44] encouraged by a combination of wages from workers in Israel – who by the 1990s constituted well over 100,000 Palestinians (40 percent of the labor force), remittances from workers abroad (particularly the Gulf states), and the growth in small firms that worked as subcontractors for Israelis.

Countering these positive trends was a decrease in the area under cultivation that resulted from a combination of expropriations and other restrictions on Palestinian access to agricultural lands, and the increasing number of Palestinians working outside of agriculture, and often outside of the Occupied Territories (most of them in Israel). This weakening of Palestinian agriculture and land tenure more broadly overshadowed the gains that had accrued with the incorporation of the Occupied Territories into the much larger and more developed Israeli economy. Indeed, the structural asymmetries between the two sides distorted the development of the economy, and made it much harder for Palestinians to resist an economic system that was geared to maximum exploitation of their markets while largely restricting their ability to penetrate the Israeli market.

4. *Growing militarization* Israel's borders, established with the 1949 Armistice Agreements, were 'more or less internationally accepted, and acquiesced in by the Arab world.' But along the demilitarized zones separating Egypt and Syria there were frequent clashes, while Palestinian guerrillas regularly infiltrated from Jordan.[45]

None of the sides was prepared to move towards compromise.

Specifically, Palestinians were unwilling to recognize Israel if it meant recognizing their present position as a nation that had lost most of its historical homeland and which had seen much of its population permanently exiled. For their part, 'Israel's leaders faced little pressure, and therefore reason, to contemplate a concession of territory or water to achieve peace,' and adopted a policy of disproportionate retaliation in order to obtain revenge against infiltrators, punish the regimes that allowed them to infiltrate, and, it was hoped, deter future attacks.[46]

The first milestone in the geostrategic landscape after 1948 was the 1956 Suez crisis, labeled by many Arabs the 'Tripartite Aggression,' in which Israel, the United Kingdom and France joined together to invade Egypt in order to weaken the increasingly powerful regime of Gemal Abdel Nasser in the wake of Egypt's decision to nationalize the Suez Canal (itself a response to the withdrawal of an offer by the United States and Britain to fund construction of the Aswan Dam).[47]

An elaborate ruse was devised in which Israel would invade, and the British and French would intervene to 'force' the belligerents to separate. At the same time the two powers would argue that Israel's invasion demonstrated Egypt's inability to control the Canal, and thus it should be placed under joint British–French supervision. Few bought the ruse, however; even the United States balked, and the three countries were forced to withdraw after US president Eisenhower supported a strongly worded UN resolution against the invasion.

During the ensuing decade Palestinian guerrillas ('fedayeen') staged increasing numbers of attacks on Israel. The growing responsibility of Palestinians in the attempts to 'liberate' their homeland ultimately led to the creation of the Palestine Liberation Organization (PLO) in 1964, and its takeover by a more activist movement, Fatah, three years later. During this time, the status quo between Israel and the surrounding Arab states continued to be one of cross-border raids, reprisals, and occasional terrorism.[48]

This balance of power would change dramatically, however, on June 5, 1967. The Six Day War, which ended on June 10, saw Israel conquer not just the remainder of Mandate Palestine – the West Bank and Gaza – but also the entire Sinai Peninsula and the Golan Heights as well. The war has long been depicted by Israel and its supporters as a fight for survival as threatening as the 1948 war. The reality was that Israeli and American leaders were both confident that in the lead-up to the war Israel would be able to defeat the combined Arab armies within one week of the initiation of hostilities.[49]

The devastating defeat of the Arab world at the hands of Israel (the war is euphemistically known in Arabic as *al-Naksa*, or the 'Setback,' compared with *al-Nakba*, or the 'Disaster' of 1948) marked the beginning of the end of the Nasser era. Soon after the conquest of the West Bank and Gaza Strip a combination of creeping annexation, creeping transfer, and a binding, colonial relationship between the two economies began to govern relations between Israel and Palestinians across the Green Line, with all forms of civil dissent and disobedience by Palestinians summarily crushed. At the international level a war of attrition began and continued for several years until Egypt believed itself to be sufficiently rearmed and trained to launch a surprise attack against Israel.

During this time, however, the seeds of the next major conflict were being sown. When Anwar El-Sadat took the reins of power after Nasser's death in 1970, he began planning for a new attack, with the goal of regaining enough prestige to force Israel to enter into negotiations on a more equal footing. In one of the greatest intelligence failures in Israeli history, a surprise Egyptian and Syrian invasion was launched on the holiest day of the Jewish year, Yom Kippur (October 6) 1973, which was also the tenth day of the Muslim holy month of Ramadan.

The strong early showing of the Egyptian army in the war of 1973 achieved Egypt's primary strategic goal of beginning a negotiating process that would ultimately lead to the return of the Sinai Peninsula.[50] The Arab world, however, saw its position vis-à-vis Israel weakened considerably by the resulting peace agreement between Israel and Egypt, which removed the most powerful Arab state from the military balance of power between the two sides.

In the wake of the 1973 war the Nixon administration, led by Secretary of State Henry Kissenger, began a process of 'shuttle diplomacy' aimed at bringing about a long-term truce between Israel

and its neighbors, particularly Egypt. That prospect led Palestinian leaders to re-evaluate both the end goal of their struggle for
independence and their strategy for achieving it. On the one hand,
the reliance on armed struggle as the primary means of securing
independence began to be questioned, while the notion of 'total
liberation' of Mandate Palestine began to give way, first, to a slightly
more open notion of a 'secular democratic state' in the late 1960s,
and then to a two-state solution in the mid-1970s, beginning with
the 12th Palestinian National Council (PNC) meeting of 1974, which
called for the creation of a *sulta wataniyeh*, or national authority, on
any territory that could be 'liberated.' At the 13th PNC in 1977 this
principle was modified further to the creation of a *dawla wataniyeh*,
or national state on any liberated lands.

The goal of these changes was to keep the PLO from being shut
out of the negotiating process, but they met with stiff resistance
from more militant members of the Palestinian leadership. The
Popular Front for the Liberation of Palestine (PFLP) and other
militant groups established a Rejectionist Front to continue armed
struggle as the only method of dealing with Israel. In a sense the
militants had a better understanding of the weakness of the Palestinian negotiating position (although their reliance on violence was
no more successful in achieving core national objectives), as became
clear when Palestinians were shut out of the negotiating framework
established with the Egyptian–Israeli negotiations that produced
the Camp David Accords. Indeed, peace with Egypt strengthened
Israel's strategic position against the Palestinians even more than
its position vis-à-vis the surrounding Arab countries.

Among the most important pressure points deployed by Israel was
the rapidly increasing number of Jewish settlements established in
the wake of the peace treaty with Egypt. Until 1977 only several dozen
settlements had been established, which housed approximately ten
thousand settlers (with another forty to fifty thousand by then living
in East Jerusalem). When the Likud came to power, however, settlement construction exploded, seven major settlement blocks were
established, and large bypass roads were built to connect them.[51]
Hundreds of settlements were established by the time of Oslo, culminating in a system in which, as of 2008, well over 400,000 people

lived in 121 settlements throughout the Occupied Territories, with upwards of half of them within the borders of 'Greater Jerusalem' alone.

5. *The rise of political religion* The final pre-Oslo dynamic that had a profound impact on Israeli and Palestinian societies was the rise in religious sentiments among large segments of both populations. It is clear that Judaism, and particularly the religious and historical ties to 'Eretz Yisrael,' were the the primary motivating factors in the development of Zionism and its focus on Palestine as the logical place for settling the world's Jews. Yet as a social and political movement Zionism – and particularly the socialist Zionism that came to dominate the movement by the first decade of the twentieth century – was largely secular (and in some ways anti-religious) as it evolved in Palestine.

Religion and religious sentiments were tools to further explicitly modern and nationalist aims of state-building and independence. This would change, however, when Israel 'miraculously' conquered the Old City of Jerusalem, home to the Western Wall, Judaism's holiest site, and along with it the biblical heartland of the West Bank, which together reawakened the latent religious identity at the core of Zionism. The first settlers in the West Bank – in the holy cities of Jerusalem and Hebron – were religiously motivated, and by the early 1970s the expansionist ideology and security concerns of the Labor establishment and the religious desire to settle and 'reclaim' the country's biblical heartland came together, leading to the tacit (and ultimately open) support for settlement activities. The settlements quickly took on religious and even messianic, rather than merely nationalist, significance, with repercussions to this day, as I explore in Chapter 5.[52]

Islam and religion more broadly have been central to almost every national identity in the Middle East, but its role in Palestine was intensified by the important role played by annual religious festivals, the religious centrality of Jerusalem, and the vast number of saints and their tombs that were pilgrimage sites within the popular forms of all three religions in the country – all of which were central to the early formation of Palestinian national identity.

The fact that the most important leader of the pre-1948 period was the Grand Mufti of Jerusalem – that is, the supreme Muslim religious figure in the country – increased the prominence of religion and Islam particularly within Palestinian identity. Two other factors that contributed to the importance of Islam within the developing Palestinian nationalism were the role of Izz al-Din al-Qassem, the Syrian preacher turned guerrilla fighter who organized the first sustained guerrilla movement in the country (Hamas's military wing takes its name from him), and the presence of the Muslim Brotherhood in Palestine, beginning in 1936.

Qassem was killed by the British in 1936, becoming the first celebrated 'martyr' to the Palestinian cause. In the wake of 1948 the role of the Muslim Brotherhood became increasingly important, especially in the West Bank, where in contrast to Egyptian oppression of the Brotherhood that carried over to Gaza, the movement had good relations with the Hashemite region in Jordan. The Brotherhood became well integrated into the Jordanian political system, which allowed it to play a strong role in West Bank society, laying the groundwork for its development across the Occupied Territories after 1967.

Israeli policies during the occupation further encouraged the rise of Islamic politics in the West Bank and Gaza, as the government believed that a religious identification would clash with and undermine the radical secular-national politics represented by the PLO. As the rise of Hamas makes clear, however, this assumption would prove to be quite wrong; yet until the 1980s religious forces were unable, politically, to offer any alternative to the program of nationalist armed struggle epitomized by the PLO, and so had little political power.[53]

This dynamic was reinforced by development across the Arab world as well. Indeed, the upsurge in religious sentiments across the MENA in the 1970s was an unanticipated effect of the 1967 and 1973 wars. The first greatly weakened the ideology of secular Arab nationalism, as Muslim activists argued that Israel won in good measure because it stuck to its religious beliefs while the Arabs had abandoned theirs. The surge in oil prices after the 1973 war provided unprecedented funds to be used for the spread of the ultraconservative, and potentially extremist and violent, Saudi-style Islam that would inspire movements such as the Egyptian and Palestinian Islamic Jihad and the Palestinian Hamas.

From the beginning of Zionist colonization until the 1960s, Zionism and then Israeli nationalism were characterized by both a frontier and a collectivist ethos; the former provided a rationale and a structure for the ongoing project of 'reclaiming' or 'redeeming' territory in Palestine that was not under Jewish control, the latter helped solidify the high level of social cohesion and willingness to sacrifice for the greater good made necessary by continual conflict with the inhabitants of the frontier – the Palestinians. With the closing of Israel's frontier in 1967 and the move towards a neo-liberal political-economic system that promoted individualism and consumption, these two core components of Israeli identity began to recede among a large share of the Israeli population.

Yet at the same time this process produced among a growing proportion of the Israeli population reaction that mirrored similar developments across the globe, in the United States as much as the Arab world; namely, the rise of socio-religious movements in both Israeli and Palestinian societies which regrounded citizenship within a larger, collective system of meaning in which territory and identity were resacralized. In the process, land and competing religiously grounded claims to the right to rule Israel/Palestine regained their centrality for a large proportion of the two populations, even as Israeli culture was, on the surface, becoming more globalized – and therefore less nationalist – in outlook.[54] These movements fed off, energized, but ultimately were not dependent on the existing state-centered nationalist political identities for their justification. At the same time, the increasingly 'global political economy of Israel' (as the economists Jonathan Nitzan and Shimshon Bichler term it) saw the country become a node of the US-dominated world economy which was determined in growing measure by a combination of moderately high oil prices and massive arms purchases, both of which were only feasible in the environment of continual conflict and occasional war made possible by a seemingly intractable Israeli–Palestinian conflict.

In short, by the time Menahem Begin and Anwar Sadat shook

hands in 1979, peace between Israelis and Palestinians had become structurally impossible – as much because of the prevailing dynamics of the world political and economic system as because of the solidification and intensification of the Occupation. Exacerbating this paradoxical situation was the fact that it occurred at the moment when new social forces, such as the socio-religious movements described here, emerged to challenge the drive towards 'peace' within the cultures of the two nations. We'll explore the impact of the various intersections of all the dynamics in the remainder of the book.

2 | From handshake to security state

Defining Oslo

The Israeli sociologist Amnon Raz-Krakotzkin has written that 'Oslo is a peace without history.'[1] In fact, it was the burden of history, not its absence, which doomed the peace process. But Raz-Krakotzkin is certainly correct in the implications of this argument: instead of grounding the peace process in an honest assessment of the historical processes that produced the current situation, Israelis, Americans, and to a certain extent the PLO elite that negotiated the accords and benefited from them operated within a series of myths – about the ability to escape history, about the ability of economic processes to render political and territorial issues 'irrelevant,' about the viability of 'ending' a conflict without fairly addressing its underlying causes. These misperceptions made it inevitable that history would come roaring back with a vengeance as soon as negotiators had to translate the lofty rhetoric of the peace process into substantive and enforceable agreements.

The dynamics that produced the Oslo process are many and complex. It's hard to imagine today, but the series of events that spurred the peace negotiations – beginning with the eruption of the intifada in December 1987, then encompassing the PLO's renunciation of violence a few months later, the dismantling of the Berlin Wall and the demise of the Soviet Union a year after that, and the growing public consciousness that the world was entering a new era of globalization – created significant hopes that a permanent resolution of the Israeli–Palestinian conflict was on the horizon.

The reality was rather different. Israel's primary benefactor, the United States, had triumphed in the cold war. Israel's most dangerous enemy, Iraq, had been vanquished in the Gulf War of 1991. Palestinians were in a weakened position after several years of the intifada, not least because Arafat's seeming support for Saddam alienated the wealthy Gulf rulers, who had previously provided financial support to the Palestinian struggle. With these factors in place, Israelis saw an opportunity to reach a peace agreement on terms that were favorable to them. Palestinians were in a much less favorable strategic position, but at the same time there was a perception among many in the Occupied Territories that Israelis were ready to recognize some form of Palestinian independence in return for full recognition of Israel's right to exist by Palestinians and the surrounding Arab world.

These sentiments of optimism reflected the general optimism among so many people (especially elites) in the developing world during the early post-cold-war years, when it seemed that in the New World Order being constructed around them, everything was possible. Somalia, Bosnia and Rwanda and various global economic crises during the 1990s would eventually put the lie to such hopes, but in the early part of the decade Palestinians and Israelis could still hope that they were moving towards the endgame of their bitterly connected histories.

Officially known as the Declaration of Principles on Interim Self-Government Arrangements, the first Oslo agreement, signed in Washington, DC, on September 13, 1993, was also the first agreement between Israel and the PLO. The goal of the agreement was to establish a framework for negotiations towards a permanent settlement, and to map out relations between the two sides during an interim period while the parameters of the final peace agreement were devised.

The substance of the accords was agreed to in Oslo, Norway, in late August 1993, after over a year of secret negotiations between the two sides which began with 'unofficial' discussions between lower-level representatives and culminated with a high-level meeting led, on the Israeli side, by Foreign Minister Shimon Peres. The document, along with letters of mutual recognition signed by the two sides, recommitted the PLO to a recognition of Israel's right to exist (it had already explicitly recognized Israel with the 1988 Algiers Declaration). The PLO also renounced terrorism, while Israel recognized the PLO as the legitimate representative of the Palestinian people.

The Oslo accords committed the parties to final-status negotiations over the next five years, based on UN Security Council Resolutions 242 and 338. They created a Palestinian Authority (PA) and a Legislative Council chosen by election, which would have varying levels of responsibility over Palestinian territory depending upon whether that territory was under full, partial or limited Palestinian control. While interim self-government would be granted in phases, the most important issues – Jerusalem, refugees, and settlements – were left to be determined by negotiations at a later phase in the process. Various committees would be established to deal with issues such as security, environmental, and economic cooperation, while a 'strong' police force would maintain security in areas vacated by the withdrawal of Israeli military forces.

With the framework for negotiations established, the Oslo negotiating process would continue until its collapse in July 2000 at the ill-fated Camp David negotiations. In the interim, almost a dozen agreements, memorandums and declarations would be signed by several Israeli governments and the PLO and Palestinian Authority, each one under slightly more duress than the last. The reason for the increasing tension was, in good measure, because each document moved farther from the original conception of the negotiating process.

However important the announcement of the Oslo Agreement was to the future development of the peace process, in substance rather than style the ideas and negotiating processes they initiated were not new. Indeed, Palestinians and Israelis were already engaged in detailed negotiations on almost every issue that would be dealt with during Oslo in the preceding years, much of it in simultaneous 'tracks' through the Madrid framework of negotiations which continued right into the summer of 1993, and which sought to produce precisely the kind of 'Declaration of Principles' that constituted the historic first Oslo Agreement.

These earlier discussions should also have prepared Palestinians for some of the pitfalls of peacemaking. PLO negotiators had already warned about Israeli negotiating tactics during the Madrid talks before Oslo, and their insights explain why Oslo was so attractive to the senior Palestinian leadership: 'The Israeli negotiator uses three languages: The first, behind the scenes, which is very generous. The second, at the negotiating table, which is more cautious. The third, in the documents, which is very intransigent and hard-line.' Echoing a complaint that would often be heard by Palestinians during Oslo, Palestinian diplomats felt that Israel was using the 'great convergence' between its own and the American position to 'continue [its] refusal to engage in substantive negotiations and violation of the agreements reached before the talks.'[2]

Not surprisingly, Israelis and commentators in the United States would offer similar complaints about Palestinian negotiating positions and tactics.[3] Both represented a lack of trust that severely strained the negotiating process and made it impossible for each side to take the leap of faith that would have been necessary to complete a permanent agreement at the final stage of negotiations, in Camp David in July 2000 and Taba, Egypt, in January 2001.

As I explained in the Introduction, during Oslo Palestinians were told that states and the institutions they controlled were going to be less and less important in the future. From this vantage point, the Palestinians should be less militant and inflexible in their demands for full independence and robust sovereignty. As Shimon Peres explained in a keynote address at the 2000 conference of the Washington Institute for Near East Policy, 'Governments are becoming irrelevant to modern societies,' which meant that as long as Palestinians could obtain better education and jobs, the details of their political situation would become increasingly irrelevant.[4]

The problem was that the new Middle East was not much different from the old one, and specifically from the Middle Eastern political and economic orders that were forged under decades of European rule. Indeed, only months after the signing of the Declaration of Principles, Sara Roy would write in the *Journal of Palestine Studies* that Gazans were 'numb, beyond despair' because of the continued occupation and the chaos and political disintegration it had produced in Palestinian society.[5] While PLO and Israeli negotiators were celebrating their agreement, roving groups of *mutaradin*, young men wanted by the Israeli security services, were unleashing random violence across the Strip. Only a few years earlier the *mutaradin* were a disciplined, ideologically motivated, and integral part of the political and social system of the Gaza Strip. But two and a half decades of occupation and the repression of the intifada had turned them into little more than criminal gangs feeding off of the economic and political decay that characterized life in the Strip before, during and after the Oslo process.[6]

Touching an illusion: looking back from Oslo

The core policies of economic neoliberalism, such as the privatization of state-owned industries, opening up of domestic trade regimes and markets, the shifting of manufacturing jobs to unprotected 'free-trade' zones, and the gradual erosion of fundamental civil and political rights, were all embodied in various ways in the Oslo agreements. Together they would have a profoundly negative impact on the chances that the process would bear anything but bitter fruit. In order to understand the specifics of these processes, we need to get a general understanding of the timeline and major events of the 'Oslo era.' Although the Declaration of Principles was signed in 1993, I will argue that the 'Oslo era' actually began in the late 1970s, when the possibility of direct negotiations between Israelis and Palestinian leaders first became imaginable.

In 1977, the recently formed Likud party defeated the previously dominant Labor Party in the Israeli national elections, and Likud's victory enabled important shifts in political, cultural and diplomatic processes which prepared the way for Oslo a decade and a half later. The Likud government also introduced neoliberal policies which transformed Israeli society, and signed the Camp David peace agreement between Israel and Egypt in 1979. The Camp David Agreement effectively removed Israel's main enemy from consideration in future military actions while setting a precedent for future bilateral negotiations under the auspices of the United States. It was supposed to be the springboard to negotiations between Israel and 'the Palestinians.' The section of the agreement dealing with Palestinians actually came before the Egypt–Israel framework. As the text of the agreement states: 'Egypt, Israel, Jordan and the representatives of the Palestinian people should participate in negotiations on the resolution of the Palestinian problem in all its aspects.' The mechanism for achieving this was almost identical to the Oslo process fifteen years later, including the 'transfer of authority' to Palestinians for a transitional period not to exceed five years, the holding of elections to choose an interim Palestinian government, and the creation of a 'strong local police force' to provide security.[7]

As important as Camp David were the economic reforms initiated by the Likud, which began a long-term process of gradually dismantling the quasi-socialist, state-centric policies of the Labor Party, whose socio-economic vision had made Jewish Israeli society one of the world's most egalitarian. Heir to the ideology of the bourgeois Revisionist Movement founded in 1920 as an alternative to Labor Zionism, the Likud sought to transform the economic structure of Israeli society in a way that eager Israeli capitalists could not have accomplished under a Labor government.[8]

However strategically important the Camp David Agreement was for Israel, it did not resolve the 'Palestinian problem.' As long as Israel refused to begin negotiations on the Palestinian track the problem would fester. And while the PLO controlled what was essentially a mini-state in southern Lebanon (which bordered Israel), it could maintain some level of coordination with and control over its society in the Occupied Territories. It was precisely to break the connections between the PLO and the Occupied Territories in order to facilitate the imposition of a limited form of autonomy upon Palestinians that Israel invaded Lebanon in 1982. The pretext for the invasion was the attempted assassination of the Israeli ambassador in London, though all sides knew that this attack was the work of the breakaway Abu Nidal faction of the PLO, which was not under Arafat's control.

The first Israeli soldiers who crossed into southern Lebanon were in fact greeted warmly by much of the Shiite majority of the region, who had grown weary of the constant abuses and violence associated with Palestinian fighters and various militia groups. But the welcome did not last once it became clear that Israel had no intention of leaving any time soon.[9]

The Israel Defense Forces (IDF) quickly became bogged down in a war with various Shiite resistance groups, including by 1983 the newly formed Hezbollah, the 'Party of God.' In one of the many unintended consequences of the war, Hezbollah would go on to develop close relations with Palestinian militants during the Oslo years.[10]

The eviction of the PLO from its southern Lebanese statelet to distant Tunis in 1982 meant that the leadership found it much harder to maintain day-to-day influence over the lives of Palestinians in the Occupied Territories, or the surrounding refugee communities. This encouraged the emergence of a local leadership whose interests would not always correspond to the 'national' leadership in Tunis. Israel had hoped for this outcome and hoped to profit from it. But instead of being more malleable, the local leadership became more resilient and defiant. During the Madrid negotiations in 1991, the local leaders took a much harder line than the politically weakened PLO was willing to adopt. It was precisely the failure of the Madrid process to produce a more malleable Palestinian negotiating stance that led to the back-channel Oslo negotiations with the PLO.

The intifada years: an old wall comes down, the foundation for a new one is laid

What brought this period to a close was the outbreak of the first intifada in December 1987. The intifada – which erupted after an Israeli truck ran over and killed eight Palestinians in Gaza – may have caught Israeli and Palestinian leaders by surprise, but it shouldn't have. It occurred at the end of a painful decade of economic and political transformations in Israel, which included such reforms as the liberalization of the economy, increasing inequality and poverty and the curtailing of social services to both Israelis and Palestinians. These caused a significant increase in social and economic dislocation within Palestinian society. At the same time, a new generation of local Palestinian leaders was emerging who had come of age during the Occupation, had come to understand that no outside force would help Palestinians free themselves, and who were much less afraid of their Israeli occupiers than their parents' generation. With no one else to help them, the intifada erupted, marking one of the great periods of social solidarity in Palestinian history. Young people, women, various grassroots NGOs and other new forces reshaped the political and social landscape of Palestine.

The intifada brought together Palestinian society across class, clan, cultural and generational boundaries. While it was symbolized by the iconic image of the rock-throwing (or slinging) Palestinian youth, more influential were the hundreds of thousands of Palestinians, men and women, young and old, most of whom had little previous activist experience, engaging in militant but non-violent resistance: civil disobedience, large-scale demonstrations, general strikes, tax resistance, boycotts and political graffiti. The resistance was coordinated by 'popular committees' led by the major PLO parties active in the Occupied Territories.

In response to the outbreak of the intifada, Defense Minister Rabin ordered soldiers to use 'force, power and blows' against Palestinians.[11] From 1987 to 1991 more than a thousand Palestinians were killed by Israeli forces, over one-fifth of them children. The violence of the intifada, and the fact that for the first time Palestinians en masse were offering resistance in their conflict with Zionism and Israel, created a new sense of 'selfhood' among Palestinians, in which a cult of 'martyrdom' and a sense of 'bravery' and 'heroism' were mixed together in powerful ways that excluded the exiled Tunis leadership. This explains why 'inside' Palestinians took a much harder negotiating stance than their PLO counterparts would during Oslo.[12]

The intifada, which literally means 'shaking off' in Arabic, shook many Israelis from their complacency about the occupation. This led many self-styled liberal Israelis, particularly those who had been at the forefront of the Peace Now movement, which had been founded during the 1982 war in Lebanon, to begin a dialogue with local Palestinians. These liberals hoped to prove that there was a willing Palestinian partner for a 'land for peace' agreement along the lines of the agreement with Egypt. The position of these 'peaceniks' was strengthened when the PLO announced the Algiers Declaration of October 1988 (also known as the Declaration of Independence), which formally recognized Israel's right to exist and renounced the use of violence and terrorism as a means of achieving national liberation. The PLO forced the Reagan administration, by its own policy parameters, to recognize the organization and to begin high-level discussions. This in turn increased the pressure on Israel to open a channel with the PLO, especially after individual Israelis and peace groups discovered that many Palestinians were willing to accept a two-state solution.

The pressure was mitigated by Israel's increasingly adept management of the intifada. By 1990 most of the local leadership had been arrested, and the Israelis had managed to encourage internecine fighting (particularly between the PLO and an emergent Hamas) that would siphon energy from the larger national struggle against occupation. By the end of 1989, the intifada became as much about Palestinian-on-Palestinian violence (killing at least 250 suspected collaborators, conflicts between Fatah and the newly emerged Islamic resistance movement, Hamas, etc.) than figuring out new and more successful ways to resist an ever growing occupation.[13]

Against this backdrop, the Iraqi invasion of Kuwait in August 1990 was a watershed moment, for many reasons. Broadly, it was an early example of how the disintegration of the cold war order would lead states and non-state actors alike to make sometimes bold (and in Iraq's case, reckless) attempts to improve their regional or global strategic position. The New World Order, it seemed, could well be characterized by disorder, as the chaos in the Balkans, Somalia, Rwanda, and across Africa and Central Asia would soon make clear.

Locally, Yasser Arafat's seeming support for Saddam Hussein, coupled with the sight of Palestinians standing on rooftops in the West Bank cheering on Iraqi SCUD missiles on their way to Tel Aviv (which were broadcast repeatedly in Israel and around the world), severely weakened the Palestinians' position. As peace activist and Knesset member Yossi Sarid famously put it about his former Palestinian friends: 'Let them look for me.'[14] In other words, Palestinians had betrayed the Israeli leftists who had championed them, and in response the left was, at least for the time being, not going to push for a peace process that seemed to be rendered moot by Palestinians cheering Saddam Hussein's attacks on Israel.

Here was the immediate context for the 'peace process': the PLO had been seriously weakened by backing the wrong side in the Gulf War; Israelis were angry at Palestinians for supporting Iraq; and the United States had promised those Arab leaders who had supported the war on Saddam that it would 'do something' about the Israeli–

Palestinian conflict after an American victory in Iraq. In October 1991, the first face-to-face negotiations between Israelis and Palestinians began, under the aegis of the Madrid Conference.

The conference, co-sponsored by Spain, the United States and the Soviet Union, brought together Israel and all of its neighbors, including Syria and Lebanon. It consisted of two tracks. The first featured direct bilateral negotiations between Israel and each neighbor, in which Palestinian leaders from the West Bank and Gaza (but not PLO officials) were allowed to participate as part of a joint delegation with Jordan. The second track was multilateral and focused on how to deal with pressing regional problems such as water, the environment, arms control and refugees, with the hope of normalizing Israel's relationship with the surrounding states.

While it provided compelling theater – especially the Syrian ambassador holding a picture of Israeli prime minister Yitzhak Shamir from his days in the Jewish underground and calling him a terrorist – the face-to-face negotiations achieved little. In the case of the Palestinians, this was because their positions were much less flexible than those of the Tunis-based leadership. They understood more fully the red lines of West Bank and Gaza Palestinians in any negotiations towards a final settlement.

The deadlock was broken by three events in 1992. First, new Israeli prime minister Yitzhak Rabin expelled 415 Palestinian activists from the West Bank and Gaza to a harsh strip of open land in southern Lebanon. This led to a huge international outcry that put increasing pressure on Rabin's newly elected government to take a bold step for peace. Second, Rabin ended the legal prohibition against Israelis meeting with PLO members. And third, in the spring of 1992 Terje Rod Larson, a senior Norwegian academic with extensive PLO contacts, sought out the Labor Party's Yossi Beilin and informed him that senior PLO figures had expressed their desire to begin direct negotiations, which would effectively end the PLO's exclusion from the Madrid process.

The Israeli government chose two academics, Ron Pundak and Yair Hirschfeld, with histories of contact with Palestinians, and accorded them an unofficial mandate to begin negotiations with Arafat's senior aides, Abu 'Ala'a (Ahmed Qurei'), Hassan Asfour and

Maher Kurd. Numerous meetings were held via this back channel, and once it was clear that an agreement was possible, the negotiations were upgraded to official status. This caused some problems, according to Qurei's memoirs, because once officials of the Israeli government rather than academics became involved, the Israeli negotiating positions hardened significantly. Many promises that had been made by Pundak and Hirschfeld were disclaimed by Foreign Ministry officials such as Uri Savir, who took over the negotiations.[15] Indeed, a 'war of documents' ultimately erupted which required intensive negotiations and the personal involvement of Shimon Peres to resolve.[16] Finally, in August of 1993 the terms of the Declaration of Principles were hammered out. The Oslo back channel had seemingly established a framework for joint negotiations towards a final settlement of the conflict.

The Oslo era, from dream to reality

Amid all the celebrations about the handshakes on the White House lawn, some observers were uncomfortable. The Palestinian intellectual Edward Said was among them: 'What was most troubling is that Rabin in effect gave the Palestinian speech while Arafat pronounced words that had all the flair of a rental agreement.'[17] He was unclear about the terms of the deal that had been agreed. 'In return for exactly what' had the PLO given up so much in the Declaration of Principles, particularly when it had already made the most important concession – explicitly recognizing Israel – half a decade earlier?

The Declaration of Principles called for the withdrawal of Israeli forces from parts of the Gaza Strip and West Bank and stipulated Palestinian self-government, through the Palestinian Authority, within what was supposed to be an ever-increasing area of full autonomy. The difficult issues of Jerusalem, refugees, and Israeli settlements were put off until the 'final status' negotiations, precisely because all sides understood how deeply rooted these problems were. In a sense, there was a great leap of faith on both sides going into this process, with each hoping that the momentum of the negotiations and the prospects of real peace or independence would lead to a 'historic compromise' on core positions by the other. Failing that, perhaps both sides would be pressured into reaching an agreement. Neither happened.

The Declaration of Principles was in essence an agreement between an occupying power and a relatively powerless occupied country (especially compared with other movements that had successfully fought for independence) to discuss a potential resolution of their root conflict. As many Palestinians have commented, Oslo became a negotiation over the terms of Palestinian surrender to Israel rather than a genuine peace agreement. But few people were going to throw water on the bright fire of Oslo so soon after it had been ceremonially lit.

The following year, 1994, was perhaps the most important year of the Oslo era, but not for a positive reason. Instead, two events occurred which would be directly responsible for its downfall. The first was the massacre of 29 worshipers and the wounding of another 125 at the Cave of the Patriarchs in Hebron by the Jewish settler Baruch Goldstein in February. In response to the killings Hamas launched its first major suicide bombing campaign beginning with a bus bombing in the Israeli town of Hadera organized by Yahya Ayash, better known as 'the Engineer.'[18] The second was the signing of the Paris Protocols to the Oslo Agreements in April. As we'll discuss in detail below, the Paris Protocols set out the economic arrangements that would govern relations between the two sides. More well known, and pivotal from the standpoint of the emerging structure of autonomy, was the 'Cairo Agreement' signed the following month, also known as 'Gaza-Jericho First.' The Agreement spelled out a series of steps towards extending autonomy, based on an Israeli military withdrawal from around 60 percent of the Gaza Strip, as well as from the West Bank town of Jericho. It also laid out the specific structure of the Palestinian Authority, its legislative and executive powers, and the larger division of authority between itself and Israel within the territory to be transferred, establishing a precedent for future withdrawals. By this time, however, the difficulty in reaching a balance between feasible agreements, the more far-reaching demands of leftists and Hamas, and the desire by civil society for greater participation in decision-making were starting to stall the process.[19]

Two months later, Arafat entered Gaza, and in October Israel and Jordan signed their peace agreement, making official a half-century-long alliance of interests (however uneasy at times) between the Zionist movement and the Hashemite Kingdom. At the same time, intensive negotiations were under way between Israel and Syria, through the auspices of US Secretary of State Warren Christopher, that would have led to a full withdrawal from the Golan Heights (which Israel had occupied since 1967) in return for a full peace and security guarantees. But the talks fell apart after Syrian president Assad grew suspicious of Israeli intentions and Prime Minister Rabin refused to directly confirm to the Syrians his willingness to withdraw to the 1967 borders.[20]

The Cairo Agreement was supposed to mark the beginning of a five-year transition period that would implicitly (but still not officially) lead to the establishment of a Palestinian state. The year 1995 was similarly consequential for the peace process. The Oslo process continued in spite of these problems. In September 1995, Arafat and Rabin signed what is variously known as the 'Taba' or 'Oslo II' Agreement, which was supposed to widen Palestinian control of the West Bank and Gaza, and which mandated Palestinian elections for January 1996. Under the terms of Oslo II, the West Bank was divided into three areas: Area A, under exclusive Palestinian control; Area B, with Palestinian civilian control and Israeli security control; and Area C, under exclusive Israeli control. The idea was that as the peace process moved forward to a final agreement Israel would transfer increasing amounts of territory from Areas B and C to Area A. The hope generated by this agreement was shattered by the assassination of Yitzhak Rabin on November 4 by an extremist, ultra-religious settler, Yig'al Amir. A look at Yasser Arafat's face when he visited Rabin's widow, Leah, in her Tel Aviv apartment said it all. The only Israeli who had the stature and background to reach an agreement that Palestinians could sign was gone, and the future would be far more uncertain, and most likely more disappointing, than the first two honeymoon years of Oslo.

As Marwan Bishara has argued, while the agreements signed during the first years of Oslo were supposed to mark the coming to maturity of Palestinian politics, the reality was that they facilitated

a 'depoliticization' of the peace process. What began as construc-
tive ambiguity would quickly become deliberate deception as each
accord was essentially an empty framework that required even more
interpretation to understand, explain and clarify it.[21] Palestinian
intellectuals and journalists began to question Arafat's judgments,
though this didn't prevent Arafat from achieving a sweeping victory
in the first Palestinian presidential elections in January 1996.

The elections were the freest and fairest in the history of the Arab
world, and returned both a president and an eighty-eight-member
Legislative Assembly. But the optimistic mood was quickly dashed
by the Israeli assassination of Yahya Ayash in March of that year.
His killing has generally been considered the cause of the wave of
Hamas suicide bombings that were launched in its wake, killing
almost five dozen Israelis.

As important, however, was the perception by Hamas that with
the elections and the consolidation of the PA, it had to block the
consolidation of a PLO state and the influence of the returnees,
who were progressively undermining its influence and participating
in 'the liquidation of the Palestinian cause' by accepting a state
over part of Palestine.[22] Even the Palestinian leadership was not
completely sanguine about the situation on the ground. Hence the
official Palestinian Authority newsletter, the *Review of Events of the
Week*, began to publish articles criticizing ongoing settlement construction, Israel's failure to release all female Palestinian detainees,
and Israel's 'distortion of the history of Jerusalem.' Israeli critics of
Oslo, and the government as well, similarly criticized the ongoing
acts of violence and terrorism by Palestinians against Israelis, both
in the Occupied Territories and inside Israel.

In April 1996, the situation deteriorated further as Rabin's successor, Shimon Peres, launched a fierce war in Lebanon codenamed
'Operation Grapes of Wrath,' aimed at stopping Hezbollah rocket
attacks against northern Israel. The violence of early 1996 doomed
Peres's chances for re-election, as it reinforced the long-standing
perception of him as weak in the face of Arab threats and violence.
In a climate of increasing Israeli despondency at the failures of the
peace process to end Palestinian violence, Benjamin Netanyahu was
elected prime minister in June 1996. His promise of 'peace with

security' didn't last very long, however; a mini-intifada erupted in September in response to the Israeli opening of a tunnel under the Western Wall in Jerusalem.

Realizing that despite their hard-line rhetoric it would be impossible – under the present circumstances – simply to put an end to the Oslo process, Netanyahu and the Likud leadership tried to coopt Labor Party elites into their negotiations. This was done through an agreement between Labor and Likud on the parameters for any final-status settlement with the Palestinians. Signed by Yossi Beilin for Labor and Michael Eitan of the Likud in September 1997, the 'National Agreement Regarding the Negotiations on the Permanent Settlement with the Palestinians' established guidelines for future negotiations that should have alerted Palestinians and American policy-makers alike that the road ahead for the Oslo process would be long and likely fruitless.

The most important of these guidelines was that 'no agreement signed by the Israeli government can include a commitment to uproot Jewish settlements in the Western Land of Israel.' Yet without such a commitment, no permanent peace deal would be acceptable to Palestinians. The Beilin–Eitan agreement explained that the 'majority of settlements ... would remain under Israeli sovereignty ... the Jordan River will be the security border of the State of Israel ... Jerusalem will be a single unified city within sovereign Israel ... [and] The agreement on the issue of water usage, as it was signed in the framework of the interim agreement, will remain in effect.' All these parameters would make it very hard if not impossible to reach a viable final settlement.

Realities on the ground also revealed how difficult the situation was. By the latter part of 1996 both Netanyahu and Arafat were seriously weakened by the failure of the peace process to provide any tangible benefits to their populations. Such was the situation that commentators were arguing that Olso was 'at a dead end.'[23] Even the state-controlled Palestinian Broadcasting Network's nightly newscasts reflected the increasingly grim mood among Palestinians, with regular reports highlighting findings by the UN about increased settlement activity, World Bank reports discussing the dire situation of the Palestinian economy, and various senior officials demanding greater Israeli compliance with existing agreements in order to ensure the continuation of the peace process.

At the same time, newspapers began to criticize the United States more directly for not putting sufficient pressure on Israel; Palestinian political activists called for new elections, greater respect for the rule of law, separation of powers and anti-corruption measures; and even Fatah leaders admitted that Netanyahu had 'killed the peace process and turned the ... confidence-building phase into a confidence-destruction phase.'[24] Some of them advocated a 'possible return to armed struggles' if the lack of tangible progress on the ground didn't change.

There were even reports of several meetings between Arafat and Hamas head Ahmed Yassin, where the 'difficulties facing the peace process' were discussed. Other reports in the Palestinian media quoted Israeli sources as saying that 'guerrilla warfare' could break out because of Palestinian disappointment with both Israeli actions and the lack of progress by American diplomats in getting the peace process back on track. Increasingly, such discussions took place not merely in the major newspaper or television stations, but on local community television states located in the major towns of the Occupied Territories as well.[25]

A particular bone of contention between the two sides at this time was the three hundred or so Jewish settlers living in the middle of Hebron, who were causing increasing hardship for their tens of thousands of Palestinian neighbors and required an ever greater number of Israeli soldiers to defend them. In the Hebron Agreement of January 1997, Netanyahu transferred over 80 percent of the town to Palestinian rule. The remainder, in which several hundred Jewish settlers lived in uncomfortable proximity with 20,000 Palestinians, remained under Israeli control. (More than ten years later, the settlers and the soldiers are still in place.) Given the bad press that Benjamin Netanyahu received from many peaceniks in Israel and the United States, it is worth noting that the Hebron Agreement was perhaps the only peace accord to be fulfilled in all its terms by Israel. It did little, however, to resolve the tensions within the town.

Under intense pressure from President Clinton and the international community more broadly, the Oslo process staggered onwards in 1998 with the signing of the Wye River Plantation Agreement. The agreement was supposed to conclude the interim agreements and make way for the negotiations on final status, which, according to the terms of the 1993 Declaration of Principles, should have been completed within a year. The Wye Agreement called for the construction of an international airport in Gaza, an Israeli withdrawal from an additional 13 percent of the West Bank, and the release of 750 Palestinian prisoners.

What is important about these promises is that none of them had anything to do with sovereignty, which was still nowhere in sight for Palestinians. Instead, what Palestinians were being granted was precisely the kind of 'functional autonomy' – and nothing more – that Israelis had envisioned for them since the first Camp David Agreement in 1977. Even here, however, the terms of the agreement were not carried out by Israel; in turn, the PA failed to crack down on terrorist activities that continued to receive a limited but crucial level of support within Palestinian society.[26] While Arafat declared his readiness to restart the intifada if Palestinians were prevented from establishing a state with Jerusalem as its capital, other senior Palestinians took a more moderate tone as they tried to account for the lack of progress. They blamed the Likud and Netanyahu rather than the terms of the peace process itself, and they reassured Palestinians that 'despite all of the obstacles ... the Oslo Agreement is the ... best option available ... [It is the] highest point and the most important struggle that the Palestinian people have fought in this century.'[27]

As diplomacy began to falter at the end of the 1990s, there was 'an extraordinary increase in settlement construction' across the Occupied Territories.[28] Economically, a UN report on the economy of the West Bank and Gaza summarized the situation in the Occupied Territories during this period: 'The labor force in the West Bank and Gaza Strip grew by 8.25 percent ... far outstripping the creation of new employment possibilities. Not only are more people unemployed, but those with jobs are earning less for their working day.'[29] Continued closures of the Occupied Territories, coupled with relatively low levels of foreign investment, corruption, repression of free expression, serious human rights violations by the Palestinian Authority against its citizens, and the natural stifling of economic activity produced by the ongoing occupation all contributed to this bleak situation.[30] At the same time, inside Israel attitudes towards Palestinians, including Palestinian citizens of Israel, remained antagonistic. In one poll, half of Israelis declared their support for denying Israeli Palestinians the right to vote and for transferring them to the territory of a Palestinian state.[31]

The continued failure of the negotiating process coincided with an election campaign in 1999 which pitted Prime Minister Netanyahu against former defense minister Ehud Barak, who won by a small margin. Barak was a confusing figure. He ran on the Labor Party's 'peace' platform, yet he had opposed Oslo as chief of staff in Rabin's cabinet. Early signs from his new government were not encouraging, especially after Barak delayed implementing some of the terms of the Wye Agreement and began courting Syria in the hopes of perhaps reaching an agreement that would increase the pressure on Arafat to cut a deal.

The confusion about Barak's intentions encouraged a period of reflection among some Palestinian leaders and intellectuals about the problems within the PA. Some Palestinians who had championed Oslo began to realize that their own people saw them as 'a group of thieves' who presided over little more than a façade of democracy. Within the Palestinian territories, some voices laid the blame for the failure of Oslo with its Palestinian cheerleaders as well as its Israeli architects.[32]

Former Clinton aides Robert Malley and Hussein Agha later summarized the Palestinian perspective on Oslo at the end of the 1990s.

> Seen from Gaza and the West Bank ... Oslo's legacy read like a litany of promises deferred or unfulfilled. Six years after the agreement, there were more Israeli settlements, less freedom of movement, and worse economic conditions. Powerful Palestinian constituencies – the intellectuals, security establishment, media, business community, 'state' bureaucrats, political activists – whose support was vital for any peace effort were disillusioned with the results of the peace process, doubtful of Israel's willingness to implement signed agreements, and, now, disenchanted with Barak's rhetoric and actions.[33]

Still, Ehud Barak was the last best hope for Oslo, and for Arafat's promise to bring a tangible agreement to his people. Things looked slightly more promising after Barak's flirtation with Syria ended in failure, forcing him to refocus on the Palestinian track. Better still from an Israeli perspective was the fact that Barak convinced Arafat to sign a revised version of the Wye River Memorandum at a summit in September 1999, reducing Israeli withdrawals in the near term in return for a promise to fast-track final negotiations, which would begin in November.

The agreement called for more stringent security measures by Palestinians while dividing the Israeli redeployment from the remainder of the Occupied Territories into even more stages. But the subsequent Israeli proposals for withdrawing from the West Bank were unacceptably small for Palestinians, leading to an impasse in negotiations that all sides reluctantly realized could be resolved only by intensive direct negotiations under US supervision. By this stage, the numerous unfulfilled Israeli obligations exacerbated the imbalance of power between the two sides. Since Israel had refused to admit that it was, under international law, an occupying power, Israeli governments found it easy to render any agreements null and void. By holding back on withdrawals, Israel ensured that land that should already have been transferred to the Palestinians during the interim period remained subject to negotiation again. This would force Palestinian negotiators to compromise again on issues that had already been agreed. At the same time, the rapid increase in settlements during Barak's first year in office suggested that the Israelis were trying to consolidate their hold over key regions of the West Bank in order to prejudice the geography of the final peace settlement. A less charitable interpretation would be that Barak was ensuring that no peace agreement was possible.

A summit held in February 2000 failed owing to Barak's refusal to carry out even the smaller redeployment agreed to the previous year. Israel did hand over another 6 percent of the West Bank in preparation for the Camp David summit in July proposed by President Clinton, but this did little to assuage Palestinian feelings that they were not being dealt with fairly. Making matters worse for Palestinians, in May Israel withdrew all its troops from Lebanon, freeing it of its most costly, time- and material-consuming occupation, pressing security issues and putting it in an even stronger position vis-à-vis the Palestinians.

Camp David: what was on the table and why Arafat said no

Arafat's sense of his disadvantageous position led him initially to refuse President Clinton's invitation to travel to Camp David, the presidential retreat 60 miles north of Washington, DC, which a generation before was the site of major Israeli–Egyptian negotiations towards peace, for a marathon negotiating session to resolve most of the outstanding issues in the peace process. Whatever his faults as a leader – and they were many – Arafat well understood that he was likely walking into a trap in which he would become the scapegoat. He would either blamed for the breakdown of negotiations if he rejected the offer on the table at Camp David, or reviled by Palestinians at home if he agreed to terms that were slanted towards Israel.

If it is generally understood why Arafat was unenthusiastic about going to Camp David, it's far less certain why Ehud Barak went. In an interview with Benny Morris after he left government, Barak explained that he 'wanted to complete what Rabin had begun with the Oslo agreement,' based on the belief that an 'official peace [would] place pacific handcuffs on [both] societies' and allow the harder work of building a peace between the two people to continue. Even though his intelligence chiefs said it was doubtful that Arafat 'would take the decisions necessary to reach a peace agreement,' Barak hoped that he would rise to the occasion.[34]

Even conservative Israeli commentators have admitted that Barak did not go into Camp David willing to offer major concessions in writing in order to achieve a final agreement.[35] On the other hand, it is equally true that Barak went a long way to break most of the taboos in Israeli politics about the peace process. He went back on pledges never to consider dividing Jerusalem, swapping Israeli territory for Palestinian territory containing Jewish settlements, and agreed to a much higher percentage of territory to be ceded – 90 percent of the West Bank – than he was originally willing to give up.

Arafat agreed to come to Camp David only after President Clinton promised him that he would not be blamed if the talks failed – in fact, it was Clinton who volunteered this condition during pre-summit discussions with Arafat ('there will be no finger-pointing,' he said).[36] Barak, however, was unwilling during the negotiations ever to put a hard offer on the table or reveal his final positions (even to the USA). In fact, there was no concrete Israeli offer, with maps and hard numbers. Rather, as Clayton Swisher argues in his comprehensive review of the Camp David negotiations, there was 'outright surrender of summit control to the Israelis by the Clinton Administration,' which even more damagingly allowed the Israelis to set parameters for negotiation in which, for the first time, Security Council Resolution 242 was no longer the guiding principle.[37]

The role of the Clinton administration as an honest broker was questionable. American policy was shaped by the close relationships between senior administration officials, members of the pro-Israel policy-making community (especially the American Israel Public Affairs Committee, or AIPAC), Congress and its media allies, and Israeli officials. This made it nearly impossible for Clinton to pressure Israel to make substantial concessions during the negotiations. In fact, Clinton struggled to persuade the Israelis even to fulfill the terms of the agreements they had already signed. This dynamic became particularly important during Barak's tenure, as he wanted Palestinians to agree to forgoing implementation of the existing agreements or to demand a settlement freeze in favor of moving directly to final-status negotiations.

Given this negotiating environment, it is no surprise that during the Camp David negotiations 'Israelis always stopped one, if not several, steps short of a proposal,' while ideas were conveyed only orally and never directly. Barak was surely afraid of the domestic price to be paid if a 'generous' offer leaked out without a compensating Palestinian concession offered. But without a tangible document or set of proposals on the table that all the parties were clear about, the sides at Camp David were negotiating over a phantom, without material substance, which evaporated whenever one or more of the parties tried to nail down specific points. Fatally, there was no map with clearly delineated boundaries that would serve as the basis of a final agreement over borders.

It was here that the depoliticization of Oslo and its emptiness as a negotiating template came back to haunt the process. Ultimately the Camp David summit broke down over the inability of Israelis to put their proposals on the table – literally – and the Palestinians' inability to respond to Israeli tactics creatively enough to continue negotiations. On July 25 the summit ended, and Clinton immediately reneged on his promise to Arafat by agreeing with Ehud Barak that the Palestinians were to blame.

The memoirs of some of the key Israeli players at Camp David reveal three main strategies for explaining the summit's failure. First, the use of history to temper Palestinian demands. Thus Yossi Beilin argues in *Touching Peace* that 'in the Lausanne conference in 1949 Ben Gurion was prepared to accept 100,000 Palestinian refugees ... but it was the Arab world that rejected this; you can't come back fifty years later ... saying you've changed your mind and is the offer still open please.'[38] In other words, Palestinians lost the opportunity to achieve a fully viable state in 1948, and therefore should accept whatever agreement they can negotiate today.

Second, as we've already seen, the peace process was defined as an inevitable product of neoliberal globalization, itself an inevitable development in world history. As Shlomo Ben-Ami argues, Oslo 'was almost the byproduct of an emergent new world.' To oppose Oslo is to oppose the tide of history. This leads to some confusion as Ben-Ami is forced to 'blame' the Palestinian negotiators 'who came from Tunis and had no knowledge of the conditions on the ground. Local leaders, who'd been brought up under the occupation, would not have let this happen.' What is ironic in Ben-Ami's remarks is that they overlook the fact that the 'Tunisians' were brought in by Israel precisely because (as Ben-Ami himself admits in a previous paragraph) the natives proved to be 'too rigid' in their negotiating stance. Finally, to the extent that Israel was guilty of obstructing peace, the blame is laid at the feet of the right wing rather than Labor officials like Barak and Peres. According to Ben-Ami, it was the Likud which 'killed the peace, softly.' The Labor Party, on the other hand, has been at the forefront of peace.[39]

On the Palestinian side, critics of Oslo had by the mid-1990s come to understand the weakness of the process. In particular, Ahmed Qurei' (Abu Alaa), who was present at over a dozen rounds of secret negotiations that led up to the signing of the Declaration of Principles, realized that one of the biggest mistakes Palestinians had made was agreeing to recognize Israel without achieving a recognition by Israel of Palestinians' right to an independent state in return.[40] Indeed, in recognizing the PLO rather than the right to statehood, Israel helped set the stage for the dysfunctional relationship between the PLO and the PA, as exemplified by Arafat's role as the head of both, the increasing centralization of power in his hands, and the frustration of the democratic process within Palestinian society by the executive and security structures of the PA.

Perhaps this realization of a strategic mistake by Palestinians at the start of the process was what led Qurei' seven years later, in asking 'Who was responsible for the failure of Camp David?,' to answer candidly that, first of all, there were the serious problems with the negotiating process at the summit from the beginning – he uses the verb *khashina*, to make or be coarse or rude. He added that 'no one of the three parties [Israel, the Palestinians and the United States] planned for the failure, and no one was completely responsible for it.'[41]

The apparent failure of the Oslo negotiating process by the summer of 2000 led some members of the Palestinian political elite to recognize the need for greater emphasis on building democracy, particularly through the education system. The PLO leadership seemed uninterested in this, and critics came to believe that the PLO would have to cease monopolizing the internal Palestinian scene because its policies were not leading towards the goal of independence. Hamas in particular had offered a stinging critique of the peace process that matched the intensification of its terrorist activities on the ground. In one 1997 book drawn from newspaper articles in Hamas's London-based Arabic newspaper, *Falastin al-muslima*, Hamas supporters argued that 'the realities of the Palestinian economy are nothing like they are imagined to be ... The Israeli goals are always clear: the elimination of Palestinian and Arab and Islamic rights ... in favor of the right of return to the Israeli entity.' The book practically predicts the eruption of violence three years later because of 'the reality of Israeli power, not just over Palestinians, but over the whole region.' With a nod to the illusory nature of Oslo, the author urges his readers to focus on 'reality' – this word appears throughout the book – arguing that 'the reality of the situation in Oslo is clear when you note the continuation of the occupation and the settlement and the encircling of Jerusalem and ... the Haram Ibrahimi [the Hebron mosque which remained under Israeli occupation] and [Israeli] seizing [of] land and water ...'[42]

While the asymmetry in power between Israel and the PA was perhaps the major cause of the failure of Camp David, Palestinian commentators also identified internal problems in the functioning of the Palestinian leadership. Specifically, the PA was unable to successfully deal with the twin challenges of a continued struggle for national liberation and the need to encourage democratic transformation and state-building. According to senior Palestinians, Arafat 'willfully confused revolutionary legitimacy with constitutional legitimacy, invoking one or the other according to the circumstances and sometimes playing one off against the other.' In continuing to personalize his rule, Arafat encouraged a dynamic of power in which 'proximity to the President' rather than institutional position was paramount. As Palestinian political scientist Khalil Shikaki explained it in the months before the outbreak of the al-Aqsa intifada, 'the near absence of political accountability; the lack of clear definition of prerogatives and responsibilities ... and the weak participation of civil society in the emergence of a new political order' all contributed to these larger structural problems.[43]

Arafat's dream of presiding over the creation of a Palestinian state died the day he left Camp David. By the time the second intifada broke out in September 2000, the majority of Palestinians had in one way or another moved beyond him. Yet as Malley and Agha conclude, this orthodoxy – that it was all Arafat's fault – 'is a dangerous ... and shallow ... one,' because it fails to account for the Palestinians' view of the offer as neither generous nor, indeed, as an offer.[44] Barak, who famously said that if he were a Palestinian, he would join Hamas, understood full well that Palestinians would have to be coerced into accepting the 'hard compromises' that were the red lines of Israel's negotiating positions; it had to be clear that all other options were worse. After 2000, the options for Palestinians would deteriorate considerably.

Collapse and chaos: the Dome of the Rock, the al-Aqsa intifada and the end of the dream

With both Palestinians and Israelis still trying to recover from the failure of Camp David, Ariel Sharon, leader of the Likud, saw and seized an opportunity to remake the political landscape and put the final nail in Oslo's coffin. This came in the guise of his September 28, 2000 visit (approved by Barak and Ben-Ami, but furiously opposed by Palestinians),[45] accompanied by upwards of a thousand Israeli soldiers, to the Temple Mount in Jerusalem (Haram al-Sharif in Arabic) for the purpose of asserting Israeli claims to sovereignty over the third-holiest site in Islam. This sparked Palestinian protests, including throwing stones at riot police and Jewish worshipers at the Western Wall located below the Haram, in response to which police shot and killed seven Palestinians. The violence quickly spread to Ramallah and other towns, and within days both sides were speaking of a new intifada.

The 2000 intifada was much different than its predecessor in 1987. First, from the start the Israelis used live ammunition and deadly force against stone-throwers and unarmed protesters. By the third day, the IDF had killed twelve Palestinians and injured over five hundred. In response to this disproportionate level of Israeli violence – well over 1.3 million bullets and shells were fired by the IDF before the first week was over; soon after the IDF began using tanks, missiles, helicopter gunships and eventually F-16s against protesters and to shell neighborhoods – Palestinians moved from stones to guns and suicide bombings as primary weapons in the emerging intifada. They also targeted Israeli civilians and settlers as well as soldiers in their attacks.

At the same time, however, many Palestinian intellectuals expressed anger at the willingness of the Israeli left, their erstwhile allies, to accept if not condone the violence deployed by the IDF to repress the intifada.[46] This sentiment was also expressed among Palestinian citizens of Israel, who for the first time engaged in intense protests, which led to thirteen Palestinian Israeli citizens being killed by police.

A summit in Egypt in October failed to produce a ceasefire; the death toll on both sides (particularly among Palestinians) grew more significant each week. By the end of 2000, 300 Palestinians had been killed and over 10,000 wounded. Dozens of Israelis had died as well. Bill Clinton became desperate to wrest something positive from the deteriorating situation before turning the presidency over to George W. Bush, whom he was sure had little interest in pursuing the peace process.

Another summit at Taba in January 2001 came closer than ever before to achieving a final peace agreement. President Clinton offered a 'bridging proposal,' which laid out further negotiations, and Israeli negotiators were reported to have accepted the concept of East Jerusalem being the capital of a Palestinian state. But Barak refused to sign off on the proposal, issuing a statement that read that 'nothing is agreed upon until everything is agreed upon.'[47] For their part, Palestinian negotiators complained that the closer the two sides came to clarifying their positions in preparation for a final agreement, the larger the gap between them became.[48] During this period, the IDF was routinely shelling civilian neighborhoods throughout the West Bank. Soon after, the entire West Bank was shut down.

Both Clinton and Barak left office in early 2001. George W. Bush took over in the White House at the end of January, and Ariel Sharon defeated Ehud Barak at the polls in Israel a few weeks later. With Sharon's election as prime minister, Oslo was officially put on life support, from which it would never recover. (One NGO described 2001 as 'the year that the Oslo process finally died.'[49]) Palestinians responded with large demonstrations against Sharon's election, some of which featured calls for more suicide bombings against Israel. With the new Sharon government deploying ever harsher policies against Palestinians, a pattern of heightened violence and indiscriminate attacks on civilians was established on both sides. This pattern defined relations between the sides for much of the next five years.[50]

By April 2001, when the former US senator George Mitchell published his report outlining suggestions for curbing the violence and renewing the peace process, it was clear just how little seven years of negotiations had achieved. Approximately eighty-eight Israeli civilians had been killed, along with thirty-nine soldiers. Palestinians fared far worse: at least 500 Palestinians had been killed, including 167 children; 14,000 were injured, including 6,000 children; 559 buildings were destroyed, 25,000 olive trees were uprooted, and 900 acres of agricultural land destroyed.[51] At the same time, Israel had frozen the VAT and other customs and tax receipts it owed to the Palestinian government under the terms of the Oslo accords. The stress on Palestinian politics and the economy led Arafat, for the first time since the creation of the PA, to admit to the need for internal political and institutional reform, to fight corruption, and affirm his commitment to the rule of law. Neither reform nor liberation would prove possible in the coming years, while the authoritarian system that only a few years earlier had been the promising democratic Palestinian experiment had degraded beyond the point where the long-established pluralism of Palestinian politics could sustain itself, and the community along with it.[52]

The impact of 9/11 on the Israeli–Palestinian conflict

The terrorist attacks on the United States on September 11, 2001 inevitably changed the political and strategic dynamic surrounding the new intifada and Israel's harsh response to it. Unsurprisingly, 9/11 strengthened Israel's position. An already unsympathetic US government was still less tolerant of Palestinian violence against Israelis, and more likely to fold Palestinian resistance into the general category of 'terrorism.' At the same time, however, the Bush administration understood that in the aftermath of its invasion of Afghanistan, something had to be done to demonstrate that America did support the resolution of the Palestinian problem and wasn't anti-Muslim per se, or solely belligerent towards the Middle East (especially as Bush administration officials were already considering an attack on Iraq even before the end of 2001). Bush thus went public with his support for the creation of a Palestinian state – the first time an American president had publicly recognized that a Palestinian state would be the end result of negotiations.

There was the potential for significant progress when the Saudi government offered a detailed and far-reaching peace initiative in March 2002: by the terms of the plan, Israel would withdraw to the lines of June 1967, a Palestinian state would be set up in the

West Bank and Gaza and there would be a 'just solution' of the refugee issue. In return, Arab countries would recognize Israel and agree to a comprehensive peace and full normalization of relations. American officials, though, pursued a new policy which in some ways resembled the Oslo approach. In 2002 the Bush administration announced a 'Road Map' towards a final agreement, responding in large measure to the failed mediation efforts by George Mitchell. The Road Map, based on Bush's proposals, was elaborated and extended by a diplomatic alliance known as the 'Quartet' – the United States, the European Union, Russia and the United Nations – which was to oversee its implementation. The Road Map largely conformed to the parameters established by the 2000 Camp David and subsequent Taba negotiations. If Oslo was supposed to end with a permanent agreement in May 1999, the Road Map would culminate in 2005 with the creation of a Palestinian state with temporary borders.

The next year, with the peace process still moribund, former Labor Party foreign minister Yossi Beilin joined together with former Palestinian information minister Yasser Abed Rabbo to issue the Geneva Accords. This unofficial agreement reversed the concept of the Road Map (and Oslo), in which the growth of security and confidence was supposed to precede a political agreement. Here, the final agreement came first. The most important development in this 'agreement' was that it demonstrated a Palestinian willingness (among the PLO elite, at least) to give up the 'right of return' to 1967 Israel in return for obtaining almost the whole of the West Bank. Further, Israel would have been allowed to keep most of its major settlements, particularly around Jerusalem, in return for which East Jerusalem would become the Palestinian capital. A similar non-binding agreement was signed by former Shin Bet chief Ami Ayalon and al-Quds University president Sari Nusseibeh. This envisaged a return to the 1967 lines, an open city of Jerusalem and an end to the Palestinian claim to a right of return to former homes.

The Geneva Accords were quickly picked up by the Israeli left as a document that could provide a 'realistic' approach to ending the conflict. But they had little chance of being accepted by most Palestinians, and despite being mailed to the home of every Israeli, never had much traction. Once the USA became bogged down in

Iraq the chances of any solution to the conflict disappeared, and Ariel Sharon sensed an opportunity to consolidate Israel's position in the West Bank with a unilateral 'peacemaking' gesture. In 2004, Sharon proposed the withdrawal of all Israeli settlers and troops from the Gaza Strip; in August 2005, the evacuation was completed. Israel thereby freed itself of the burden of having to protect 20,000 settlers amidst 1.5 million Palestinians. Just as important from a diplomatic standpoint, Gaza could be offered as proof – to the Western and especially American media – of Sharon's willingness to agree to a major withdrawal from the West Bank if the violence stopped completely. Yet it is likely that Sharon understood that the violence would not stop on either side, and thus Israel would have the chance to consolidate further its presence in the parts of the West Bank that it hoped to retain in any permanent peace. A precedent for unilateral peacemaking had been established.

In order to consolidate the Israeli presence in the West Bank, Sharon pursued policies to prevent Palestinians from scoring any sort of military or political victory from the intifada. The Israeli military employed sieges and the wholesale destruction of major civilian neighborhoods in the most important cities of the intifada, particularly Nablus and Jenin. The 'Battle of Jenin' (in Arabic '*majzarat Jenin*') in April 2002 offered the first evidence of the level of blunt force Israel was willing to apply in the wake of 9/11. Responding to several horrific suicide bombings carried out by militants, Israel sent soldiers, armored vehicles, attack helicopters, and, most damagingly, armored bulldozers into Jenin's refugee camp, destroying around 10 percent of the area of the camp. While Palestinians described the battle as a massacre, reports of hundreds of civilian deaths proved wildly exaggerated. Some fifty-two people were confirmed dead, twenty-two of them civilians. Yet if the death count was far smaller than some had claimed, both Human Rights Watch and Amnesty International accused Israel of committing numerous 'prima facie war crimes' during the battle, which seriously disrupted the lives of Palestinian civilians in the city, and for a time degraded the ability of militants to work out of the town. In the long term, however, attacks on Israel continued.[53]

A similar siege and battle occurred in Nablus at around the same time, which resulted in the destruction of much of the town's historic old city and large swaths of other neighborhoods as well. (The damage was so great it took weeks for the extent of the loss of life and property to become known.[54]) Upwards of seventy-five Palestinians, fifty of them civilians, were killed in Nablus, many of them by helicopter attacks and tanks. Over a hundred houses were destroyed. One Israeli soldier died. Another siege occurred simultaneously at the Church of the Nativity in Bethlehem.

Ultimately, however damaging the military tactics, they were not nearly as important as the intensification of what Israeli geographer Jeff Halper has termed the 'matrix of control' by Israel over the Occupied Territories. As I will explain in the next chapter, the two primary components of the matrix of control since the 1980s have been the strategic placement of settlements themselves and the extensive network of bypass roads connecting them. Along with hundreds of military checkpoints, these settlements and roads have fractured Palestinian control and access to their lands, while enabling Israel to manage, and when desired prevent, the movement of the entire population of the West Bank and Gaza.

Since the outbreak of the al-Aqsa intifada, however, a new element has become central to the matrix of control: the 'separation barrier' or wall built by Israel across the 1967 border, and often deep within the West Bank. Termed the 'apartheid wall' by Palestinians and other critics (including the International Court of Justice, which issued an advisory opinion declaring its construction in contravention of international law), as of 2007 upwards of five hundred miles of the wall had been constructed, with most of the length being composed either of networks of fences surrounded by vehicle trenches, or concrete walls of up to eight meters in height.

Israel declared that the goal of the wall was to curtail Palestinian infiltration and terrorism. And indeed, terrorist attacks, and with them Israeli civilian casualties, have been reduced in the areas of Israel adjacent to the wall. At the same time, most of the international community accepts the right of Israel to construct a security wall along the 1967 border. But however effective in its stated goal, the wall has met with intense opposition from Palestinians and much of the world community because much of it is located not along the border, but instead deep into Palestinian territory. In many cases, Palestinian farmers have been cut off from their fields, children from their schools, and villagers from their neighbors. Palestinians fear that the wall is establishing a de facto final border between Israel and the West Bank which Israel will attempt to formalize whenever final-status negotiations resume. This fear was exacerbated when President Bush declared in April 2004 that 'In light of new realities on the ground ... it is unrealistic to expect that the outcome of final status negotiations will be a full and complete return to the armistice lines of 1949.'[55]

For much the same reason, some Israeli settlers have opposed the wall for creating a material separation between what they see as two inviolable parts of the Land of Israel. But many settlers have embraced the wall because it has embraced them: its course has been carefully plotted to envelop Jewish settlement blocs in the Jerusalem, Bethlehem, and Hebron regions, ensuring that the main settlement clusters remain inseparable from Israel.

The Israeli government defends the wall by arguing that its construction has enabled the IDF to lessen the number of closures and checkpoints in Palestinian areas near the wall, which in turn have eased movement in these parts of the West Bank. This has indeed occurred, but the larger price has been quite steep. Construction of the wall has necessitated the uprooting of over 100,000 olive trees and the demolishing of numerous structures, with a high cost to Palestinians on whose land it is being built. These olive trees, many of which are hundreds of years old, are not just one of the most powerful symbols of Palestinian ties to their land (and of Israeli ties to the Land of Israel as well), they are also one of the most important components of the Palestinian economy. The untold tens of thousands of olive trees destroyed before, during, and since Oslo are one of the most powerful continuities in the Israeli–Palestinian conflict.

Unless this chain can be broken, the chances of Oslo producing a legacy of peace are slim indeed. But the links that tie the past and future were not weakened during Oslo. Rather, they were strengthened, evolving into a web, or matrix, that made it even harder for Palestinians to achieve independence. Land, territory, even identity would be increasingly constrained by the same forces that promised freedom, development and a global future. It is to the mechanics of these forces, and the manner in which they reshaped the political, economic and social geographies of Israel/Palestine during Oslo, that we now turn.

3 | No land, no peace

As the discussion in the previous chapter has made clear, the trajectory of the Oslo negotiating process was set in motion and profoundly shaped by long-term historical forces that lay at the root of the Israeli–Palestinian conflict. In the remainder of the book, I will explore how these forces impacted crucial areas of the negotiating process: the Jewish settlements in the Occupied Territories, the evolution of the Israeli and Palestinian economies, the growing power of socio-religious movements in the two societies, and the role of civil societies, NGOs, and the discourse of violence in the attempts to forge a path towards peace. This chapter will explore what has according to most people been the heart of the problematic relationship between Jews and Palestinian Arabs during the last twenty years: the competition over territory.

From the arrival of Zionism in Palestine in the late 1800s until the present day, the priorities of Zionist and then Israeli leaders have been to 'unfreeze' land owned or controlled by the indigenous Palestinian inhabitants and 'refreeze' it under Jewish ownership and ultimately sovereignty.[1] This strategy has proved incredibly successful; Israeli Jews today control roughly the same amount of territory as did Palestinians before the 1948 war – roughly 90 percent of the territory of the country.

With the conquest of the remainder of Mandatory Palestine in 1967 Israel put to use a modified version of the strategies it deployed to gain control of land in pre-1948 Palestine, and within Israel between 1948 and 1967: direct expropriation or confiscation, military and planning regulations that forced the transfer of Palestinian-owned land into Israeli government control, and, when possible, purchases at well above market prices.[2] The difference in the post-1967 era is that far fewer Palestinians have been willing to sell their land to Jews; in only four out of well over twelve dozen settlements on the West Bank (not including outposts) has more than 4 percent of the land been sold by Palestinians to Jews. This has necessitated the development of an extremely sophisticated system of land acquisition by the Israeli state in the face of concerted opposition by the Palestinian population.

According to a 2006 study by Peace Now's Settlement Watch, roughly 40 percent of settlement land is composed of privately owned Palestinian land that has, according to international (and often Israeli) law, been 'illegally confiscated' from the owners. Of the remaining land, 54 percent is 'state land,' an Ottoman legal category that a century ago described land that local inhabitants could obtain rights to if they began farming it, but today refers to land under the control of the Israeli state to which Palestinians effectively have no opportunity of obtaining access or rights.[3] Here we must explore the dynamics of this system and the determinative role it has played in the collapse of the Oslo peace process.

What makes the sheer force of the settlement enterprise so interesting to study is that it has grown more powerful even though the concept of trading land for peace has been at the heart of negotiations between Israel, its neighbors, and ultimately Palestinians for two generations. It was first given international legitimacy and sanction by Security Council Resolution 242, passed in the wake of the Six Day War of June 1967, and then reaffirmed in Resolution 338 of 1973. For a generation they constituted the reference points for Israeli–Palestinian and broader Israeli–Arab negotiations, strengthened by the near-universal acceptance that permanent occupation of and settlement in territories occupied during wartime was illegal according to international law.[4]

Whatever their public statements, by the time the Madrid Process began in 1991 leaders on 'both sides knew,' as the *Washington Post* editorialized, that 'land for peace is inevitable.'[5] The question, of course, was how much land Israel would be willing to return and what kind of peace the Palestinians and surrounding Arab states were prepared to agree to in exchange for that territory. It was here that the weakness of Resolution 242 as a basis for negotiations became apparent, as it excluded Palestinians from the negotiating equation by focusing only on the right of 'all *states*' – and therefore not the West Bank and Gaza – to live in peace and security. It was a disadvantage that Palestinians have never been able to overcome.

We can see the impact of this dynamic in the statistics on settlement during the Oslo period. All told, the number of Israeli settlers during Oslo grew from 110,000 in 1993 to well over 200,000 in the West Bank and Gaza by 2001; in East Jerusalem, the Jewish population rose from 22,000 to over 200,000 in the same period. Upwards of two dozen new settlements were established and more than 18,000 new housing units for settlers were constructed, over 130 outposts were established (many of which are 'laundered' into legality by means of obtaining permits after the settlements were already established), fifty homes were demolished every year in East Jerusalem (with hundreds more during Oslo in the Territories more broadly), and 35,000 acres of Palestinian land were expropriated for roads and settlements. By the time the al-Aqsa intifada exploded, even a mainstream commentator like Ze'ev Schiff was forced to conclude that 'considerable responsibility devolves on Israel because of its deliberate foot-dragging and its disruption of the timetables contained in the agreements – for example, in the implementation of the various stages of the redeployment.'[6]

In this context, while the absence of Palestinians from the original negotiating framework did not doom the process, the reality that many of the most senior Israelis involved in fostering the Oslo process were also among the most important figures in the settlement enterprise during the entire post-1967 era made it extremely difficult for the process to arrive at a successful conclusion. Indeed, the most dovish senior Israeli official of the Oslo era, Shimon Peres, was the architect of the creation of outposts and 'work camps' that subsequently became fully fledged settlements (the settlement of Ofra northeast of Jerusalem), which Peres's successor as Labor prime minister, Ehud Barak, later declared to be 'now and forever' part of sovereign Israel.[7]

Such activities reveal the essential continuity in settlement policy between Labor and Likud governments in the post-1967 period. The only difference was that while Israel's Labor leadership was ideologically maximalist territorially,[8] historically it had demonstrated a willingness to relinquish a larger share of the West Bank to Palestinian control than would its Likud counterparts, if it meant securing the larger strategic goal of achieving peace and normalization with Israel's Arab neighbors.[9]

Allon's plan: separation or assimilation?

Of the roughly two hundred settlements and outposts in the Occupied Territories as of early 2008, fewer than three dozen were established during the first decade of occupation. Yet these settlements were crucial for laying out the architecture of settlements during the Oslo era, as they adhered closely to a strategic settlement map devised by then deputy prime minister Yigal Allon.[10] In the summer of 1967, within a month of the Six Day War, Allon outlined a plan that focused on the need for Israel to obtain 'secure borders' as the basis for any peace agreement with its neighbors. Within such parameters, the plan outlined a territorial division of the West Bank between Israel and Jordan in which Israel retained control of a strategic zone in the eastern West Bank (running from the Jordan Valley towards the Syrian border in the north, and connecting to the Israeli Negev in the south) as a buffer against any attack by an Arab army or armies from the east. Additionally, a greatly expanded Jerusalem would remain permanently under Israeli sovereignty.

The Allon plan would have left Israel in permanent control of one-third to 40 percent of the West Bank; but since most of those lands would be sparsely populated, they would not have threatened Israel's Jewish character, nor leave Israel in control of the major Palestinian population centers. With the majority of Palestinians free of direct Israeli control, Palestinian identity could then 'find its expression in a single Jordanian-Palestinian state.'

This 'pragmatic' or 'realist' vision for settling the Occupied Territories was opposed by many Israeli politicians, including General Moshe Dayan, one of the heroes of the 1967 war. Dayan preferred instead a combination of intensive Israeli settlement and free trade leading to Palestinian economic integration with Israel and political integration with Jordan. His vision was reflected in the 'Master Plan for the Development of Settlements in Judea and Samaria,' which called for settling 'not only around the settlements of the minorities [i.e. Palestinians], but also in between them' in order to 'learn to live with the[m].' Not surprisingly, his view found favor in the Likud, which won power in 1977 and literally reshaped the map of Israel/Palestine in the ensuing decade.

By 1970 three Jewish settlements had been established according to the Allon Plan: Kiryat Arba, Gush Etzion, and Ma'ale Adumim. By 1977 the number had reached about twenty-one; on the eve of the first intifada in 1987 forty-eight settlements had been built within the lands Allon said should be annexed to Israel. By this time, Israel had split the West Bank into three longitudinal strips that became most defined during the Oslo period: the eastern strip of the Jordan Valley, the central/mountain strip, and the Western strip.[11]

The Likud's goal of attracting 80,000 new settlers by 1986 was not met until six years later, at the dawn of the Oslo era. The era of peacemaking would differ significantly from the paradigm developed by Dayan and executed by the Likud in that it called for the political and spatial segregation of Palestinians rather than integration. Such a 'divorce' between the two people – 'Us here, them there' was one of Rabin's main election slogans in his victorious 1992 campaign – was seen as a prerequisite both for peace, and for the continuing successful absorption of Israel into the emerging economic geography of neoliberal globalization. That is, increased physical separation, in the context of partial political independence coupled with continued economic dependence, would solidify the advantages of Israel's economic relationship with the Occupied Territories – indeed, as we'll see in the next chapter, with the creation of maquiladora-like industrial estates it would benefit both Israeli and Palestinian capital – without the political costs, while enabling Israel to penetrate global markets that were previously closed to Israeli capital and products because of the conflict.

Yet such was the power of the Allon plan's geography that it served as the foundation for achieving the primary strategic objectives of splitting the West Bank into cantons, and creating major settlement blocs that would remain part of Israel in any potential peace deal.[12] Indeed, an examination of the data on settlement construction reveals that the number of West Bank settlements had begun to plateau by the late 1980s, at between 110 and 120 settlements (not including East Jerusalem and the outposts). If we compare the settlement map at that time with the map as of early 2008, it becomes evident that Oslo was ultimately more about finding a process in which to cement Israel's permanent hold on these settlement blocs than arriving at a land-for-peace formula that would produce a viable Palestinian state.

Settlers in the pre-Oslo era were aware of this endgame, feeling that if the population of the settlements could reach 250,000, 'that would be the end of the story.' As one leader explained in 1990, 'Even if we record the same level of growth over the next several years as we have had in the last three – and I think we will be able to do at least as well as before – we're going to come to a state where the situation is irreversible … So we don't need dramatic decisions by the new government. All we need is continuity.'[13]

In fact, as Meron Benvenisti explained in the seminal 1987 *West Bank Data Base Project*, the settlement movement's leaders had achieved their goal by this time. As Dayan had predicted, by the mid-1980s the Occupied Territories had become so integrated into Israel that it was no longer possible to consider separating them.[14] The story of Oslo was, then, already written, long before secret talks began in the Norwegian capital in 1992.

As important as Benvenisti's recognition of the depth of the Israeli occupation by the 1980s was his realization that the goals of successive Israeli governments never included annexing the whole of the West Bank. Rather, 'the Israeli body-politic is precisely where it wants to stay. The present, fluid, amorphic situation is preferable and suits everybody. A better method than "annexation" has been found to integrate and segregate at the same time: to integrate the territories for Israeli interests … and segregate the Palestinian population to avoid any burdens (citizenship, extension of Israeli welfare system, free political expression).'[15]

These are among the most prescient words ever written about the Israeli–Palestinian conflict, and they reveal that half a decade before Oslo Israel had already achieved its primary objectives in the settlement process. Israeli leaders had found a formula to maintain permanent control over the desired areas of the West Bank without fomenting overwhelming Palestinian opposition; in fact, Palestinians had been economically integrated into Israel. Two events would, however, challenge the integrationist view of Moshe Dayan and re-energize the separate-and-segregate strategy of Allon and his successor, Yitzhak Rabin: the intifada and the rise of neoliberal globalization.

The ongoing intifada led Defense Minister Moshe Arens to initiate the first large-scale closure of the Occupied Territories in 1990. This policy would become a central strategy for managing Palestinian resistance to ongoing settlement and occupation during the Oslo process. At the same time, globalization was transforming the economy of Israel and the Occupied Territories, and in many ways opening it up to foreign penetration. The collapse of the Soviet Union, the large-scale immigration of Soviet Jews, the liberalization of the Israeli economy, and the possibility of replacing Palestinians with safer, less expensive and more exploitable 'foreign' workers all conspired to create a situation in which closing off the Occupied Territories more or less permanently from Israel became a feasible, and even desirable, option for Israeli policy-makers in their pursuit of peace.

With neoliberalism and corporate-sponsored globalization now firmly entrenched as guiding principles in the administration of Israel's economy, a set of territorial and economic policies that could be described as 'separate-segregate-integrate' came to characterize the system of Israeli rule in the Occupied Territories. This system made it impossible to separate economic, nationalist, and territorial considerations, and it ensured Israel's control during and beyond the Oslo process.

The shape of things to come: settlements during the Oslo period

Despite an intense, decade-long program of settlement, expectations were high for a settlement freeze when the Oslo process commenced in 1993.[16] The freeze would not come. Instead, during the seven years of Oslo (1993–2000) successive Israeli governments allowed a doubling of the settler population to occur, while the number of housing units increased by 50 percent (from 20,400 to 31,400, excluding Jerusalem). The sharpest increase actually occurred under Ehud Barak's tenure as prime minister, just as final

TABLE 3.1 Population and number of settlements in the West Bank excluding Jerusalem during the Oslo period

Date	No. of settlements	No. of settlers (in '000s)
1977	31	4,400
1987	110	57,900
1993	120	110.9
1994	120	122.7
1997	122	154.4
1999	123	177.5
2000	123	191.6
2001	123	198

Source: Central Bureau of Statistics, *Israel Statistical Yearbook* (various years), not including a 'number of settlements' for the years 1967–81

status talks were under way in 1999 and 2000. To understand how and why there was such an increase during a period of ostensible peacemaking, we need to recall the provisions of the various accords and how they dealt with either settlements or the relinquishing of territory by Israel.

During Oslo, Labor-led governments were responsible for well over 51,000 new settlers, while under 40,000 new settlers would move into the Occupied Territories during the Likud governments of Benjamin Netanyahu (1996–99) and Ariel Sharon (2001–06). Palestinians were aware of this fact early on in the negotiating process; the same year the two sides signed the 1995 Taba, or 'Oslo II', Agreement, which set out the three main geographical parameters for the withdrawal of Israeli forces, Palestinian leaders were complaining that Israeli settlements were 'insurmountable obstacles' to the implementation of the agreement.[17]

The initial Oslo withdrawal mandated in the Declaration of Principles constituted roughly 60 percent of the Gaza Strip, along with the town of Jericho and its immediate environs (about 65 square kilometers of territory). This agreement seemed like a good way to begin the land-for-peace process; the structure of the remaining withdrawals, as laid out in Oslo II, was, however, so disadvantageous to Palestinians that Shimon Peres would famously remark to the Chinese ambassador to Israel not long after the agreement was signed: 'We screwed the Palestinians.'[18] So telling was this remark that it has also been attributed to President Ezer Weizmann and to Yitzhak Shamir.

How were the Palestinians 'screwed' by the A-B-C format embodied in Oslo II? To understand this, we need to understand how much territory was actually turned over with each redeployment, and compare it to what was supposed to happen based on the terms of the agreements. To begin with, the initial Gaza–Jericho pullback was an exceedingly small, and in many ways meaningless, withdrawal, since Israel retained full military control over the Strip, and the population of the area around Jericho, which was ringed by some nine settlements, was only about 25,000 people.[19]

The next withdrawal, the first under the terms of Oslo II, occurred in 1995 and released to the newly established PA full control over only 3–4 percent of the West Bank, comprising some 31 percent of the population (the West Bank's seven Arab cities minus the area inhabited and used by the Jewish residents of Hebron). Area B was considerably larger, comprising nearly all of the remaining 460 Palestinian population centers: towns, villages, refugee camps, and hamlets, which together constituted 24 percent of the West Bank. Finally, Area C was 73 percent of the West Bank, and consisted of the remaining territory, covering Israeli settlements, military locations, and uninhabited rural land. Israel retained full authority over both public order and internal security in these regions.

A main problem with the threefold division of control over Palestinian territory was that land remained in play 'on the ground'; that is, Israelis continued to gain control over land by various methods: direct military or other official confiscation or expropriation, settlers 'illegally' occupying hilltops and other strategically important lands, expanding settlement borders to allow for 'natural growth,' and even, according to Palestinian sources, via the services of several hundred Palestinian land brokers who mediated (sometimes fraudulently) the sale of lands from Palestinians to Jews.[20]

A 1997 article from the *al-Quds* newspaper described one such event, in the village of Ya'bad. Based on eyewitness testimony, it

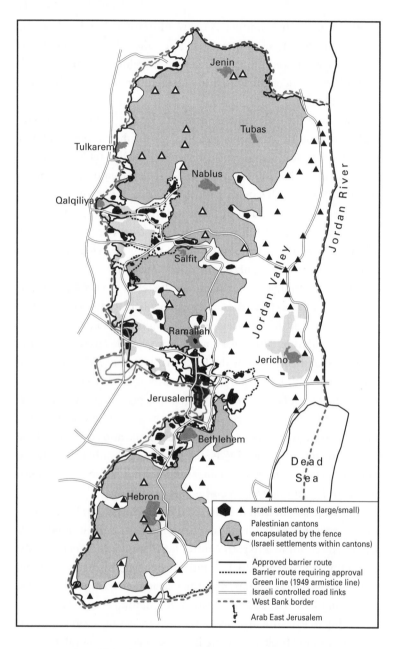

The political geography of the West Bank in 2008

quoted residents explaining that as part of the expansion of the neighboring Dotan settlement, built on land belonging to the town, Israeli bulldozers began to clear the ground and uproot their crops in order to open a new road linking Dotan to the nearby Hermesh settlement. The land in question amounted to several thousand dunams (at least 500 acres), and owners had papers and documents proving their ownership of the land. Despite, or perhaps because of, complaints from the townspeople, Israeli military vehicles began carrying prefabricated houses to the site as soon as the ground was cleared.[21]

On the same day, near Qalqiliya, Israeli bulldozers, amid strict military measures, closed off over four thousand dunams of agricultural land belonging to twelve families bordering the Alfey Menashe settlement southeast of Qalqiliya. Near by, bulldozers blocked several agricultural roads, while settlers from surrounding settlements cleared Palestinian-owned land and then filled it with caravans. In Tulkarem, heavily guarded bulldozers cleared around twenty dunams planted with olive trees and uprooted 600 olive trees belonging to 'Arif Sabir Ya'qub and Ahmad 'Abd al-'Aziz Durubi in the Wadi Jamus area of the village of Shufah, which borders the Avney Hefetz settlement, under the pretext that it was state land.

They also erected a military checkpoint on the road leading to that site and declared it a closed military area, thus preventing Palestinians from reaching it. Several other confiscations, bulldozings and clearings were also going on across the West Bank and Gaza on the same day, which led Palestinians to complain that Israelis were trying to 'Judaize' more and more land to connect nearby settlements.[22]

Palestinian leaders were fully aware of what was occurring on the ground. As early as 1994 Arafat was dismissing self-described bold moves against the settlers by the Rabin government as 'hollow' gestures.[23] During 1997 and 1998, lead negotiator Sa'eb Erakat would complain that the peace process was in 'deep crisis' because of the ongoing settlements; a Fatah Central Committee member and the mayor of Hebron would each warn of a 'new intifada' and a 'complete explosion' (*infijar shamil*) if the settlement building didn't stop. Another senior official declared that the peace process had been 'killed' and that negotiations were 'worthless.' The PA warned

Palestinians of a 'colonial onslaught aimed at forcing faits accomplis' around Jerusalem (particularly with reference to the expansion of Ma'ale Adumim) and more broadly called attention to the attempt to make Palestinians a minority in East Jerusalem through expanding settlements in the area. The PA even sought to build thirty-five new roads across the West Bank to counter Israel's construction of settler bypass roads across the Occupied Territories.

At the grassroots level, villagers from Jayyus and Falama tried to perform Friday prayers on 5,000 dunams of recently confiscated land; villagers in a dozen satellite villages of Ramallah vociferously protested groundbreaking for settlement expansion on lands belonging to their villages; the 'National Institutions Council' (*majlis mu'asasat wataniya*), representing fifty-seven Palestinian NGOs, would declare that there could be 'no peace without Jerusalem'; Palestinian newspapers demanded that the United States pressure Israel to remove 'obstacles' to successful negotiations; activists held sit-ins and planted upwards of twenty thousand fruit-bearing trees on land threatened with expropriation.[24]

None of these and innumerable other warnings and attempts to stop continued settlement expansion succeeded in stemming the process. As long as expansion occurred in the context of the Oslo II Agreement, which explicitly excluded settlements and military locations from the process and gave Israel so much latitude in 'gradually transfer[ring] powers and responsibilities relating to territory … to Palestinian jurisdiction,' Israel could continue to expand the settlements with little fear that the United States would force it to stop, still less the Palestinians.

Most important, as the Oslo process moved towards its endgame the Israeli government focused on cementing control over as much territory in the West Bank as possible. As Ariel Sharon exhorted settlers: 'Move and take over more and more hills. The time is coming when whatever we take will be ours and whatever they take will be theirs.'[25] Such an attitude negated the positive impact of the withdrawals that did happen, such as from 80 percent of Hebron, as per the Hebron Agreement in January 1997, or the Wye River Agreement, in which Israel transferred authority from approximately 3 percent of territory.[26]

Indeed, in the wake of the Wye Agreement the Israeli paper *Yediot Aharonot* reported 'non-stop building' in the Occupied Territories, saying that 'what was done until now in secret has come out into the open.' A thousand new units were tendered not long after Wye, and all told, the paper reported that 'thousands of new dwelling units have been authorized in recent months,' in addition to new hilltop outposts and bypass roads.[27] At the same time, population growth within the settlements was almost four times greater than that of Israel itself, which gave the lie to the argument that the increase in their population was due to natural population growth.[28]

The next Israeli redeployment took place in early autumn of 1999 as part of the Sharm al-Sheikh summit, which set out a timetable for a permanent peace settlement. The month before, however, the Barak government announced fourteen new military orders sealing off large parts of the agricultural land of seventy-nine Palestinian villages, totaling a land area greater than the 7 percent of the West Bank transferred to Palestinians a week earlier, on 13 September.[29]

Indeed, at a cabinet meeting the next day, Barak laid out Israel's positions at the final-status talks: 'No return to the 1967 borders; all of Jerusalem as Israel's capital; no foreign army west of the Jordan River; most Israeli settlement blocs to remain under Israeli sovereignty.' At the West Bank settlement of Ma'alei Adumim the same day, he told residents that 'Every tree you plant, every house you build is part of the State of Israel forever. Period.'[30] It is not surprising, then, that in November *Ha'aretz* would editorialize about Barak's removal of several outposts that they were little more than 'an optical illusion ... The evacuation of a few patches of temporary structures is totally insignificant in the face of the steps the government has taken recently to bolster the Jewish settlement enterprise in the territories.'[31]

In March 1999, the third and last stage of Israeli redeployments in the West Bank during the interim period set forth in Oslo II transpired; 5.1 percent of Area B and 1 percent of Area C were both transferred to full Palestinian control (Area A). With this transfer, the Palestinian Authority fully controlled 17.2 percent of the West Bank (Area A), and had civil control over 23.8 percent (Area B) when the two sides began their fateful final-status talks at Camp David in July 2000. At the same time that some land was transferred to Palestinian control, however, settlers from Ofra and Bet El purchased 250 dunams along the projected route of a road that would connect the two West Bank settlements.

By the time of the Camp David meeting, the allocation was as follows:

TABLE 3.2 Allocation of land in the West Bank, 1999

Region	Thousands of dunams[32]	Area of WB by %
Area A	1,008	18.2
Area B	1,207	21.8
Area C	3,323	60
Total	5,538	100

What these numbers clarify is that even at the end of the Oslo period Palestinians only had 'full' control over less than 20 percent of the West Bank, and civil control over only 40 percent of that territory. Sixty percent was still under full Israeli control, including 41.9 percent of the West Bank directly controlled by settlements.[33]

The fortress mountain and the encirclement of Palestinian Jerusalem

Perhaps the greatest clue to the synergy between Labor and Likud governments during Oslo concerns the Har Homa (in English, the Fortress Mountain) settlement in East Jerusalem. Known as Jebal Abu Ghneim in Arabic, groundbreaking for the settlement by the Netanyahu government in March 1997 caused an international outcry as well as severe Palestinian criticism. The land of Jebal Abu Ghneim was located on a hill along the southern edge of Jerusalem, between the Arab village of Um Tuba and Bethlehem. It had long been declared a 'green area' by the Jerusalem municipality, in order to prevent its development by the land's Palestinian owners (most of whom lived in Bethlehem). While Shimon Peres initially approved plans for construction on the site as a 'legitimate extension' of Jerusalem, he postponed groundbreaking for political reasons.

Elected on Likud's pro-settlement platform, Peres's successor

Benjamin Netanyahu did not have such considerations to worry about. The initial plan was to have upwards of 6,000 homes and 40,000 residents; the plan itself was used to justify the creation of another settlement, in the Palestinian neighborhood of Sur Bahir, which faces Jebal Abu Ghneim, featuring 3,000 new apartments and 400 government-financed housing units. The goal was to provide aesthetic and demographic 'balance' to Har Homa.

By July 1998 the Israeli government had completed the confiscation of all the land, which was being held as 'absentee property' – a designation first created by the newly created State of Israel to appropriate land and property of Palestinians who were forced into exile in 1948. The goal was to prevent the owners, who as non-Jerusalem residents could be stripped of their rights to the land, regaining control of it (the land was farmed by about six hundred families from nearby Bethlehem before being confiscated).

In 2000 it was announced that construction in Har Homa was 'proceeding along at full steam and sales [of the settlement's 6,500 units] are booming.'[34] Taken along with the announcement that more than twenty new settlements had been approved by Barak – the first such approval of new settlements in years – the continuity in Israeli policy during the Oslo period and after, across the political divide, becomes clear.[35]

Har Homa's expansion continued throughout the decade. In January 2008 the construction of 1,000 new units was announced. According to *Ha'aretz*, when completed they would 'isolate Bethlehem completely from the Palestinian neighborhoods south of Jerusalem.'[36] What the narrative of Har Homa reminds us of is the centrality of Jerusalem in the settlement process during the Oslo era. As I explained in the last chapter, if there was one issue which sealed the fate of Oslo more than the others it was the inability of the two sides at Camp David to agree to an arrangement for Jerusalem.

In the context of the settlement process, what made Jerusalem so difficult to address was that there are several layers of conflict surrounding the city. The first concerns sovereignty; that is, who will control the city and what are the limits of its borders. The second concerns access to it; that is, who has the right to visit and otherwise move through it. And the third involves residency; who has the right to live within its boundaries.[37]

Within this general scheme, the layers proceed outward from the core conflict: the religiously explosive issue of who should have sovereignty over the Haram al-Sharif or Dome of the Rock, over the surrounding Old City, the neighborhoods of East Jerusalem, and then the 'suburbs,' or settlements built outside the traditional boundaries but which the municipal boundaries of the city were expanded to encompass.[38]

The expansion of a Jewish presence in East Jerusalem had as one of its primary goals physically severing East Jerusalem and its Palestinian neighborhoods from the remainder of the West Bank through the use of constant closures, the construction of four settlement blocs and with them bypass road construction during the Oslo period. The municipal boundaries of East Jerusalem were expanded to over ten times their pre-1967 area, with the twofold goal of maximizing the open land area available for settlement while minimizing the number of Palestinians included within the boundaries. So well understood has this 'maximum land, minimum Arabs' strategy become that Israel's most well-known rap group, Dam (whose members are Palestinian citizens of Israel from the working-class Palestinian town of Lydda), made this a refrain of one of their most famous songs, 'Born Here.'

Ultimately, the settlement process in and around Jerusalem would 'blur the distinction ... between Israel and the West Bank, and make the Green Line irrelevant.' It is worth noting in this regard that it was 1993 when West Bank and Gaza Palestinians were first prohibited from entering Jerusalem without a special permit. That is, the formal separation of Palestinian Jerusalem from the remainder of the West Bank began the same year as the commencement of the Oslo peace process.[39] A decade later, in 2003, the Israeli government would announce the construction of at least 3,500 new units in and around Ma'alei Adumim, which essentially 'sealed the fate of the Palestinian state.'[40]

Almost as soon as the al-Aqsa intifada erupted Israel began expanding settlements at a faster rate than in previous years. In January 2002, the first families moved into Har Homa. In April,

Israel reasserted direct security control over the entire West Bank, 'irrevocably undermining' Oslo in the process.[41] At the same time, Prime Minister Sharon won approval from the Bush administration of a 'security map' that closely resembled the 'Allon Plus' plan he helped devise for Netanyahu five years earlier. By late summer 2002, the settlers' council would announce a net gain of 17,000 settlers since the collapse of Camp David, while outposts continued to be built or transformed into civilian settlements.

By this time, it was clear, as the Israeli human rights organization B'Tselem wrote, that 'the drastic change that Israel has made in the map of the West Bank prevents any real possibility for the establishment of an independent, viable Palestinian state as part of the Palestinians' right to self-determination.' Indeed, since the Gaza 'disengagement,' the overall population of West Bank settlements had expanded some three times as fast as that of cities in Israel proper, creating a virtual 'population boom' in the West Bank.[42]

Symbolizing the extreme deterioration of the situation, in October 2002 the last group of Palestinian families abandoned the village of Yanun after succumbing to years of settler harassment. This marked the first time in recent memory that Palestinians had abandoned an entire village.[43] By the next year, according to the *Settlement Monitor*, 'The territorial division of historical Palestine has entered its most decisive stage since Israel's occupation of the West Bank and Gaza.' At this point, little more than an 'ersatz Palestine' could hope to be created, which led settlement expert Geoffrey Aronson to conclude that Sharon's almost completed master plan for a geography of Israeli settlement in the Occupied Territories had become a 'historical contribution ... on par with David Ben Gurion's creation of the state in 1948 and Menachem Begin's peace treaty with Egypt in 1979.'[44]

The matrix of control

As already noted, Palestinian leaders and citizens alike were well aware of the impact of the ongoing settlement program on their chances of establishing a viable state. As a senior Palestinian official admitted in 1995, 'If anyone looks at the present map of the West Bank ... he will find that the homeland looks like a body infected by smallpox.'[45]

It was during this period that successive Labor and Likud governments established a 'matrix of control' over the very territories that
Israel was obligated to hand back to Palestinians as part of Oslo.
According to Jeff Halper, the Israeli geographer who coined the
term, the matrix of control has 'virtually paralyzed the Palestinian
population' by creating several overlapping layers of Israeli control
of all aspects of Palestinian movement.

The first is the 'actual physical control,' that is, settlements and
their extended master plans, bypass roads, military installations,
industrial parks, closed security zones and control of nature reserves
and aquifers. The second layer is the bureaucratic and legal systems
that entangle the Palestinian population in a tight web of restrictions
that makes it difficult to buy, build on, develop or even have access
to their lands. Finally, the third layer involves the use of violence to
maintain control over the matrix, particularly the military occupation itself, and the large-scale imprisonment and violence that go
with it.[46]

Halper concludes that 'the only meaningful way to dismantle the
matrix is to eliminate it completely.' But already by the late 1980s
the West Bank was so integrated spatially into Israel proper that
separation was all but impossible. This is perhaps why then speaker
of the Palestinian Legislative Council, Ahmed Qurei', offered to solve
the settlement issue by leaving the settlements in place and treating
their residents as foreigners subject to Palestinian law.[47]

Another reason for the power of the matrix of control has been
the crucial role it has played in the normalization – at least to Israeli
and American eyes – of the occupation and the continued existence
of Israeli settlements inside the West Bank which it was meant to
ensure. The matrix enabled Israel to establish near-complete control
over the Occupied Territories through its interlocking mechanisms
with a minimum of brute force. With this web of control points
and corridors criss-crossing the West Bank – including hundreds of
roving roadblocks and checkpoints – the matrix became extremely
elastic and hard for Palestinians to map out, allowing Israel to rely
largely upon actions defined as 'proper administration,' 'uphold-
ing the law,' 'keeping the public order' and, of course, 'security' to
maintain and expand its hold on Palestinian territory.[48]

The last aspect of the matrix of control, involving the deployment of violence, has been investigated by Israeli architect and urban theorist Eyal Weizman. Through extensive research into the 'architecture of the occupation,' Weizman has demonstrated how Israel prepared to capitalize on the opportunity to degrade Palestinian capabilities for a viable state once the intifada began. This preparation involved not only conventional military planning but also an element of theoretical training that might seem more suited to graduate school than to war college. According to Weizman, Israeli commanders and cadets have been reading up on classic French post-structuralist thinkers like Michel Foucault and Gilles Deleuze.

From the insights of these seminal thinkers of contemporary left-wing politics, military strategists created a new 'art of war' in the Occupied Territories, adopting concepts such as 'inverse geometry' and 'infestation' to develop the much-criticized but militarily successful tactic of moving horizontally through walls and vertically through holes blasted in ceilings and floors in order to find and kill Palestinian fighters during the sieges of Nablus, Jenin and other locations.[49] Less overt but equally important have been the more or less permanent closure of the West Bank, home demolitions, large-scale imprisonment and torture of younger men, pressures on families to sell land, the use of collaborators, and in response to Palestinian violence the targeted killings and occasional reinvasions of territory formally ceded to Palestinian authority.[50]

Roads and walls

Settlements by themselves would not have been as effective in securing Israel's control over the territory of the West Bank. Two more spatial mechanisms of segregation have been crucial to the functioning and effectivity of the matrix of control: the bypass road network and the Separation Wall. The bypass road network was upwards of 500 kilometers in 2008, and has necessitated the confiscation of 40,000 dunams of Palestinian land for its construction and to maintain security along it. The network is crucial to the matrix of control because it divides the West Bank into 'cantons' (as Sharon has described it),[51] cuts off villages from their farmland, and allows for easy military movement throughout the territories while making it difficult for Palestinians to attack Israeli settlers as they drive to and from their homes and Israel. And supplementing this measure of control are the hundreds of checkpoints (more than five hundred as of 2006) on Palestinian roads, which control movement within and between Palestinian-controlled areas.[52] Most important, the bypass road network renders it nearly impossible to expand Palestinian towns, and, as important, access and utilize local water resources;[53] in so doing it effectively prevents the construction of a contiguous state and undermines the Palestinian economy by restricting Palestinian movement and impeding the flow of commerce and workers from area to area.

The power of the matrix of control was evident in the parameters of the only map presented to Palestinians by Israel during the Oslo period, in Stockholm in May 2000. The map cut the West Bank into thirds horizontally, while a vertical strip along the length of the eastern border of the West Bank (the Jordan river and Dead Sea) would remain in Israeli hands, much as it was intended to do in the original Allon plan.[54] The settlement blocs and bypass road network made this division not just possible, but inevitable.

The Stockholm map reveals how settlements occupied the core spatial nodes of the matrix of control, linked together by bypass roads that eased movement for Israelis, while various types of checkpoints (from mobile roadblocks to apparent international borders, such as the massive checkpoint at Qalandiyya) impeded Palestinian movement within 'their' territory. Israeli control over the vast majority of the remaining territory of the West Bank (60 percent of which was still Area C in 2000) ensured the permanent immobilization of the greater part of the Palestinian population.

This was the reality that confronted the two sides as they came to Camp David to begin their negotiations for a final agreement. In this context, as Halper explains, the popular impression that Barak made a 'generous' and even 'unprecedented' offer of 95 percent of the West Bank, plus considerable parts of East Jerusalem and all of Gaza, and that the Palestinians made a 'historic mistake' when Arafat rejected it, is, as I discussed in the last chapter, misguided. Viewed through the lens of the matrix of control, to the extent that Barak actually made a concrete offer several points must be considered.[55]

First, that offer did not include a final map, which made it hard for Palestinians to accept it as concrete. Second, when the amount of territory encompassed by the broader territory of settlements and roads, and with the area of the Dead Sea falling within the West Bank as part of the total area, is taken into consideration, Barak's offer was closer to 88 percent of the West Bank. Moreover, the territory under consideration included non-contiguous territory that would make it nearly impossible to establish a viable state; East Jerusalem would be a nearly unnavigable patchwork of neighborhoods surrounded by Israeli settlements, while a 'Greater Jerusalem' of some 250 square kilometers (just under 100 square miles) would dominate the entire central region of the West Bank.[55]

The wall and the end of Palestine

The ultimate expression of the matrix of control is the so-called 'Separation' or 'Apartheid' Wall, which is gradually creating the de facto border between Israel and the portion of the Occupied Territories upon which it desires to allow Palestinians to establish a state. In fact, the West Bank wall was the second wall in Palestine; the first had already completely surrounded Gaza and cut it off from Israel, the West Bank and Egypt a decade before.

The fragmentation of Palestinian society and economy was tied to the expansion and consolidation of Israel's settlement geography, and the wall was crucial to this process.[56] The idea for constructing a separation fence in the West Bank was first envisioned during Rabin's tenure, in 1995. True to the ideological divide between Labor and Likud governments, the Netanyahu government objected to the fence on ideological grounds because it would implicitly acknowledge the partition of at least part of the West Bank from Israel.

The Barak government pressed forward with it after the eruption of the al-Aqsa intifada. In 2002 the Sharon government approved the construction of a permanent barrier to effect a physical separation of the parts of the West Bank Israel was willing to cede to Palestinians from those that Israel intended to keep in any final agreement. Because the route of the wall repeatedly enters deep into Palestinian territory, the International Court of Justice declared on July 9, 2004 that it violated international law, an opinion that, at least in principle, the Israeli Supreme Court recognized a little over one year later, when it required the government to adjust the route of the wall to have less of an imprint on Palestinian territory.[57]

The wall's impact is not just territorial. In cutting off the expanded municipality of Jerusalem, and particularly East Jerusalem and the Jewish settlements built throughout it, from the rest of the West Bank, the socio-economic motor of a future Palestinian state has been permanently separated from the rest of its territory, turning much of the rest of the West Bank into peninsular dead-end areas that cannot achieve economic sustainability.[58] This is not hard to understand when the sheer size of the wall is taken into account: at well over two hundred kilometers long and placing over 8 percent of the West Bank on the Israeli side to the west, the wall will succeed in locating approximately 88 percent of settlers on the west side, while leaving 89 percent of Palestinians on the east, or inside, section of the wall.

As Palestinian sociologist Salim Tamari describes it, 'The problem is that the wall does not separate the Israelis from the Palestinians or the Jews from the Arabs, but it separates many Arab communities from the rest of the West Bank and it leaves the rest of the West Bank surrounded by Jewish settlements. So the wall is not between Jews and Arabs but between Arabs and Arabs.'[59] In that way, the wall will fulfill the long-term goal of the matrix of control – securing the main settlement blocs to Israel – but at the price of turning the West Bank into a larger version of the prison that has been erected in Gaza.[60]

Almost every Palestinian town or village lying in the vicinity of the Green Line or near a Jewish settlement has experienced the impact of all of the technologies associated with the matrix of control – settlements, bypass roads, home demolitions and land confiscations, and ultimately the wall itself. It is hard to appreciate the full impact of the matrix unless you've attempted to move through it. For example, driving from Jerusalem to Abu Dis, purportedly the future 'East Jerusalem' and capital of Palestine, used to take ten minutes. Today it can take more than three times as long, because an 8-meter-high wall has been erected at the entrance of the town from Jerusalem.

In the first phase of the wall's construction, in the early 2000s, it was about half its current height, and Palestinians used the rubble surrounding the wall to build a makeshift stairway that allowed them to climb to the top, and, if they were agile and thin enough, fit through a hole and get to the other side. Israeli soldiers standing guard near by normally didn't stop the movement of people across (taxis would wait to pick people up and drive them to Jerusalem), nor did they offer assistance to the many old women carrying heavy groceries or young women with babies on their backs who had to climb through it one or more times a day to buy food or conduct business on the other side.

But as more than one Palestinian would explain to me, 'at least then we could still get in and out of Abu Dis and to Jerusalem.' After the full wall was constructed it became impossible to move through it. Today it requires significant planning, and luck, for a Palestinian from Abu Dis, one of Jerusalem's historic villages, to make it to the city without a permit. Getting caught can result in arrest, fines and jail.[61]

The farming town of Jayyous (population about four thousand) is located in the Qalqiliya region of the West Bank, not far from Ramallah, approximately three and a half miles from the Green Line. Its situation is in many ways even more precarious than that of Abu Dis. In 1988 the Israeli military governor of Qalqiliya first declared 2000 dunams (500 acres) of Jayyous's agricultural land 'state land'; after eight years of appeals, an Israeli court confirmed much of the expropriation, which led over two dozen farmers to lose part or all of their land.

According to Sharif Omar, of Jayyous' Land Defense Committee, in 2002 the Israeli government began building its wall in Jayyous, which involved annexing 75 percent of the village's land (6,800 dunams or 1,700 acres), including six underground wells, for the neighboring settlement of Zufim. The land to be cut off was used to grow fruits and vegetables. In completing the wall around the village 520 dunams (130 acres) of land were destroyed, 4,000 trees were uprooted and 75 percent of the land was no longer accessible to villagers.

Moreover, 419 residents were subsequently denied permits to pass through a gate in the wall to access their land, while IDF soldiers regularly harassed villagers trying to enter their lands, also preventing them from grazing their flocks of sheep. But the most onerous burden was the demand by the military government that years of back taxes be paid (the residents had stopped paying after the PA took administrative control of the village and no longer required this income, and the declaration of parts of the land as a 'Seam Zone' – that is land located east of the 1967 border but west of the (proposed) route of the wall, which was considered a security zone and thus further constricted their access to the land, and, as important, its water resources.

The Israeli government has advocated the construction of industrial parks in the Seam Zones, which could employ farmers who lost their lands. The advantage from Israel's perspective is that Palestinians and Israelis could each enter the industrial park from their side of the Seam Zone but Palestinians would not have access to the other side, with, as I describe in Chapter 4, great benefits for Israeli and Palestinian (and in some cases foreign) owners of these factories.

Conclusion: the demise of the Second Israeli Republic

As we saw in the last chapter, one of the main bones of contention at Camp David was precisely how much land was going to be transferred to Palestinian sovereignty in the final peace deal. A range of percentages has been put forth by Israeli, Palestinian and American participants, and then commentators who have interviewed the main players, ranging from the low 90s to upwards of 100 percent (when land swaps for territory annexed to Israel are included in the figure) for the area of the West Bank being offered to Palestinians as part of the final deal. The discussion in this chapter, however, makes clear that even a 100 percent Israeli withdrawal with land swaps would not enable the creation of a viable Palestinian state because the 5 to 8 percent of the West Bank taken up by settlements and bypass roads have created a canton system that prevents the territorial contiguity which is the foundation for political and economic independence.

In light of this reality, Palestinians were right to conclude that Barak's '95 percent offer' at Taba in January 2001 was not viable on the ground, because it would not have dismantled Israel's matrix of control over the Occupied Territories. In its failure to do so, the independent Palestinian state that would have been established at the end of the peace process would have been mortally wounded at birth, if not stillborn. Palestinian negotiators understood this, which is why, as Ahmed Qurei' retells it, they displayed such *'summud'* – a highly charged word that when used by Palestinians has come to stand for remaining steadfast on the land no matter what the pressure to force them off – in the face of American and Israeli pressure to sign up to the final negotiating positions being suggested by President Clinton.[62] Arafat and his negotiators well understood that the 'day after Camp David' would be harsh indeed, but they also understood, finally, that at this late stage there was no longer any hope or possibility that structural problems in this agreement could be fixed in the next round.

In concluding his seminal 1987 study on the West Bank, Meron Benvenisti argued that 'on the seventh day of the Six Day War the Second Israeli Republic in the Land of Israel was established.'[63] What he meant was that Israel had by the eruption of the first intifada consolidated its control over the West Bank and Gaza in so tight a manner that the Israeli government effectively ruled the entire territory of Mandate Palestine, which could no longer be imagined as separate units politically or geographically, despite this being achieved through a complex combination of separation, segregation and integration.

Benvenisti describes the Second Israeli Republic as 'a bi-national entity with a rigid, hierarchical social structure based on ethnicity. Three and a half million Jewish Israelis hold total monopoly over governmental resources, control the economy, form the upper social stratum and determine the education and national values and objectives of the republic ... It is a "Herrenvolk Democracy." The only reason this has not been universally acknowledged is that the territories have not been formally annexed.'[64]

Herrenvolk Democracy is a termed coined by sociologists to describe a 'parliamentary regime in which the exercise of power and suffrage is restricted, de facto and often de jure, to the dominant [ethnic] group.'[65] The paradox of having a democracy that excludes some groups from participation is achieved by labeling those outside the *herrenvolk*, or 'the people,' as dangerous outsiders and even subhuman. Historically, the two countries most frequently associ-ated with this phenomenon are the pre-civil-rights-era United States and apartheid-era South Africa.[66]

While Israelis have been making the comparison between Israel and South Africa for decades, including in the country's leading newspapers, such a juxtaposition remains a politically charged enter-prise in the United States, as former president Jimmy Carter learned when he published his provocatively entitled book *Palestine: Peace Not Apartheid*. Carter defines apartheid as the 'forced separation of two peoples in the same territory with one of the groups dominating or controlling the other.' Under that definition, he admits, the United States practiced a form of apartheid during its 'separate but equal' years of segregation, and indeed, such segregation in many ways defined the situation of Aborigines in Australia, and other countries established as white European settler colonial movements. In most of these cases, settler states came into being in which millions of members of the indigenous population remained without political and civil rights, saw much if not most of their land confiscated, were spatially segregated from much of the space controlled by Europeans while being economically exploited by them, and were subject to a different and usually harsher set of laws than their European counterparts.

Each one of these components of apartheid exists in the Occupied Territories today. Indeed, the physical separation of Palestinians from Jewish-controlled territory is far more complete than what occurred in apartheid-era South Africa. This is crucial to the success of Israeli policies vis-à-vis Palestinians, because while in the pre-civil-rights-era American South, or apartheid South Africa, segregation occurred in the context of black movement through white spaces – thus there were colored drinking fountains or toilets, etc., next to facilities reserved for whites in locations through which both could move – in Israel non-citizen Palestinians are so successfully segregated from Jews inside the Green Line that such micro-segregation of people occupying the same broader space is not necessary. Palestinians are for the most part simply not part of the everyday physical and demo-graphic landscape of Israelis (and, as important, tourists).[67] And this reality points to another important fact – that Israel remains the only country of the pre-twentieth-century colonial settlement enterprises that still retains essential features of that paradigm.[68]

Israeli geographer Oren Yiftachel has developed the idea of Herrenvolk Democracy with his discussion of Israel as an 'ethnocracy,' or 'ethnocratic state.' According to Yiftachel an ethnocracy is a political system in which 'the dominant nation appropriates the state apparatus to further its expansionist aspirations while keeping some features of formal democracy.'[69] Basing his analysis on a detailed study of Israel's political, social and economic geography, Yiftachel concludes that the situation in Israel/Palestine is one of 'creeping Apartheid' that has produced 'a new phase in the evolving geography of Israel/Palestine ... that will entrench Israel/Palestine in a state of "neither two states nor one"' – exactly the kind of ambiguity that Benvenisti pointed out a generation ago was central to the achievement of Israel's goals in the West Bank.[70]

In this context, Yiftachel describes the post al-Aqsa intifada phase of the history of Israel/Palestine (particularly after the withdrawal from the Gaza Strip) as one of 'oppressive consolidation' that has followed 'decades of unabated Zionist demographic and spatial expansionism ... and uncompromising attempts to judaize the entire Israel/Palestine space.'[71] Despite its laudable rhetoric, the Oslo process could not bring an end to Israeli colonialism in the Occupied Territories. Zionism remains a 'deeply ethnocratic movement,'[72] while Palestinian nationalism, as exclusivist in its vision of territorial sovereignty as almost every other nationalism, is too weak to force a substantive transformation in Zionist/Israeli identity, whether by violence or by non-violent means. As long as these competing visions continue to dominate Israeli and Palestinian identities, the dreams of Oslo will be buried by the ongoing war over small seams of territory in the West Bank.

4 | The economics of failure: neo-liberalism and the new Middle East

Near the end of August 2007 President Shimon Peres, elder states-man of Israel and still Oslo's biggest booster, went on al-Jazeera's Arabic channel to discuss the potential for improving economic rela-tions between the two parties as part of a larger push to re-energize the peace process. He was asked by the interviewer whether there was a back channel for economic discussions in the manner of the political back channel that led to Oslo. 'The economic issue is an open issue,' he explained. 'In the world the only secrets are related to wars, not to development. In the past we heard but did not listen. Now we are listening because we have to do it.'[1]

It was not clear what motivated the president's admission that Israel had not paid much attention to the needs of Palestinians during the last decade and a half of negotiations. But now that Israelis – and presumably the Arab world – were listening, Peres wanted to discuss his plan to build an agricultural complex in the form of a Qualified Industrial Zone, near Jericho, another one for IT production near Jenin, and a joint Israeli–Jordanian international airport at Aqaba. These and more new endeavors could produce at least 135,000 news jobs for Palestinians, he explained; double that number if the service jobs that would be created along with them were counted.

As the quote from Peres above suggests, as long as the al-Aqsa intifada defined relations between Israel and 'the Palestinians,' Israel felt compelled to return to a war footing in which discussions about the future of the country would be made unilaterally and in secret. Now that negotiations looked set to begin anew, Peres argued, both sides could return to an open and honest discussion of the future of the country, particularly as it related to the Palestinian economy.

This chapter will show why, however sincere the president's intentions, the future of the Palestinian economy is likely to be determined in as closed and confusing a manner as it was during the Oslo period, when the lofty rhetoric of open borders and free trade was belied by much less comforting and claustrophobic realities on the ground.[2] To be sure, during the 1993–2000 period the Israeli and Palestinian economies became more integrated, in line with the global agenda of neoliberalism that guided the Oslo process. But along with greater integration came greater separation, and greater dependence of Palestinians on the far larger and more robust Israeli economy.[3] Indeed, the evidence presented in this chapter will demonstrate why, *pace* the rhetoric of Peres and the other architects of the Oslo process, the continued globalization of the Israeli economy during Oslo was accompanied, and in many ways made inevitable, by the continued de-development of the Palestinian economy. Indeed, the very economic mechanisms that were supposed to lead to greater integration of Israel into the larger MENA economy would weaken the economic position of most of the Palestinian workforce.

Globalization and the transformation of the Israeli and Palestinian economies

From the first accord signed in 1993 to the failed negotiations at Camp David seven years later, the Oslo process was as much about economics as it was about politics.[4] Indeed, the 1993 Declaration of Principles can accurately be conceived of as primarily an economic document, as two-thirds of it was devoted to describing the functions of eight PLO–Israeli committees, whose job it was to 'harness a degree of mutual economic interests that exceeds any agreement signed between the two states.'[5]

In the last chapter we explored the territorial component of Oslo and the continued conflict. Here we will see how the conflict's economic dynamics have interacted with its territorial dynamics, a reality that most powerfully hit home to me one day in late 2006 when I was driving to the Qalandiyya checkpoint, which is the main access route from Jerusalem to Ramallah and has the look and feel of an international border. As I drove along the wall about one kilometer from the checkpoint I passed an elderly woman walking along the road next to the wall, with a giant basket filled with vegetables. I offered to give her a ride and, after much discussion, she accepted. When we pulled up at the checkpoint and she opened the door to get out, all of a sudden the dozen or so guards who were standing around leisurely joking and smoking cigarettes grabbed their automatic weapons and, pointing them nervously at us, screamed at her in Hebrew mixed with Arabic to drop the basket and put her hands up.

On the one hand, the guards were no doubt afraid that she might have had a bomb, as a few months before a sixty-eight-year-old Palestinian grandmother had blown herself up at a checkpoint, injuring three Israeli soldiers in the process.[6] On the other hand, however, the idea of this Palestinian woman moving between Israeli and Palestinian space with goods to sell from one side to the other was equally threatening, if not to the soldiers, then to the larger system that they represented. The threat is indeed a long-standing one; as I sat frozen, trying not to move my hands off the steering wheel while soldiers ran up to the car, I remembered a discussion I came across between various Zionist officials over seventy years ago, in which the deputy mayor of Tel Aviv threatened to 'blow up with bombs' a Jewish-Palestinian market the British had opened on the border between Tel Aviv and Jaffa because it would be a conduit for 'Arab' goods to penetrate into a self-described 'closed' Jewish space and economy.[7] Despite half a dozen wars and intifadas, and hundreds of kilometers of walls, checkpoints and other barriers, the threat remains impossible to contain.

The distorted development of the Israeli and Palestinian economies

The roots of the political economy of Oslo can be traced to the late 1970s when, after almost three decades of state-led, quasi-socialist economic policies, Israel began a transition towards a neoliberal economy with the election of the Likud. The transformation did not start smoothly; indeed, during the next half-decade inflation spiraled into triple digits while Israel suffered other economic problems such as reduced growth and increased deficits as Israeli capitalism became realigned within the framework of globalized capital.[8]

A combination of the continued power of the labor movement

(through the Histadrut Federation), badly planned and executed policies, and the rapid increase in military spending brought on by the
invasion and occupation of Lebanon in 1982 caused unprecedented
stress to the Israeli economy.[9] By the end of 1984 the inflation rate
had skyrocketed to 950 percent, which forced significant budget cuts,
currency devaluation, wage cuts and price freezes.[10]

This structural transformation of the Israeli economy was cem-
ented by the Economic Stabilization Plan of 1985, which would mark
a 'turning point' for the Israeli economy.[11] The goal of the plan was to
bring down crippling triple-digit inflation, while taking a page from
Reagan and Thatcher by using the crisis to weaken the organized
labor movement in Israel. By adding an unprecedented degree of
fiscal austerity regarding social spending, privatizing state-owned
and Histadrut-owned firms, and deregulating the labor market and
broader economy, a structural shift in the political economy of Israel
was completed in which the business community had an unprecedented level of power to shape state policies.[12]

Better news was on the horizon, as during the period of Israel's
'closed war economy' the major state-owned industrial conglomer-
ates, such as Koor, Hapoalim, Leumi, Clal, and Israel Discount Bank
Holdings, had moved into military production, and as the cold war
was winding down, into the burgeoning Israeli stock market and
other sectors of the emerging liberalized economy. As Israeli economist Jonathan Nitzan explains, 'The intensification of the Israeli–
Arab conflict contributed to rising military spending and growing
arms exports. This burdened the aggregate economy, but much like
in the US, the ensuing "military bias" was highly beneficial, both
relatively and absolutely, to the leading arms contractors of the big
economy.'[13] As important, it led ultimately to a radical transformation
of Israel's political and economic structure, in which the government
gradually lost its central role in the economy. In this way, different
sectors of the Israeli economic elite were impacted by, and thus
responded to, the war economy in contradictory ways. But in the
final analysis, the most globalized sectors were able to adapt to and
even capitalize on both trends depending on the larger geostrategic
environment in which Israel was functioning.

It was during the latter half of the 1980s that the capitalist class in Israel underwent a metamorphosis, with global capital playing an increasingly prominent role in the economy compared with local capital and state investment. During this period, foreign firms increasingly replaced a purely 'Israeli' capitalist class as the dominant economic force in the country, at the same time as the momentary collapse of the military bias encouraged a reconcentration of capital and innovation into the country's soon-to-be-famous high-tech economy.[14]

This process was impacted powerfully by two events in the late 1980s: first, the outbreak of the first intifada in 1987, and second, the arrival of at least one million new immigrants beginning two years later with the collapse of the Soviet Union. Both put strains on the Israeli and Palestinian economies, although not surprisingly Israel was in a much better position to absorb the shocks, and ultimately was able to use both to strengthen its position vis-à-vis the Palestinian economy.

While Israeli economic indicators began trending upward in this period, the intifada and the post-cold-war immigration fed an increasing schizophrenia in Israel. An emerging Israeli 'yuppie' class began to push for a peace agreement that would expand their economic and cultural opportunities at home and abroad; while settlers channeled the full weight of the Israeli state towards realizing their religio-national interests through expanding the settlement system and deepening the occupation it entailed.[15]

Creating such a 'peace economy' had become a concern for Israeli, American and international academic and policy-making institutions, with the primary goals being to help end the Arab boycott and open lucrative emerging markets such as China's and India's. All of this reflected the needs of the new yuppie class and the increasing power of Israel's business sector and consumer-oriented middle class.[16] At the same time, however, Yitzhak Rabin, whose friendship with Israeli industry helped launch Oslo in 1993, well summarized the Israeli position vis-à-vis Palestinian development as defense minister in 1985: 'There will be no development in the occupied territories initiated by the Israeli government, and no permits given for expanding agriculture and industry which may compete with the state of Israel.'[17]

But there was another reason, little discussed by scholars, which was probably behind a change in Israeli policies towards the separation-segregation-integration model I introduced in the last chapter: after a generation of working in Israel, Palestinian workers were beginning to have enough savings to buy land in the Occupied Territories for themselves, which threatened the project of settling across the West Bank.[18] Closing them out of the higher-priced jobs in Israel while intensifying expropriations in strategically sought-after territory would together ensure that Palestinians would have tremendous difficulty regaining, and, as important, maintaining control over, their territory during Oslo. This process was exacerbated by the changing basis of the Palestinian economy from its historic agricultural basis to services (especially the public sector) and other non-productive occupations, whose prominence reflected the inability of the private sector to take a lead role in economic development during Oslo.[19]

More broadly, while some members of the Palestinian business class profited from this emerging dynamic, as a whole Palestinians were not part of the considerations involved in the transformation of the Israeli economy, and most Palestinian workers were impacted negatively by it. The Israeli establishment saw the Palestinian sector as existing primarily to serve its economic interests, and so 'Israeli authorities discouraged Palestinian business initiatives that might compete with Israeli firms.'[20] The absorption of surplus Palestinian labor into an increasingly liberalized Israeli economy created a two-way economic flow: cheap labor and commodities produced by intensive labor would be 'exported' to Israel, while in the other direction flowed more advanced and higher-value-added commodities produced by capitalist investment.[21]

In this model, no independent development or planning was allowed, leaving the Palestinian economy to rely on worker remittances from Israel and the Arab world, agriculture for local and Israeli consumption, and non-tradable services and construction, as the main contributors to the economy of the West Bank and Gaza Strip. There was little opportunity for Palestinians to put forth their own development strategies, determined by their own national interests. This situation would not change during the Oslo period.[22]

As Israel's economy became more integrated into the emerging architecture of neoliberal globalization, developing a 'peace economy' became a concern for Israel's business and policy-making elite. At least for the time being, and for those most closely aligned with the early 1990s vision of economic liberalism as the panacea for many if not most of Palestine's ills, the 'war economy had run its course' (as the CEO of Israel's Koor Industries put it).[23] There was a general understanding by the emerging generation of Israeli capitalists, and their government allies, that the conflict with Palestinians would have to be 'economized' – that is, transformed from a zero-sum conflict over territory, into a series of ultimately economic problems that could be addressed with the right policy prescriptions.

It is this need which led the Declaration of Principles of 1993 to do much more than establish a 'framework' for future negotiations between the two parties. A significant portion of the September 1993 accord dealt with economic issues, such as describing the functions of eight PLO–Israeli committees whose job it was to harness a degree of mutual economic interests that would help provide a foundation for a final settlement in the uncharted future.[24] The importance of the economic dimensions of Oslo is further indicated by the fact that the Paris Protocol on economic relations, which we'll describe in detail below, was signed before the Gaza–Jericho agreement that laid out the framework for Israeli withdrawal from Palestinian territories during the peace process.[25]

The problem was that in the process of being liberalized in the lead-up to, and during, the Oslo years, Israel was transformed from one of the world's most egalitarian advanced economies into one of the most unequal. And so, as Israel became wealthier, the economic well-being of a large share of the Israeli population deteriorated, particularly for Palestinian citizens and Jews from Muslim countries.

By the 2000s, the richest 20 percent of Israelis would earn twenty-one times more than the poorest, compared with only three times their income in the 1950s; indeed, from 1990 to 2004 only the top 20 percent of Israelis saw their income go up – but that rise was substantial enough to allow economists to argue that the 'Israeli economy' was growing, even though in reality it was only their economic position which carried the rest of the economy – but not the population – towards growth.

It is hard to overestimate the importance of the deterioration in the economic position of so many Israelis – particularly Mizrahim, new immigrants, and Palestinian citizens, each of whom in their own way had rebelled against the peace process by the end of the decade – in shaping the contours of Israeli identity during Oslo, and through it, in making it much harder for the ideology behind the peace process to bear fruit. If the success of the Oslo discourse within Israel depended on a large proportion of working- and middle-class Jews experiencing a gain in their economic position, then the reality of increasing poverty and inequality, coupled with a whittling away of the country's once-strong social safety net, would leave many of the supposed beneficiaries of the peace process unimpressed with its results economically, while remaining skeptical, at best, about the arguments for increased security and the value of exchanging a significant share of the country's biblical heartland for a vague concept of peace.

This problem emerged as a direct result of Oslo's economic rationale, which lay in the belief that economic cooperation and development would spearhead political understanding and ulti-mately peace, replacing 'antagonistic nationalist identities' with a larger identity shaped by 'a common enemy: poverty ... the father of fundamentalism.'[26] As important, the sound and 'clear' principles of the market economy would lead the way to this transition, proving that 'a high standard of living for all the people is the best promise for the stability in our midst.'[27]

To achieve this goal Israelis had begun planning for a 'new' Pales-tinian economy at the same time as the Madrid process began. Liberal academics such as Yossi Beilin and Yair Hirschfeld set up an 'Economic Co-operation Foundation' in 1991 to study how to move the Palestinian relationship with Israel 'from dependence to inter-dependence' as part of a 'new regional order' that would accompany the larger New World Order called for by President Bush.

In hindsight the grandiose plans for upgrading the Palestinian economy were never actualized in Israeli or international policy; but there was no surprise that such rhetoric should have been very attractive at the time, when asymmetric trading relations, regulatory and budgetary constraints, and declining access to natural resources dominated the horizons of Palestinian economic life. By 1993 the economy was in absolute disarray. The intifada had wiped out the modest yet steady gains of the 1970s and 1980s, which were in any case vulnerable since they relied on remittances from workers in Israel and the oil-rich Gulf states rather than on the success of Palestinian industries. As the first Oslo agreements were confirmed, Israel was strongly placed to continue using the Territories as a captive market in which to sell its products.

It would take the explosion of the first intifada, whose roots were strongly economic, for Israel's security establishment to consider the need to foster some level of Palestinian development and to allow more than a trickle of Palestinian agricultural products into Israel proper.[28] We can only really talk about the beginning of a 'national economy' in Palestine, however, in the sense of public infrastructure, state bureaucracy and a public sector, after the creation of the PA in 1994.[29]

After half a decade of the intifada, the birth of the Oslo process coincided with an intensive need to generate employment and improve productive capacity, especially in agriculture and industry, through heightened investments; enhance private sector growth; improve the quality of education training and health; and end the dependency on Israel. Palestinians held high expectations that the Oslo process would mark a transformation from economic dependence to 'cooperation' with Israel.[30] The problem, of course, was what cooperation would mean. As I alluded to above, many Israeli economists, following Rabin's political rhetoric, saw peace as entailing a 'separation' from Palestinians that would result in far fewer Palestinians working in Israel. On the surface this desire could be interpreted as reflecting security concerns, but this is only part of the story, and perhaps not the most important one.[31]

Another model for integration/separation presented itself around this time: the maquiladoras of Mexico, which were given a huge boost by the signing of the North American Free Trade Agreement in 1994. The establishment of maquiladora-like industrial estates on the borders of 1949 Israel would allow Israeli businesses to reap the benefits of having a captive, malleable foreign workforce located only miles from its main cities.

There were three primary reasons for the lack of development in the Palestinian economy during Oslo. At the most basic level, the problem lay in the powerful role of neoliberal policy prescriptions in shaping the development agenda in the Occupied Territories. Indeed, the new economy of the Palestinian Authority had the distinction of being one of the first economies 'designed from its very beginning by the policies and prescriptions of globalizing institutions.'[32] And these institutions, most notably the World Bank, saw the development of an independent Palestinian economy as a 'contradiction' of the signed economic agreements between the two sides.[33] Such thinking complemented the views of international institutions such as the World Bank and the IMF that the leadership could 'pursue "good policy,"' develop an 'independent macroeconomic policy,' and encourage private investment without ending the Israeli occupation.[34]

Not surprisingly, then, throughout the Oslo years 'the facts on the ground show[ed] that the Palestinian economy remained completely under the control of the Israelis.'[35] This brings us to the second problem, that the economic structure of the Oslo process clearly favored Israeli business interests at the expense of Palestinian (and Israeli working-class) interests. That globalization tends to favor the capitalist class over workers is not unique to Israel/Palestine, but its occurrence in the context of an ongoing occupation exacerbates the problems it causes because workers, and the colonized people more broadly, have much less power to resist and reshape the agenda than workers in a non-colonial setting.

The final and perhaps most devastating blow to Palestinian economic development was the frequent closure of the Occupied Territories during the Oslo period, which not only destroyed Palestinian exports, but also led to a severe decline of trade within the West Bank and Gaza. Below we'll discuss whether the closures were initiated primarily for security or economic reasons. Here it needs to be understood that they became increasingly a fact of economic life during the Oslo period, both comprehensive closures that restricted all movements into and out of PA-controlled areas, and internal closures, which restricted movement between Palestinian cities.

Without any substantive development, then, the billions of dollars pledged in international aid and investment during Oslo's first four years produced a situation in which more than two-thirds of Palestinians believed that the peace process had harmed the economy and produced only 'disappointing' results.[36] On top of the pressure from Israel, Palestinians continued to confront the emerging globalized system at a distinct disadvantage, as the terms of the accords, coupled with the advice of international aid institutions such as the IMF and the World Bank, further constrained economic development. The problem was well summarized by a 1997 IMF report, which explained that 'the economic agreements between Israel and the PLO in 1993–95 largely regularized the existing trade regimes of the West Bank and Gaza Strip.' In other words, the existing and highly unequal system of relations between the two sides was reinforced, rather than transformed, by Oslo.

In fact, the economy of the PA 'collapsed' in the wake of the first agreement, both because of the terms of the accords, and because the PA was corrupt, prey to nepotistic and monopolistic practices by its leaders, and saw its budget skewed significantly towards the payment of tens of thousands of members of various security services rather than towards developing the economy.[37] As another IMF report from 1998 explained, 'the revival of private investments hoped for at the time of the Oslo accords has not materialized.'[38] A year later, the average income in the Occupied Territories was 10 percent less than in 1993, and despite considerable external assistance, living standards were lower too.[39] By 2000 unemployment and poverty rates were estimated at 23 percent and 62 percent respectively, 350,000 children under five were suffering from chronic malnutrition, and personal income was dropping precipitously.[40]

Oslo and the birth of the new Palestinian economic elite

All told, during the Oslo years, far from reducing its power to subordinate or suppress Palestinian trade and agriculture in favor of its own producers and exporters, Israel actually enhanced its position in this regard.[41] This is why Palestinian exports fell more than 10 percent during the Oslo period, at the same time as expatriate Palestinians increasingly squeezed out and even displaced local entrepreneurs to create a new elite that was not rooted in the local scene. While Palestinian leaders committed themselves to promoting a free market economy that guaranteed a primary role for the private sector, what arose instead was a new state-made economic elite that had little incentive to create a sustainable, truly free market economy.

Overall, Palestinian economist Adel Samara concludes, the PA's 'unquestioning adoption of neoliberal economic policies favoring foreign capital at the expense of local capital has further weakened the local private sector and resulted in a kind of "development" that does not serve the population.'[42] Historically, the composition of the Palestinian elite was based on religious affiliation by certain families with the holy places and religious personalities. Service to the Ottoman state in various capacities as well as ownership of land and control of key local industries such as soap and citrus were also important. With the emergence of the PLO in the 1960s, however, a new elite emerged that was qualitatively different from the older 'notable class,' as it was composed of mostly middle and lower middle classes and included people from refugee camps and rural areas as well.[43]

The trend picked up speed after 1967 and into the 1980s, especially as the PLO's control over the Occupied Territories weakened after its ousting from Lebanon in 1982. With the 1993 Oslo accords, however, the stage was set for the demise of the emergent 'inside' elite as the 'returnees' from Tunis, who'd been marginalized during the intifada, reasserted their authority.[44]

A new class of entrepreneurs and businessmen began to emerge with various companies operating 'at a national level,' often as near or total government-approved monopolies, such as Padico (Palestine Development and Investment Limited) and Paltel, the telephone company. Indeed, at least ten different sectors of society participated in the emerging political and economic elites. Together they created an 'evolving kaleidoscope of linkages and social forces that included academic, security, government, political, industrial-financial-commercial, religious, local-municipal, tourist, real estate and traditional-family ties on the one hand, working within the framework of political, policing, bureaucratic, NGO and business

elites, and cross-cut by the often competing agendas of local, government sponsored and expatriate Palestinian capital.'[45]

Most important, under Oslo a new transnational regime emerged
within the Palestinian economy. On the one hand, wealthy diaspora
Palestinians dominated the economic sphere – in fact, the total
GDP of the members of Padico was about $20 billion, almost seven
times the $3 billion GDP of the Occupied Territories. But gradually
local business interests gained a foothold in the new Palestinian
bourgeoisie through the marriage of local family businesses and
expatriate capital investments, as well as from the establishment
of new incorporated companies and the creation of a Palestinian
stock exchange in 1996, many of whose original listing companies
had more than $200 million in capital.

It has yet to be satisfactorily explained how this much wealth
could fail so thoroughly to develop the economy and reduce poverty,
even with the ongoing problems associated with the occupation.
But some of the reasons are clear: a lack of rootedness on the part
of the expatriate capital that returned during the peace process; the
growing authoritarianism and personalization of power of the Arafat
government; the inefficiency, and in some cases corruption, of the
monopoly system; and the larger relationship between the PA, state-
owned companies, and the economic elite, which saw senior Palestinian politicians like Mahmoud Abbas and Ahmed Qurei' also function
as economic principals in a number of concerns, such as cement,
dairy and other basic consumer and commercial commodities.

With all these problems, however, what ultimately emerged in
Palestinian society during Oslo was not a typical comprador bourgeoisie that owed its existence entirely to the capitalist class of the
imperial/colonial power (in this case Israel). This is largely thanks
to the efforts of local business people, who quickly understood
that they needed to pool their resources, know-how, and political
strength. By the end of the 1990s, they had created various business
associations and joint enterprises in order to compete with the state
and the expatriate capital. But just when the local business sector
began to acquire political and economic clout, the outbreak of the
al-Aqsa intifada shattered their dreams of a more equitable business
environment.

TABLE 4.1 Real GDP growth in the Occupied Territories (percent)

1993	1994	1995	1996	1997	1998	1999
8.00	−3.00	1.00	3.00	8.00	7.00	−1.00

Source: Sébastien Dessus, 'A Palestinian growth history, 1968–2000,' unpublished research paper, World Bank

Whatever the structural problems of the emerging economic elite, Palestinian leaders understood their weakened position vis-à-vis Israel during Oslo and attempted to formulate various strategies in response – from boycotting Israeli-made goods to trying to amend the Paris accords unilaterally. At the same time Palestinian economic officials tried to 'orient [their] efforts in the direction' of greater trade with the Arab world, even though they understood that there was 'Israeli dissatisfaction with any Palestinian–Arab rapprochement.'[46] What did not seem to be recognized at the time was that the whole point of the economic component of Oslo was that Palestinian economic relations with the surrounding Arab world were to go through Israel, not independently of it.

This was clear from the terms and implementation of the 1998 Wye River Memorandum, which contained economic provisions recognizing the 'need to actively promote economic development in the West Bank and Gaza,' but which sought to make the closures system an 'economic fact of life' rather than ameliorating the hardships it produced, or allowing for a more equitable Palestinian participation in the partnership between Israel and Jordan in the industrial estates program.[47]

Not surprisingly, in the years after the signing of the 1993 framework agreement, the 'central story of the Palestinian economy' became one of deterioration. The situation was bad enough that already by 1995 Dr Hisham Hawartani, a delegate to the Paris accords, declared that the economic agreement had 'failed,' and called on the PA to demand its reopening. The next year Ahmed Qurei' would declare that 'an explosion is approaching,' explaining that 'the situation is very bad. The poverty is dangerous.' When the interviewer asked what had changed as a result of previous economic conferences, he replied, simply, 'Nothing' – a succinct but accurate summary of the situation three years after the commencement of the peace process.[48]

Two years later senior Arafat advisor Nabil Sha'ath would argue that Israel was 'seeking to destroy' the PA's economy; other officials and economists accused Israel of having 'blown up the Paris economic agreement' because of continued closures, and the secretary-general of the Council of Ministers called for the separation of the two economies. As one official explained by way of an example of the obstacles Palestinians faced, 'Israel's repressive policies are creating problems for us daily. With regard to the industrial estate in the al-Mintad area in Gaza and the agreement signed with the Israelis on the details, the Palestinian company implementing the project is hampered daily in order to delay the construction of the infrastructure needed for this project.' Together, such actions gave the impression that 'there are clear Israeli actions designed to create an atmosphere unsuitable for investment in Palestine.'[49]

Things looked different on the Israeli side, at least among Israel's political and business leaders. At around the same time Sha'ath was complaining about Israel's intentions towards the Palestinian economy, Peres exclaimed in an interview that Israelis were 'content' with the pace of the peace process, specifically because there was 'hardly any Israeli citizen who has not benefited from [it].'[50]

As the 1990s drew to a close, the Palestinian economy did improve somewhat because of reduced closures, returning to its historical growth trend of about 5 percent per year.[51] The situation would not improve much before the outbreak of the al-Aqsa intifada in September 2000 (although some commentaries claim that the 'economy' was improving before the al-Aqsa intifada erupted). And the fighting itself would produce disastrous results for the Palestinian economy; according to an IMF report, the situation was described as the 'worst … shock experienced … in 30 years … the recession is among the worst in modern history,' and as a whole the economic disasters would be sure to 'alienate a generation of young Palestinians.'[52]

By 2003 the economy was experiencing losses of over $5.4 billion in its gross national income, significant losses in the stock market and higher government deficits, and extremely high levels of unemployment, increasing poverty from 21 to about 60 percent across the Occupied Territories.[53] There was a 33 percent drop from 1999 to 2002; per capita GDP in 2006 ($1,130) was 40 percent less than in 1999. An already fragile economy was transformed from a track geared to investment and private sector productivity, to one sustained by government and private consumption, and donor aid.[54] In sum, during the 2000s the Palestinian economy entered a phase of sharp deterioration and then stagnation that exacerbated a social and political situation in which insecurity was a defining feature of life.[55]

Text and structure: why the economic vision of Oslo was bound to fail

Why did Oslo produce such a bleak economic outcome? There are two interrelated reasons; the first relates to the texts and terms of the accords, the second to the structure of the agreements as they were implemented on the ground. In both regards, the most significant economic document of the Oslo process was the Paris Protocol, officially known as 'The Protocol on Economic Relations between the Government of the State of Israel and the PLO, Representing the Palestinian People,' negotiated in Paris in the interval between the Declaration of Principles in September 1993 and the agreement on its implementation in the Gaza Strip and Jericho in May 1994.

According to the World Bank, 'The experience under the Paris Protocol illustrates the degree to which political and economic factors are intertwined ... favoring Israel in several ways.'[56] Specifically, both as a document and in terms of developments that occurred in its wake, the Protocol preserved the unequal relationship between Israel and the Territories. But at the same time, it was described as 'representing [the] new order' of neoliberal globalization in the Middle East. In order for this order to function, however, Palestinian as well as Israeli leaders and economic elites had to play their role, which the latter did by declaring their commitment to 'promoting a free market economy ... that guarantees the cardinal role for the private sector.'

What was not realized at the time was that the private sectors designed to benefit most directly from the accord were Israeli,

Jordanian American, and other foreign sectors, not the Palestinian economy.[57] Moreover, such was the contradiction between the Protocol's language and its impact on the ground that the purported 'new' era of 'open borders' was brought into being through the regular closing of Israel to Palestinian workers.

Such contradictions helped to preserve and even exacerbate the unequal relationship between the two sides during the Oslo years.[58] Specifically, this dynamic is what made it so difficult for the PA to achieve its 'highly cherished goal' of reducing dependency on Israel (a goal which, paradoxically, the World Bank still believed in 2007 was 'more accessible following the signing of the Paris Economic Protocol'). A modified customs union with Israel, established by the Paris Accord, was supposed to help realize this goal by enabling increased trade with neighboring economies, but the anticipated income convergence with Israel did not materialize because it limited Palestinian imports to relatively expensive Israeli goods, while taxes collected by Israel on the PA's behalf were not transferred to the PA (often in retaliation for continued Palestinian violence).[59]

Because of these dynamics, scholars exploring growth trends in the Occupied Territories could not detect a 'structural break with the pre-Oslo period' as a result of the Paris Accord, noting that what growth did take place in the Palestinian economy was tied largely (aside from international aid) to continued work in Israel and the number of closures imposed on the Occupied Territories each year, two processes on which Israel and the Palestinians had very different views and in which Israel held almost all the cards. As a 2002 World Bank paper described it, as a result of continued 'asymmetric market relations,' regulatory restrictions, institutional underdevelopment, and restricted access to natural resources, 'Palestinian growth under occupation was transitional rather than sustainable, as mostly driven by factor accumulation. Conversely, technological transfers from Israel, economies of adaptation and innovation, and economies of scale that could have been encouraged by a larger potential export market remained extremely scarce all over the period of occupation.'[60]

Since the status quo at the start of the negotiating process was 'highly disadvantageous to the Palestinians,' progress would come

only if Israel, the stronger side by far, made the majority of concessions in order to allow Palestinians to 'restructure our economic
relations with Israel, to separate as much as was possible in an
interim period, and to link our economy, as much as we could,
to that of the international community and to the Arab world.'[61]
Naturally, Israel had little interest in supporting these goals, since
they would seriously undermine its dominant economic position
in the Territories.

Palestinian leaders did not think that Paris was irredeemably
against their interests. As Sai'b Bamiyah, director of the Palestinian
Economic Ministry, explained in 1997, 'What is more important is
Israel's honest and sincere commitment to and implementation of
all the agreements, first and foremost the Paris agreements, which
contain numerous positive and negative points.'[62] 'The problem,' he
continued, was that 'there are Israeli measures which we experience
daily, especially with regard to the economy. The aim [of these] is
to destroy any positive aspects of the agreements and to place obstacles in the Palestinian Authority's way in order to prevent it from
achieving any direct trade plan or program with the world, initiating
internal development or developing the private sector.'[63]

Indeed, the path towards Israeli–Palestinian cooperation was not
just marginalized in the Paris Protocol; as important was the relega-
tion of the discussions of the mechanism of future cooperation to
the fourth annex of the 1993 framework agreement, which 'ma[de]
the entire process of development contingent on joint action of the
two sides and places development funds in a joint framework – which
is tantamount to subordinating development to Israeli control.'[64] One
clause in particular reflected this dynamic particularly well: Article IX,
paragraph 3, states that 'Each side will do its best to avoid damage
to the industry of the other side and will take into consideration the
concerns of the other side in its industrial policy.'[65]

While this sounds reasonable on its face, when one considers
the huge disparity in development between the two sides, in which
a de-developed Palestinian economy was facing one of the most
developed and powerful economies in the world (and certainly in the
region), what this clause meant was that Palestinians were prevented
from developing any new industries that could compete with existing

Israeli industries. Palestinians desperately needed economic autonomy, but this would have been 'inconsiderate' of Israeli interests,
and was therefore off the negotiating table from the start. This left
very little room for autonomous industrial development aside from
small-scale industries, usually agricultural in nature, that were considered 'amenable to Palestinian development' without threatening
existing Israeli industries.

One can ask whether the economic failures of Oslo were intentional
or the result of ill-conceived, naive policy prescriptions by the negotiators of the various agreements. It is not possible to answer such a
question definitively; what is clear, however, is that relations between
the two sides after Oslo remained 'strikingly similar' to the situation
before: Israel's dominance as a trading partner, the preservation of
the one-way trade structure that insured unimpeded Israeli access
to Palestinian markets, the continuing lack of Palestinian access to
Israeli markets, the excess of imports over exports, and the continuing limited access to international export markets.[66]

Hamas leaders well understood this dynamic, and in their 2006
election platform specifically argued that 'the economy and monetary system should be independent from the Zionist entity and its
economic and monetary system ... International economic agreements will be reconsidered and revised so as to serve the interests
of the Palestinian people, chief among them ... the Paris Economic
agreement, the Free Trade Agreement with the USA, the Partnership
Agreement with the EU, and the Economic Agreement with Egypt
and Jordan.'[67]

Here was another, less well-publicized reason for Israel to be
wary of an incoming Hamas government: its stated desire for greater
economic autonomy. Yet whatever their critique of the underlying
economic dynamics of Oslo, once in government Hamas was unable
to offer an alternative economic vision; indeed, the imposition of
international sanctions led by the United States and the European
Union against the government, along with Israel's continued refusal
to turn over a large share of VAT and other revenues owed to the
Palestinian government, meant that Palestinians' economic woes
grew even worse in the period between the Hamas victory in 2006
and mid-2008, when this book was going to press.[68]

Closing off the future

If the texts of the Paris Protocol and other agreements made it difficult for Palestinians to achieve the goals of greater economic development and autonomy, if not independence, Israeli policies on the ground during the Oslo period made it impossible. We saw in the last chapter how important the control of territory was to Israel's ability to strengthen its position in the Occupied Territories during the transitional period. From a strictly economic perspective, however, of greater importance than continued settlements and bypass roads was the policy of more or less continual closure imposed on the Occupied Territories through the entirety of the Oslo period.

Israel has long argued that the policy of closures was enacted and continues to be deployed in response to Palestinian violence. Yet closures began at least as far back as 1990, and were imposed more or less permanently to some degree beginning in March 1993, half a year before the Declaration of Principles was signed (and more than a year before the first suicide bombing).[69] They have never been lifted, although their intensity varies within the larger framework of three forms: the overall or general restriction on all movement of labor, goods and people, total closures that ban any movement in relation to terrorist attacks on Jewish holidays, and internal closures that restrict movement between Palestinian localities inside the West Bank.

The closures have served numerous purposes. They have helped reduce the risk of Palestinian attacks on Jews, although even here senior military officials have admitted that the extensive system of closures and hundreds of checkpoints have in many cases been 'useless' from the standpoint of security.[70] More broadly, 'The route of the Barrier, the expanding settlements and the closure regime and associated controls are severely damaging the social and economic structures of the West Bank and contributing to increased aid reliance, poverty and unemployment.'[71]

At the same time, the closures, along with checkpoints and other aspects of the 'matrix of control', kept continual pressure on the Palestinian population by increasing poverty and continuing the expropriation or destruction of land and natural resources.[72] More important, closures have been crucial mechanisms for ensuring the successful regulation of labor flows when other policies, such as the issuance of work permits, have failed to do so on their own. In this way closures have had an impact on the territorial dimension of the negotiating process, as the closure system has served as 'the most effective means of restricting the mobility of workers and demarcating boundaries between Palestinian and Israeli areas.'[73] Perhaps unwittingly, a 2007 World Bank report succinctly captured how, for example, the uprooting of an olive tree signaled both the 'grasping' of Palestinian land and the destruction of the economy, when it entitled its map of the West Bank 'Break up of economic space: West Bank Fragmentation Map.'[74]

Here we see how the various aspects of the 'matrix of control' serve both economic and territorial functions, in the process demonstrating their interrelationship within the larger Israeli strategies for managing the negotiating process and the ongoing conflict in a manner that strengthens its position. Specifically, the closures have most often not been about closing out Palestinian workers from work in Israel per se; rather, they are an important tool in the management of the Palestinian labor force.

What made closure work, from an economic perspective, was the arrival in the early 1990s of what would become hundreds of thousands of foreign migrant workers in Israel. Coming from around the globe – from Thailand, Romania, and the Philippines, as well as Africa and other eastern European countries – these workers had many advantages over Palestinians. First, when working within Israel they were cheaper and more reliable (because they would live inside and not have to commute from the oft-closed Territories), and second, like illegal workers everywhere, they were more easily exploitable than Palestinians, who received some benefits and were protected, at least on paper, by various labor laws.

They did not replace Palestinians completely, but they did shift the function of the workforce dramatically. Palestinians had been Israel's primary low-wage, manual labor force, especially in construction and agriculture, where they constituted between 40 and 60 percent of the workforce. Now they became a reserve labor force, or 'tap,' that could be turned on when labor demand was high, and otherwise could be left idle or used primarily in the settlements and industrial estates along the 'Seam Zones' between the wall and the 1967 border. According to Histadrut chairman Amir Peretz, they might even work for Israeli defense contractors as a low-wage labor force that could remain under Israel's security control. These policies would make the Palestinian workforce complicit, however unwillingly, in the cementing of Israel's territorial and economic dominance of the West Bank and Gaza.[75]

Palestinian labor flows during the Oslo years evolved in a way that reflected a process of redefinition of economic and territorial boundaries between the Israeli and the West Bank and Gaza Strip economies. And because the Palestinian component of trade between Israel, the Occupied Territories and the outside world did not change that much, the economic agreements worked more to manage labor flows to the economic and political advantage of Israel. As important, the policies of closures and restricted work permits kept a high level of social, economic and political pressure on the Palestinian population, which allowed Israel to continue to take a hard line in negotiations without fear that Palestinians could force a better deal.

Replicating foreign geographies in the Holy Land? Scholars and activists have long tried to make analogies between Israel's actions in the Occupied Territories and those of other settler colonial states, such as the United States or South Africa. I explored the latter comparison in the last chapter; here I would like to discuss two interrelated concepts applied to the Occupied Territories: cantonization and Bantustanization. If one takes them as strategic goals of the Israeli government during Oslo, then it becomes clear that from an Israeli perspective Oslo did not die with the eruption of the al-Aqsa intifada; instead, it has remained very much alive in that the core processes behind it – settlement, separation and then integration – have continued unabated during the last decade.

The idea of cantonization comes from the word canton, whose several meanings share a common notion of dividing one, larger and usually national territory into smaller units, as epitomized by the Swiss canton model, and most recently by the division of the former Yugoslavia into ethnically determined national cantons. In the case of Palestine, however, the cantons would be far too small, geographically isolated and economically dependent on Israel to support a viable state.

As important, all goods moving into Palestinian areas would also pass through one of three transit points under the control of the Israeli military. These three points help define the cantons – in the north, center, and south of the West Bank – that have been created during Oslo; and all movement of goods and people between these areas is under the control of the Israeli military. What this process reveals is how interconnected the economic and territorial components of the matrix of control have become.

Because of the unequal political dynamics involved in the creation of these cantons, scholars also use the term Bantustanization to describe the evolving political and economic geography of the Occupied Territories; this comes from the Bantustans, or homelands, set aside for South African blacks to live in during apartheid.[76] Adopting the term 'emphasizes the economic dimension of Palestinian "cantonization," especially the role of regulating labor flows in shaping the nature of the Palestinian entity.' Moreover, the idea of the Bantustan underscores both the ethnic homogeneity of the cantons, and their forcible closure from each other and the outside world, except as permitted by the occupying power.[77]

Getting the 'miller's share'

In essence, Oslo was built on an irresolvable paradox: both increased physical separation and increased economic integration. Of the many possible solutions the most appealing was that of the maquiladora-style factories along the borders of Israel and the West Bank and Gaza Strip (but located on the Palestinian side), where Israeli, foreign and to some extent Palestinian capital could profit from the labor of relatively skilled, educated and low-priced Palestinian laborers.

Palestinians too wanted separation from Israel – but for them it meant removing most Jewish settlements and soldiers from the Occupied Territories, while maintaining their ability to work inside Israel proper (among the biggest single sources of employment for

Palestinians). Both peoples naturally wanted greater integration with the surrounding Arab world.

In the maquiladora scenario, capitalists from both societies would grow rich, with Israeli industrialists getting the 'miller's portion' ('*maquila*') of the profits. The word maquiladora comes from colonial Mexico, where millers charged a '*maquila*' for processing other people's grain. Today the same term is used to describe companies that process (assemble and/or transform in some way) components imported into Mexico, which are, in turn, exported, usually to the United States. The managers and owners of the maquiladoras would earn the greater share of the profits gained from turning the border regions between Israel, the Occupied Territories, Jordan and Egypt into sites for low-wage and low-cost production of commodities for the US and European markets.

The germ of the idea of Palestine becoming Israel's Mexico emerged during the waning years of the first intifada, when the Association of Israeli Industrialists began to advocate for a peace deal with Palestinians as a way of stimulating and helping to globalize the Israeli economy. On the ground, the 'maquiladora scenario' began to appear even before 1993, as for much of the previous decade Israeli companies had been meeting with and even subcontracting their production to Palestinian firms.

A team of Israeli economists concluded that 'many of the economic ratios between Israel and the Palestinian economy are of the same order of magnitude as those between the US and Mexico,' as were many of the dynamics between them – including the low wages and excess labor supply in Mexico and the West Bank and Gaza Strip. And it seems that both Israeli and US exports to their respective partners grew significantly in the 1990s (actually doubling in Israel's case from 1987 through 2000 from $961 million to $1.8 billion). This was on top of Israel's increasing access to the Jordanian, Egyptian, Turkish, Central American, and Asian markets, which opened up as a result of the ending of the Arab boycott.

Indeed, the motivations of the Israeli political and economic elite in supporting Oslo were quite similar to those of their American counterparts in supporting NAFTA.[78] Both agreements emerged to deal with the aftermath of painful structural adjustments in the economy of the larger and more powerful neighbor – the United States and Israel. And so it is not surprising that Peres visited Mexico in September 1995 to learn more about NAFTA, or that soon after talk began of a new acronym, 'MEFTA,' the Middle East Free Trade Area.[79]

The main idea chosen to ameliorate this situation was that of a maquiladora-style 'industrial estate,' which would be financed by the European Investment Bank, USAID, and the World Bank. The first industrial estates were established in the Occupied Territories in the 1970s as a way for Israeli and Palestinian businessmen to engage in joint ventures and provide local employment for Palestinians. As recently as 2004, the estate at Erez, between Gaza and Israel, employed around four thousand workers in more than two hundred enterprises, half of them Palestinian owned.[80]

Many of these estates would be located in 'qualifying industrial zones,' or QIZ, areas designated and recognized by the US government as enclaves whose merchandise may enter US markets with duty and tax reductions or exemptions.[81] The first QIZ was the Gaza industrial estate at Erez in 1995. What is most important about the QIZ from our perspective is that through them the Occupied Territories served not just or even primarily as a market in and of itself, but more important as the conduit to the rest of the world – not just Egypt and Jordan, with whom Israel established QIZ, but even more so Asia, Africa and Europe. In this respect, we can see that if the Paris Protocol helped produce the QIZ, the QIZ in effect made the strategy of continual closure possible, and in so doing helped to create a new kind of space in the Occupied Territories, within the 'Seam Zones': gray zones that are neither fully Israeli nor fully Palestinian, to which each side has various levels of access and over which they exercise different and unequal measures of control.

Ultimately, the very act of closing the Occupied Territories off from Israel, and the world, enabled the opening of new, global markets for Israeli (and to a lesser but important sense for Palestinian) capital. This is why the QIZ were vigorously promoted as a model for the development of the Palestinian economy and a template for its integration into global markets.[82] They epitomized the Labor Party/Oslo concept of 'divorcing' Palestinians through the peace

process – what one study euphemistically termed 'friendly separation'[83] – except that here separation became segregation. With the
maquiladora idea, then, Israelis could 'Get Gaza out of Tel Aviv' (as
Rabin's 1992 election slogan put it) by bringing Tel Aviv, or at least
its businessmen, to Gaza.

Even at the height of the al-Aqsa intifada there was talk of reopening some of the zones. But even had they reopened, there was not
much chance that they would improve the lives of most Palestinians
because Israelis were also engaged in similar QIZ agreements with
Jordanians, against whom Palestinians would have a hard time competing. As one Jordanian expert on the QIZ explains, 'Palestinians
are worse off' because jobs that could have gone to them were now
going to Jordan. Not to Jordanians, however. Instead, in a perfect
example of how neoliberal policies so often have the opposite of
the intended effect, Jordanian capitalists have found it more cost
effective to bring in even cheaper and more malleable workers from
Bangladesh and other extremely poor countries. 'Two thirds of the
labor force in the QIZs is non-Jordanian, mainly from Far Eastern
countries. There are virtually no linkages between the QIZs and the
rest of the economy.'[84]

Conclusion: the spectacle of the Oslo economy

Traditionally, the failure of the Palestinian economy has been
blamed on Palestinian terrorism and the closures Israel imposed
in response to them. The dynamics of the QIZ zones and industrial
estates, and the larger political economy of neoliberalism in Israel/
Palestine which they reflect, demonstrate more complex processes
at work. These processes ensured the preservation and in many
cases intensification of the imbalance of power between Israelis
and Palestinians within a system of global and local interests that
were incompatible with the needs of the majority of Israelis and
Palestinians, whose lives were determined by them on both sides
of the Green Line.[85]

All these problems were elided, however, in the optimistic read-
ing of the Paris Protocol and the larger economic component of
Oslo made by the international community, as well as Israeli and
Palestinian negotiators, all of whom assumed that the two economies

would develop in tandem in a manner that transformed economic autonomy into political sovereignty.[86] And here the failure of the Protocol to account adequately for the problem of sovereignty on the Palestinian side only reflected the larger failure of the Oslo process in the same regard. It also reflected the PA's unquestioning adoption of neoliberal economic policies favoring foreign capital at the expense of local capital in pursuance of a kind of 'development' that does not serve the population.[87]

Perhaps the best discussion of the economic dimensions of Oslo and the commingling of the discourses of globalization and peace is offered by Palestinian economist Adal Samara. Samara argues that Palestinian experiences of globalization were determined by two factors: first, Israel's prevention of the development of the Palestinian economy, and second, the embrace by Palestinian elites of neoliberal globalization, to which they – if not the population at large – 'adapted with ease despite the problems of other countries.'[88] This created a situation in which the West Bank and Gaza Strip saw an economy 'without a center,' and 'without the ability to place restrictions on capital,' completely open to the outside, dependent on Israel and its products.

Globalization, as defined by Israeli capital, has dangerously weakened the economic and political fabric of Palestinian society, making the prospect of independence and a viable state harder to imagine even without the territorial conflict. As we'll see in the next chapter, the donor industry – from the international financial institutions like the World Bank, the IMF and USAID, to many major American and European NGO funders – has, intentionally or not, facilitated this negative process. The process this reflects was grounded in a 'myth of Palestinian development' that made possible both the Oslo process and its innumerable failures.[89] This myth doesn't just mask a lack of development of the Palestinian economy; it obscures a process of 'de-developing' Palestine in order to ensure a weakened Palestinian polity for the foreseeable future.[90]

Naef Hawatma, founder of the guerrilla/terrorist group turned political party, the Democratic Front for the Liberation of Palestine, points out that few if any of the developments described in this chapter were unknown to scholars and activists on the ground. In fact, they were predicted from the start of the process. Borrowing – perhaps subconsciously – concepts from the Frankfurt School founder Theodor Adorno and the French postmodern philosopher Jean Baudrillard, Hawatma argues that 'perhaps one can say that Oslo was a spectacle, produced for the consumption of the very yuppie classes whose interests it was meant to serve.' Hawatma believes that, like the culture industry Theodor Adorno and Max Horkheimer excoriated more than half a century ago for feeding the addiction of 1950s consumerist American culture, the neoliberal peace process 'perpetually cheated its consumers of what it perpetually promise[d].'

Yet it had them coming back for more, all the while reminding Palestinians that 'the PA will need to take steps to create preconditions promoting private investment in order to reduce the high rate of unemployment.' In the spectacle that was Oslo, no one bothered to ask whether such an action, to the extent that it was even conceivable, could compensate for the structural violence of the Oslo accords and the continued occupation and violence during the peace process.

5 | Religion, culture, and territory in a globalized context

As we saw in the last chapter, perhaps the most important political division within Palestinian society during Oslo emerged between the PLO, and particularly Fatah, and Hamas. The opposite positions on the peace process were the primary reason for the split between the two groups, but their divergent views on the place of Palestine and Palestinians within the emerging neoliberal global system – its cultural as well as economic aspects – also played a role in the conflict between them which emerged during the 1990s, and became increasingly bitter and even violent in the mid-2000s.

We have already explored Hamas's military and economic response to the unfolding negotiating process. This chapter looks at Hamas, the Israeli settlement movement and the ultra-Orthodox Israeli political party Shas. All three have been religiously grounded social movements that seek to bring about transformative change in their societies. While existing on opposite sides of the religious and national divide, the three movements represent perspectives on the New Middle East that are held by Israelis and Palestinians for whom the upbeat vision of Oslo's boosters was either contradicted by economic and political realities on the ground, or violated fundamental religious tenets regarding the right to sovereignty in Israel/Palestine and what kind of culture should ground each society in the future.

Hamas and the settlement movement contributed directly to the violent confrontation and hostility between Israelis and Palestinians, although each at moments laid out visions of the future that could include coexistence between the two peoples (for the settlement movement pioneers of Gush Emunim, Palestinians could receive full civil rights, including the right to vote, hold office and serve in the IDF in a greater Israeli state, while for Hamas Jews could live as a protected minority in Palestine without fear of being 'thrown into the sea'). Shas's impact on the peace process and Israeli society more broadly has been more oblique, shifting several times during the last two decades, with significant differences in the attitudes of the leadership and the rank and file.

Ultimately, all three movements have contributed in important and ultimately negative ways to the history of Oslo: Hamas with its opposition to the peace process and use of terrorism, the settler movement in pushing for unrestricted settlement throughout the Holy Land and the violence attendant on that process, and Shas with its change of heart against the peace process after initially providing the crucial political cover that allowed the Rabin government to sign the first agreement. In this chapter we will explore the role of globalization in shaping the attitudes and policies of all three, based on the reality that religion constitutes a foundational culture response to the experience of globalization throughout the world today.

Culture, religion and globalization

Israel/Palestine is often seen simply in the light of political violence and unilateral policy. Yet culture and cultural globalization have also been crucial. They shaped Hamas's ideology and justifications for opposing the peace process, and to various degrees would, as part of the larger experience of neoliberal globalization in Israel/Palestine, impact the development of the settlement movement and Shas as well.

What scholars term 'political Islam' – that is, Islam specifically engaged in trying to bring about social and political transformation in society based explicitly on Islamic principles – emerged as a source of political discourse and action in the Muslim world began in the late Ottoman period, and picked up steam after the establishment of the Muslim Brotherhood in Egypt in 1928 (the movement spread to Palestine in the 1930s). Islam was a handmaiden to the nationalist ideologies and identities that emerged in the Middle East during this period; particularly in Palestine, where the Grand Mufti of Jerusalem, Haj Amin al-Husseini, was the putative leader of the nationalist movement during the Mandate period.[1]

But however important, Islam was only one component in the larger nationalist identities that were being forged during this time. Christians (and in Iraq even Jews) played a role as well in developing what were for the most part secular nationalist movements in which religion would be used instrumentally, when at all, to justify ideologies and policies that had little grounding in Islam. Three events helped Islam to become the defining characteristic of most identities in the MENA. The first was the humiliating defeat of Egypt, Jordan and Syria in the Six Day War of 1967, which discredited the secular Arab nationalism of the regimes in Egypt, Syria and Iraq. The second was the spread of Salafi doctrine and influence financed (through mosques, universities and other social institutions) by the oil-rich Gulf regimes after 1973. Finally, the success of the Islamic Revolution in Iran inspired Palestinian militants, who have received steady financial, moral and (indirectly, through Iran's relationship with Hezbollah) logistical and military support from the country since the Khomeini period.

The rise of the Islamic Resistance Movement – Hamas

If Islamism is a global phenomenon, Palestine still has a unique character, resulting from nationalist considerations that developed in the face of occupation (first British, then Israeli). I discussed the role of Islam during the late Ottoman and Mandate periods in Chapter 1. Hamas was clearly inspired by the Islamic politics of this period. Not only does it define itself in Article 6 of its charter as a 'distinct Palestinian Movement,' as opposed to referencing the global *umma* (Islamic community), as do many other Islamist groups (ideologically if not in practical political terms), Hamas is also directly inspired by the Islamic-grounded resistance movement started by Iz al-Din al-Qassem in 1935, whose attacks on Jews and British forces, and subsequent 'martyrdom,' inspired the movement's military wing (which bears his name).[2]

Hamas grew out of the Palestinian Muslim Brotherhood, whose Gazan and West Bank branches had very different experiences under Egyptian and Jordanian rule between 1948 and 1967. During the first two decades of the Israeli occupation, the Palestinian Brotherhood worked to build its infrastructure and organization within

Palestinian society, 'preparing the liberation generation'[3] according to a cultural-educational model. The goal of such preparation was 'to launch a comprehensive effort at cultural renaissance designed to instill true Islam in the soul of the individual and, following that renaissance, to embark on the path of liberation.'[4]

These words are from a book entitled *Signposts along the Road to the Liberation of Palestine* (*Ma'alim fil-tariq ila tahrir filastin*), a clear allusion to the activist/militant philosophy of Muslim Brotherhood ideologue (and spiritual godfather of al-Qaeda) Sayyed Qutb, which was itself based on a strongly cultural politics. To further this end, the al-Mujamma' al-islami (Islamic Center, Gaza) was established by Hamas founder Sheikh Ahmed Yassin in 1973. Al-Mujamma' provided a network of social services that functioned as a parallel system to the meager (or absent) Israeli occupation services, which were reduced even further with the liberalization program of the late 1970s.[5]

The Mujamma's focus on religious and social activities allowed it to garner public support without appearing to threaten either the PLO's hegemonic position among the Palestinians or the Israeli occupation authorities.[6] So successful was this strategy that the Israeli intelligence services secretly funded the movement – including, in its early days, Hamas – as a way to counterbalance the hegemony of Fatah, whose explicitly nationalist agenda was a more direct threat to Israeli control of the Occupied Territories.[7]

The 1980s, especially after the eviction of the PLO from Lebanon in 1982, witnessed the reassertion of Islam in Palestinian society through several avenues: the provision of a vast range of important social and educational services on the one hand (about which more will be said below), and 'more disturbingly, through the use of force, beatings, public hate campaigns and acid attacks.'[8] Victims included not just women dressed 'immodestly' but academics who were considered atheists or 'communist and immoral.'[9]

This attitude changed with the eruption of the first intifada. The more militant activists in Gaza recognized their opportunity to seize the initiative within Palestinian society, and Hamas as an organization was established in December 1987 by Yassin and several other members of the Brotherhood who wanted to take a more activist stance against Israel. With its grassroots base, religious grounding and militancy, the movement quickly challenged the Tunis-based PLO's attempts to manage the intifada on its traditional nationalistic terms. Eight months after the intifada started, in August 1988, the organization presented an Islamic platform that blatantly appropriated the PLO's national values, as set forth in its charter, cast in Islamic terminology and an Islamic belief system.[10]

Hamas's structure In the five years between its founding in 1988 and the dawn of Oslo, Hamas constituted a growing and unprecedented threat to the hegemony of the PLO on the ground in Palestine. Its popularity went through several ups and downs – lows in the first three years of Oslo, an upturn after Netanyahu's election, a downturn again in the years leading up to the al-Aqsa intifada and then a growing popularity that culminated with its unprecedented election victory in the 2006 national elections.

Hamas's activities could broadly be divided into two spheres: jihad and public activities. In pursuance of these two broad agendas, the movement developed a multi-part structure: *Da'wah* – that is, recruitment of new members and gaining broader public support; popular violence and terrorism, first through the *mujahidun falastinun* (Palestinian holy warriors), and later through the Iz al-Din al-Qassem brigades (whose first victims, in 1991, were not Israelis, but rather Palestinian collaborators); security, or *Aman*, which involves gathering intelligence on suspected collaborators and the use of 'shock troops' (*al-Suad al-Ramaya*) both to interrogate and kill suspects, and to enforce strikes and boycotts of Israeli goods; and finally a publications bureau, *al-'Alam*, which produces and distributes leaflets and propaganda.[11]

Hamas's leadership structure is complex, and has usually been shrouded in some degree of secrecy. The movement has always had a two-part leadership structure with responsibilities – usually with coordination but sometimes with tension – divided between the 'inside'/West Bank–Gaza leadership and the Damascus-based exile leadership. This dynamic became more complicated when Israel killed long-time leader Ahmed Yassin, and then his successor, Abdel Aziz Rantisi, within a month of each other in 2004.

After their assassination a loosening of Hamas's previously rigidly hierarchical structure occurred. When it finally decided to join the Palestinian political process, Hamas even published the names and photos of its new senior leadership, during the 2006 election campaign, in order to demonstrate its seriousness about governing Palestinian society.[12] By early 2008 it was hard to tell who had the ultimate decision-making power between PA prime minister Ismail Haniya and the Palestinian branch, and the Damascus-based Khaled Meshal, who is known to be more extreme, and whose attempted poisoning by Israeli operatives in Jordan in 1997 led to Israel's releasing Sheikh Yassin from his Gaza prison in order to avoid a diplomatic incident with Amman.[13]

As I explain in more detail in the next chapter, a broad network of charity associations (Jamayath Hiriya) and committees (Lejan Zekath) operates in the Territories, on the basis of two Jordanian statutes: the Charity Association and Social Institutions Law, and the Charity Fund-Raising Regulations. Hamas makes extensive use of many of these charity associations and committees, which (together with the mosques, unions, etc.) also serve as the overt façade of the organization's activity, operating parallel to and serving its covert operations. Ideologically and pragmatically, the movement places great emphasis on charity (*zakat*), which serves to bring the people closer to Islam and, as a result, to broaden the ranks of Hamas.[14]

Hamas devotes much of its estimated $70 million annual budget to an extensive social services network, which includes schools, orphanages, mosques, healthcare clinics, soup kitchens, and sports leagues. According to Israeli Hamas expert Reuven Paz, 'approximately 90 percent of its work is in social, welfare, cultural, and educational activities.'[15] Together, they have provided crucial aid to Palestinian society in the context of the failure of either the Israeli government or, since Oslo, the PA to provide adequate levels of any of these services. Moreover, such activities enabled Hamas to increase its power within Palestinian society at the expense of the Palestinian Authority, which could not reconcile the objectives of fulfilling its security commitments to Israel (which demanded a sprawling police sector that ate up much of its budget) and containing any viable opposition to Oslo (peaceful as well as violent), while continuing to press for an independent Palestinian state.

Ultimately, Hamas's social activities laid the groundwork for its still-unfinished transformation from a resistance movement into a political party. They also served as good propaganda to convince the foreign press of its strong social base, and for the arguments of its leaders that the movement was far more than just a terrorist organization, as reporters or researchers who've gone on 'Hamas tours' in Gaza or the West Bank will tell you.[16]

However important its social activities, however, Hamas always perceived its central role as being to direct violent resistance to the Israeli occupation. This is clear from Hamas's earliest leaflets, where it justifies its violent strategy by explaining that 'it is necessary that the Jews understand: despite their chains, their prisons and their detention centers ... despite the ordeals that our people are enduring under their criminal occupation ... the uprising constitutes the manifestation of rejecting the occupation and its pressures ... rejecting the politics of expropriation of land and the creation of settlements ... rejecting the politics of repression conducted by the Zionists.'[17] Such language reflects the movement's overt antagonism towards, if not 'blind hatred' of, Jews, who are seen as synonymous with Zionists.[18] At the same time, however, Hamas's rhetoric usually stops short of advocating mass murder (as does al-Qaeda), and its discourse explicitly makes a place for Jews to remain as a protected minority within the movement's vision of a democratic Islamic state.

Hamas's violent opposition to Israeli rule has never been justified solely by nationalist considerations. Religious references, such as to 'Muslims in the land of the night voyage of the Prophet,' or 'Descendants of Ja'far and of Abu Abayda,' as well as the frequent discussions of the USA and its role as a global imperialist and 'crusader' power bent on destroying Arab/Muslim unity, all demonstrate that culture – and specifically a kind of cultural discourse typical to Arab/Muslim writings on globalization – was always a central component and driving force behind Hamas's identity, ideology and strategies. Indeed, in the same way that the PLO reshaped the goals and strategies of Palestinian society a generation before, Hamas also, beginning in the late 1980s, 'sowed the seeds for a markedly significant political transformation in the society.'[19] For some observers, it seemed that Hamas appropriated wholesale the fabric of Palestinian nationalism;

others believed its use of that language was merely tactical, and that its larger aims still revolved around creating an Islamic state in the more universalist mode of traditional Islamic thinking.[20]

Yet whereas the PLO stressed 'national liberation' as its *raison d'être*, Hamas from the start described itself as struggling in order to defend the 'Muslim person, Islamic culture, and Muslim holy sites ...'[21] Hamas's Islamization of Palestinian nationalism, and by extension of Jewish claims on Palestine, was accompanied by nationalizing and territorializing the movement's pan-Islamic ideals, producing an integration of religion and nationalism that was a common response to the lack of security – economic, political, territorial and even 'ontological' – associated with the onset of contemporary globalization in many societies, including Israel/Palestine.[22] This tendency was uniquely inflected, however, in serving as a clear riposte to the Israeli strategy of integration through separation and segregation as it developed during the Oslo period.[23]

Another militant group, Islamic Jihad, was founded several years prior to Hamas by a breakaway faction of the Brotherhood. While also focused explicitly on Palestine, its ideology is closer to that of the Egyptian Islamic Jihad, whose founder, Ayman al-Zawhiri, is today the second-in-command of al-Qaeda. It is not surprising that it is considered even more extreme than Hamas, as leaders argue that 'it is futile for the Islamist to dream of complete independence of a comprehensive civilizational revival while the center of colonial operations remains fully entrenched, fully fortified and fully equipped in Palestine to do what it pleases, and hell-bent on imposing "the Israel era" in our region.'[24] This thinking joined the battle for Palestine with a battle against the colonial legacy. In this sense it was also against the nationalism that inherited this legacy; and in a sense against a modernity that could not have been born apart from colonialism, and cannot be continued except through globalization.[25]

During the Oslo period (1993–2000), Hamas's polemics were directed not just at Israel or Arabs who didn't support its actions. Its ideologues also hurled accusations of 'infidelity' against Arabs or Muslims who had abandoned their culture, and, like other Muslim critics of globalization, have warned Palestinians about the need to raise Palestinian morals to defeat Israeli attempts to create a 'corrupt ... effeminate and sluggish young generation.'[26]

And so it is not surprising that the argument that the 'peace process' intends 'to Zionize the Palestinian problem and the Arab nation as well as the Islamic world' is also a staple of such literature; particularly of critiques of Shimon Peres's vision for a New Middle East in which Israel is the spearhead for the renewed 'cultural invasion' of the region by amoral hyper-consumerist capitalism.[27] The 'new American order' was of equal concern; one of the first Hamas leaflets argued that anyone who looks towards America 'won't reap from America and its policies anything but a mirage because it [supports] Israel with money and weapons and [is] against us in everything.'[28]

Together, these arguments created a potent cultural brew that raised public/popular consciousness about the severity and scope of the threat facing the people. They concerned more than just the Israeli usurpation of Palestinian land. The United States, described as the 'world policeman' of the new global order, was also a threat to Palestinians, and to Muslim civilization more broadly, through its desire for human, economic and military power. Against the potential for 'unbelief and apostasy against faith,' Palestinians were urged to transform 'the process of education' (as a leaflet critiquing the Balfour Declaration described it) in order to 'unify the national leadership' through religion.

For Hamas leaders, as part of its 'mechanisms of domination,' imperialism 'seeks to establish its hegemony over the region in order to serve its own political and economic interests and to nip in the bud threats to its hegemonic position emanating from the cultural aspects of the Arab nationalist movement and from a potential cultural renaissance in the region.'[29] Most interesting in this regard is the explanation of one senior Hamas figure that 'we know that Palestine will become a bridge for Israel to penetrate the Arab world economically, politically and culturally and we worry that one of the secret provisions is that the PLO have accepted to be a tool of oppression against the Islamic current as is now the case in Tunis, Algeria, Egypt and throughout the world ...'[30]

The notion of 'penetration' is crucial in Arab/Muslim critiques that focus on culture because it reveals the intensity of the feeling of being invaded. Indeed, the act of penetration was crucial to the mechanism of imperialism across the Middle East, as Europeans sought to penetrate the cultures, and the very bodies, of the peoples they colonized with new ways of living and behaving.[31] Viewed from this perspective, Hamas's call for a *'Falastin Islamiyya min al-bahr ila al-nahr'* (Islamic Palestine from the sea to the [Jordan] river) can be seen not just as a nationalistic or religious slogan, but also as representing a cultural stand against the forces of secularism and globalization.[32]

If all these arguments provide only circumstantial evidence of the important role of culture in the Hamas discourse and ideology, its introductory memorandum specifically states that 'the struggle ... in Palestine is a *cultural struggle* for destiny that only can end when its cause, Zionist settlement in Palestine, stops. The belligerent Zionist settler movement complements the Western design to separate the Islamic ummah from its *cultural roots* and to impose Zionist-Western hegemony over it through the realization of the Greater Israel plan, so that it then can dominate our entire ummah politically and economically.'[33]

The focus on cultural struggle is important here, because it demonstrates the understanding by Hamas ideologues of the relationship between the continued struggle over territory and the newer struggles over identity, particularly of the attempt by Israeli leaders to convince Palestinians that independence was less important than creating a neoliberal economy and its attendant consumerist culture. In this regard culture is seen as the engine or vehicle for Western – and through it Israeli – political and economic hegemony.

Indeed, the memorandum quoted above also describes Israel as 'the Zionist enemy, who is associated with the Western project to bring the Arab Islamic ummah under the domination of Western culture, to make it dependent on the West, and to perpetuate its underdevelopment.'[34] Thus Hamas argued at the signing of the Oslo accords that the PLO had 'relinquished all our lands, traditions, holy places and culture which Israel has usurped.'[35] In a period in which the dominant political discourse was one of a peace process, it is not surprising that culture – and the perceived loss of identity and the intellectual and ethical invasion of the West – would become more central given its original understanding of the Palestinian struggle as being culturally rooted, and because of it being 'a question of life or death and a cultural struggle between the Arabs and Muslims on one side and Zionism on the other.' Even more, it was a 'fateful civilization struggle ... Th[e] aggressive [Zionist] enterprise comple-ments the larger Western project that seeks to strip the Arab Islamic nation of its cultural roots,' against which a 'wide comprehensible reform' and a 'renaissance of the Islamic spirit' among Palestinians were desperately needed.[36]

Hamas's spectacular attacks, whether suicide bombings or the more recent strategy of rocket attacks against Israel launched from Gaza, have usually been undertaken for one of several reasons: to avenge Israeli attacks, maintain its profile within Palestinian society, demonstrate its continued relevance to Israel and the outside world, or more broadly to force Israel to pay some price for the ongoing occupation. The organization has always justified the use of terror-ism as being a 'legitimate' or 'justified' response to continued Israeli occupation, settlements and repression of Palestinian nationalist aspirations.[37] Such use of the 'weapons of the weak' has been been supported even by so-called 'moderate' (*wassatiyya*) Muslim jurists such as Egypt's Yusuf al-Qaradawi, but it has garnered little sympathy in Israel or the West, particularly in comparison with the acceptance of Israel's use of systematic violence – whether direct physical vio-lence or the structural violence of closures and other collective forms of punishment – based on the similar logic of justified self-defense.

Indeed, since September 11, 2001, Hamas's use of terrorism has led it to be considered in the United States as little different than al-Qaeda. Yet despite its intensity, destructiveness, and terroristic impact, the use of violence by Hamas is not equivalent analytically to that of al-Qaeda or other militant Salafi groups for a host of reasons: it is specifically directed against an occupying power; the underlying ideology is more nationalist than supra-national religious; despite its Islamization of Palestinian identity, and the deployment of anti-Jewish tropes from the Koran and classic European anti-Semitic tracts such as the *Protocols of the Elders of Zion*, Hamas has shown much more pragmatism and tolerance for non-Muslims than have al-Qaeda and other extremist Sunni Salafi groups.

Moreover, generally it has not defined its jihad against Israel as part of a larger worldwide jihad; nor does Hamas declare other Muslims apostates and engage in theological justifications for targeting them, as do al-Qaeda and other extremist groups. Indeed, the movement's leadership – although not all its members and certainly not all Muslim Palestinians – has generally been supportive of Palestinian Christians in its communiqués and actions, replacing the Koran with a map of Palestine as the centerpiece of its logo to broaden its appeal, and running a Christian, Hosam al-Taweel, on its slate in the 2006 elections. Christians do come under attack by Muslim activists in the Occupied Territories, but this has rarely or ever been on the orders of Hamas leaders, unless it was in specific retaliation for actions deemed traitorous or anti-Islamic, such as selling alcohol or missionizing.

Equally important is the fact that Hamas has almost always limited its activities to the territory of Mandate Palestine – as we saw at the beginning of this chapter, the liberation of Palestine, rather than the restoration of the caliphate, is Hamas's 'end product.' However broad its ideological appeal, and its declared genealogy within the Egyptian Muslim Brotherhood tradition, Hamas has used religion to serve the interests of Palestinian nationalism – indeed, many Hamas activists I have encountered do not exhibit outward signs of religiosity in dress or demeanor, expertly weaving together the 'common symbolic order' in which both partake.

Finally, like the Muslim Brotherhood and Hezbollah, but unlike al-Qaeda and other pure jihadi groups, the vast majority of Hamas's activities have always been geared to the provision of the large array of social services already described – clinics, schools, day care and related needs that the Israelis, and after 1994 the PA, have been unwilling or unable to provide. Today, Hamas and Hezbollah are the only Middle Eastern militant resistance groups to participate in elected government.

Most important, whereas many if not most al-Qaeda *mujahidun* come to the movement from afar, often leaving their home countries to join jihads in foreign lands, the use of violence by Hamas is born almost entirely out of a sense of desperation, a belief that no other tactics of resistance are viable within the context of an ongoing occupation of their own land.[38] As one of the leaders explained to me, desperation is the key, even at the elite level. 'We know suicide bombings don't work [i.e. won't achieve the desired goal of ending the occupation], but we don't know how to stop them.'[39]

In other words, the continued dominance of suicide bombings, and more recently rocket attacks from Gaza, reveals a strategic myopia by Hamas as much as a fanatical disposition against Israel, with which most Hamas leaders accept the inevitability, if not desirability, of reaching some kind of settlement, if it recognizes 'the right of the Palestinians to live peacefully in their own state within the borders of the territories occupied by Israel in 1967.'[40]

In discussion with Hamas leaders, when I have raised the issue of the movement advocating a binational position like that being adopted by many Israeli and Palestinian activists and intellectuals, one exclaimed to me, 'We don't want to live closer to Jews, we want a divorce. Just leave us alone already.'[41] When I mentioned that he was using the same language as former Israeli prime minister Ehud Barak, he smiled and shrugged his shoulders slightly. Indeed, Hamas has been heavily criticized and even accused of treason and of having 'betrayed Islam and turned its back on Jihad' by al-Qaeda leaders, for its willingness to negotiate with Israel, and to agree to a long-term truce and even, under certain conditions, peace.[42]

From civil society to electoral power to civil war

As far back as the 1980s there was evidence that Hamas, and the Mujama'a before it, would not hesitate to use violence against other Palestinians to achieve and enforce power. If in the 1980s and during the first intifada members of the movement attacked supposed collaborators or inappropriately dressed women, during the al-Aqsa intifada opponents of Hamas were shot, saw their houses blown up, and even had acid poured on their children (Fatah is also guilty of assassinating Hamas officials).[43] Together, these actions demonstrate a kind of schizophrenia that questions, if not belies, Hamas's stated goal of working towards national unity (a goal that was exemplified during the al-Aqsa intifada by Hamas's participation in the National and Islamic Higher Committee for the Follow-Up of the Intifada, and in the staging of joint attacks with the al-Aqsa Martyrs brigades).

This schizophrenia is equally evident in the manner in which Fatah (and through it the PLO) and PA officials began to adopt language resembling that of Israel – calling Hamas 'murderous terrorists' who are trying to build an 'empire of darkness,' for example.[44] This came to a head in 2006. It was then that Hamas and Fatah began what many Palestinians and outsiders have described as a 'civil war' for control of the Palestinian Authority, and through it of the future of both resistance to the occupation and the negotiations to bring it to an end.

When the al-Aqsa intifada first erupted, Hamas saw it as a means to revitalize resistance across the Palestinian political spectrum by bringing all the various Palestinian factions together under the shared leadership of Hamas and Fatah. But fairly quickly, Fatah's strategic weakness was exposed, as seven years of power – however limited – through the PA had put it in a position of having to decide whether to allow the PA to be destroyed by joining an all-out resistance war against Israel, or attempting to crush Hamas in order to preserve whatever international legitimacy it had through the PA. Hamas–Fatah tensions increased in 2005, following Arafat's death in November of the previous year.

The violence came to a head on January 25, 2006, when the first elections for the Palestinian Legislative Council were held since 1996. Hamas had already given indications of its strength with victories in the municipal elections of the year before. Running on a platform that barely mentioned resistance (aside from 'safeguarding it') in favor of a good governance discourse, Hamas won the election, with seventy-four seats to the ruling-Fatah's forty-five. This provided Hamas with the majority of seats and the ability to form a majority government on its own. Immediately, however, the Western powers, exemplified by the 'Quartet' (the USA, the EU, Russia and the UN), threatened to cut off most aid to the Palestinians, a threat carried out to some degree by the USA and the EU soon thereafter when it became clear that Hamas was not going to renounce violent resistance.

By the spring of 2006 there were tit-for-tat attacks between Hamas and Fatah, and Palestinian officials were warning of a civil war. By the end of the year, as I drove around the Occupied Territories, the atmosphere and scenery reminded me more of Somalia or Sierra Leone than the Palestine of even a year or two earlier – roving bands of young men, armed with automatic rifles, packed like sardines into the back of pick-up trucks with seemingly little aim other than to find an adversary to fight. Meanwhile senior Hamas leader Khalil al-Hayya accused President Abbas of 'launching ... a war ... first against God, and then against Hamas.'[45]

By early 2007 the situation was so bad that on the same day Gaza suffered attacks by IDF helicopter gunships and street battles between Hamas and Fatah. The Occupied Territories by this time had been largely, if not completely, divided in a manner that saw Fatah and the PA president Abbas in charge of the West Bank, and Hamas and Prime Minister Ismail Haniya in charge of Gaza. This situation continued even after Abbas dissolved his government and appointed former finance minister Salam Fayyad in his stead.

The sometimes violent stalemate between Hamas and Fatah as of early 2008 was reflected in the spate of rocket attacks, usually with locally produced Qassem rockets, from Gaza on the Israeli town of Sderot, less then five miles from the border with Gaza. The attacks succeeded in terrorizing the town's 24,000 people, and even led its Likud mayor publicly to declare his willingness to talk with Hamas leaders to try to arrange a ceasefire. But from a political and strategic perspective the rockets achieved few if any gains for Hamas or Palestinians more broadly (indeed, polls showed that the movement's popularity went down as a result of them), since, as they had to the suicide bombings, Israel retaliated with massive force, killing dozens of Palestinians and laying a months-long siege to Gaza that left residents so desperate that the Hamas government of the Strip blew up the border wall separating Gaza and Egypt so that residents could escape, at least for a day, to the relative freedom of Rafah, where supplies of gas, food and drugs quickly ran out.

Hamas's 'tearing down of the wall' between Gaza and Rafah was lauded by Palestinians, and symbolized to the world their desperate plight fifteen years after Oslo began. Yet the fact that Hamas or Palestinians more broadly have never made a similar effort to destroy the wall to the Israeli side of Gaza, or to tear down the sections of the wall lying within the West Bank, points to the political and strategic myopia of the leadership, and the fatigue of the people, after so many years of fruitless negotiations and violence. Hamas remains unable to move beyond rockets or suicide belts, while Fatah and PA president Abbas have little more to offer than criticizing the militarization of the intifada and advocating a return to some mythical 'popular origins.'[46] In twenty-first-century Palestine, violent resistance against Israeli occupation, whether religiously or secular-nationalistically inspired, remains as divisive and unsuccessful as it was in the previous century. I'll explore what other options remain open to Palestinians in the conclusion.

The Israeli settlement movement

The defeat in the 1967 war profoundly reshaped Arab politics and Islam throughout the Middle East. Its impact on Israeli politics and Jewish religious expression in Israel was just as profound, and ultimately negative from the standpoint of achieving the goals laid out by Oslo. Indeed, 1967 changed the contours of Israeli society as much as it did those of the Arab/Muslim world, similarly encouraging the growth of what Ehud Sprinzak terms 'Zionist fundamentalism.' By the 1980s this trend had become 'the most dynamic social and cultural force in Israel,'[47] its dynamism owed in good measure to the fact that, like its Islamic counterpart, Jewish fundamentalism was a reaction against globalization and a 'search for wholeness in a materialistic world' at the same time that it was a response to territorial imperatives after the conquest of the West Bank and Gaza.[48]

Of the many reasons for the importance of the victory in the Six Day War for Israelis, the 'reopening of the frontier' that occurred with the conquest of the West Bank and Gaza helped recharge a somewhat moribund Jewish nationalism at the moment a new Israeli-born generation, for whom traditional Labor Zionism held less attraction than it had for its parents, was coming of age. It was out of this milieu that Gush Emunim (Block of the Faithful), the pioneering organization of the settlement movement and 'the most successful extraparliamentary movement to arise in Israel since the state's establishment in 1948,' was born in 1974.[49]

The movement was founded in the settlement of Kfar Etzion, with about two hundred people participating, but its ideological roots derived from the writing of Abraham Yitzhak Cook, the spiritual father of the Revisionist Zionist movement, and his son, Zvi Yehuda. Both men argued that Zionism, even that of secular Jews, was actively contributing to the redemption of the Jews; because of this, religious Jews should work with their secular compatriots to resettle and retain the land. Gush Emunim's development helped reignite the flame of maximalist Zionist ethno-religious nationalism at a moment of significant stress to Israeli society, fusing together Zionist, religious and secular ideologies and beliefs to gain popularity across the spectrum of Israeli politics, and once again uniting Labor and Revisionist Zionism in a shared focus on permanently retaining as much of Eretz Yisrael as possible.

By the early 1980s Gush Emunim comprised 10,000–20,000 activists, yet soon thereafter the movement began to fade from view, as events on the ground caught up with the desire of the leadership to settle throughout the West Bank to the point that Gush was no longer as important as before. Particularly once Ariel Sharon became a dominant figure in the Likud government, Gush Emunim had no need for noisy extra-parliamentarism. The outside instigator had effectively taken over the direction of government policy on the country's most crucial issue. In this sense Gush Emunim's power only grew during the Oslo period.[50]

Gush Emunim first emerged as an organized faction within the National Religious Party (NRP), known in Hebrew as *Mafdal*, which itself was established in 1956. The NRP focused primarily on heightening the status of Judaism within Israeli society. In its early years the focus was on personal-status issues, education, culture and kosher food provisions. But after the Six Day War a messianic trend was spawned among more religious Israeli Jews which moved the party towards the right, and many members to Gush Emunim.

By the time Ariel Sharon removed the settlers from Gaza in 2005, the NRP had left the government rather than cooperate. By then the NRP had become the most important right-wing party in Israel. It took a hard line against any relinquishing of territory to Palestinians in exchange for peace, and advocated dismantling the PA and 'sending the PLO back to Tunisia'; yet unlike the more extreme parties the NRP did not advocate transfer, and unlike ultra-Orthodox parties did not advocate a religious state.[51]

Three other right-wing parties have emerged since the 1980s which reflect a similar settlement orientation to the NRP's: Tzomet, established in 1988, is both militantly secular and militantly maximalist territorially; Moledet and Tehiya advocate an even more extreme 'Jordan is Palestine' option, which would involve the transfer of most Palestinians across the Jordan river 'under an international agreement.' Until that time, they call for the cancellation of all work permits for Palestinians, in order to 'encourage them to immigrate' to other Arab countries.[52]

The dynamics of Gush Emunim's growing power in this period were clearly influenced by the same processes of globalization that have influenced other social movements around the world, particularly those grounded in ethno-nationalist identities, and the larger rise of religious movements worldwide during the 1970s. It is thus not surprising – although rarely mentioned in the non-Israeli media – that most of the hardcore Gush settlers, who live in the smaller and remoter settlements, are extremely religious. Although there was – and remains – little love lost between the settler movement founded and inspired by Gush Emunim and the religiously traditional ultra-Orthodox non-Zionist Haredim (most of whose members choose not to settle outside annexed East Jerusalem's Jewish neighborhoods because of a theological belief that Jewish sovereignty in Eretz Yisrael should not occur until the coming of the Messiah), they share a similar antipathy for secular Jews and 'Arabs,' while also believing themselves to be creating a 'religious, ethnocentric, anti-liberal and anti-universalist "new society" ordered by God.'[53] As important, religiously inspired settlers appear as the opposite of the corrupt politicians willing to sacrifice principles for expediency, and the self-indulgent, hyper-consumerist contemporary generations of Israelis, whose yuppie lifestyle and individualist credo are seen as the antithesis of the founding ethics of Zionism.

This viewpoint is given greater power because the theology of the settlement movement has increasingly veered towards that of Sayyed Qutb and contemporary Salafi thought. Like their Muslim counterparts, hardcore settlers have come to believe that any values that go against their interpretation of Jewish law should be suppressed, and that 'real Jews would have to segregate themselves into ghettos to keep from being corrupted by, and even prepare to fight against, the rest of their society.' Even the Israeli government could be stripped of its legitimacy and its leaders declared apostates when they engage in activities or policies that go against their settlement goals. This was indeed the justification for the assassination of Yitzhak Rabin, who was labeled a *rodef* (pursuer), who could be killed (the Sixth Commandment notwithstanding) to prevent him from murdering other Jews. Indeed, so extreme was this belief – which closely mirrored Hamas's intense anti-Jewish ideology in its fervor and seeming irrationality – that by 1995 there was widespread public discussion in ultra-Orthodox circles, including the press, about whether Rabin and Peres deserved death and how they could be executed.[54]

What is important to consider here is that these views are less marginal than their seeming extreme tone suggests. By the time Oslo was launched the IDF had been so deeply penetrated by the settler movement (many and perhaps most of whose members trained and served in 'Hesder Yeshivot' units comprised only of ultra-religious yeshiva students), and the 'settler Judaism' it was fostering, that it became increasingly hard to imagine how the Israeli state could take decisions that would uproot a significant number of settlers.[55]

This reality doomed the entire Oslo exercise from the start. What is surprising is how few people noticed the signs. More astute observers, such as Oslo architect Yossi Beilin, had at least an inkling of the problem facing them, as is clear in a September 27, 1995 *Maariv* interview when, in response to an accusation that Rabin had abandoned the settlers, he responds that 'the situation in the settlements has never been better than that created following the Oslo Accord.'

The birth and history of Shas

If Hamas wants to 'abrogate' Israel's existence as an independent state and the settlement movement sought to annex the remaining part of Mandate Palestine to Israel, Israel's *haredi*, or ultra-Orthodox religious, communities have a more ambiguous position towards a state that, from their theological perspective, should not exist before the coming of the Messiah. Indeed, Ashkenazi ultra-Orthodox movements have long combined official opposition to Zionism with a willingness to participate in politics in order to obtain necessary social services and secure the passage of favorable legislation on issues such as control over conversions to Judaism, avoidance of military service, and personal status.

In the last two decades the political power of the *haredim* has grown dramatically, as exemplified by the meteoric rise of the Shas movement. Shas – the name is an acronym both for the Shisha Sidrei Mishna, the standard book of Jewish oral law and Talmudic commentaries, and of the longer name 'Shomrei Torah Sephardim,' or Sephardic Torah Guardians – is without doubt the most talked-about yet least-understood political phenomenon of contemporary Israel. There are many reasons why this is so, chief among them the movement's paradoxical identity: at once Zionist and non-Zionist, Mizrahi and Western, *haredi* and traditional, sectarian and integrationalist towards Israeli society at large.[56]

In the first four decades of Israel's existence, neither the Israeli political left nor the right, both dominated by Ashkenazim, succeeded in integrating Jews from the Middle East and North Africa into Israeli political, social, and economic life. When Shas was created in 1984, the Israeli political and journalistic establishment literally had no idea how to categorize the movement. It quickly established itself as a force in Israeli politics with a strong showing in the 1983 municipal elections in Jerusalem and then in the 1984 Knesset elections.

The party became a kingmaker in 1990 and 1992, when Shas toppled the government of national unity and ultimately joined a Labor Party-led coalition. All told, from 1984 to 1999 Shas's representation in the Knesset jumped from 3.1 to 13 percent, stabilizing at between 8 and 10 percent of the electorate since that time.

Shas clearly posed a major challenge to Ashkenazi dominance with its attempt to delink Jewishness and Europeanness in order to make the former the sole marker of Israeli identity and basis of citizenship, rather than the ethno-nationalism of Ashkenazi Zionism.

Of course, while more inclusive from a Zionist perspective, it still left non-Jewish citizens outside the bounds of Israeli identity, and therefore undeserving of full civil and political rights. With respect to Palestinians across the Green Line, Shas's 'dovishness' had always been largely an 'optical illusion,' since while its leaders were relatively dovish, its working-class and poor Mizrahi constituents were among the most hawkish in the Israeli political spectrum.

Looking back, it is clear that the Shas's emergence and rapid rise were part of a larger phenomenon in Israeli, and indeed world, society, of increasingly powerful ethnocentric and sectarian politics and culture coming to the fore. Indeed, the same year that Shas won its first seats in the Knesset, Meir Kahane's explicitly racist Kach party (outlawed in 1988) also won seats; the two movements competed for the votes of Israel's poor Mizrahim.[57]

What made Shas so powerful as a movement ultimately was that it stood on the fault lines of three crucial divisions within and between Israeli and Palestinian societies: Jews and Palestinian Arabs, Ashkenazim and Mizrahim, and secular versus religious Jews. Class cleavages based on ethnic prejudice – both culturally and as a matter of state policy on the part of Israel's Ashkenazi elite – have traditionally been underplayed in Israeli politics in favor of the hegemonic narrative of a unified Jewish nation (*'am Yisra'el*). But they have been particularly important to the emergence of Shas. The socio-economic situation in the development towns in which so many Mizrahim lived verged on the deplorable in the decades after their mass immigration, beginning in the 1950s. As I demonstrated in the last chapter, inequality grew even more pronounced in the 1980s as a result of the neoliberal policies of the Likud (who had attracted the support of Mizrahim since the late 1970s by promising, but not delivering, more of the national economic pie to their sector). To maintain the loyalty of this crucial electoral constituency, however, the Likud borrowed a page from the US Republican 'southern strategy' vis-à-vis race, and played off the ambivalence of MENA Jews towards their Arab/Middle Eastern identity by emphasizing their distinctiveness from and superiority to Palestinians.

Shas picked up on this strategy, but used it to build an ethnic 'brand' in which MENA Jews would come to see Shas as the true reflection of their cultural, economic and political interests. And once the Ashkenazi elite understood Shas to be a reflection of Mizrahi ethnic assertiveness, the movement began to be represented as a 'strategic threat' to Ashkenazi cultural, political and economic dominance; this fear was represented discursively as a threat to the core of Israeliness.[58]

Such a strategy worked, but only up to a point. In fact, the shared focus on economic and ethnic issues explains why neither rich Mizrahim nor poor Ashkenazim have supported Shas.[59] That is, Shas's natural constituency wasn't just based on ethnicity – being a Jew of Middle Eastern or North African heritage – but also on being from a working-class or poor background, which together produced an 'ethnoclass' of cultural and economic marginalization that can move between hardcore nationalist and more ambivalent supranational identities depending on the larger political context. One stark example was the remark by the movement's religious leader, Rabbi Ovadia Yosef, an Iraqi-born Jew, that culturally he felt closer to Khomeini than to most secular and Ashkenazi Israelis.

The Labor Party was not unaware of this dynamic; in response Ehud Barak placed the social problems of the MENA Jews at the top of the party's agenda, even holding the 1997 party convention in the Sephardi development town of Netivot.[60] This would lead to Shas's broad support for his election. But Prime Minister Barak reneged on these promises and the economic situation of the MENA Jews deteriorated further.

Shas's securing of an unheard-of seventeen seats in the 1999 elections was dubbed by many commentators as the 'catch 17,' because with such a large presence in the Knesset Shas could no longer define itself merely as a haredi or 'ultra-Orthodox' movement. It now had to address larger social issues, such as continued and even worsening inequality and poverty among its constituents, as demanded by the 200,000 additional voters who in 1999 chose Shas in protest against the Ashkenazi–Zionist hegemony rather than out of support for the larger, ultra-Orthodox religious program of the party (polling revealed that at least 50 percent of Shas voters did not consider themselves particularly religious; only 25 percent did).

In order to maintain their support Shas would have had to steer the government away from neoliberal policies and towards a serious redistribution of resources. Like its Labor counterpart, however, Shas also failed to deliver on its promises of focusing the government's attention on Mizrahi issues, and the party lost six seats in the 2003 elections. At the same time, perhaps understanding that its inability to effect economic change necessitated appealing to the baser political instincts of voters long tapped into by Likud and the right, by 2002 Shas had firmly moved into the right-wing camp, as epitomized by the visit of Spiritual Guide Yosef to a Jewish settlement in the West Bank, and his praising of the residents there.

The many forms of resistance in Israel/Palestine

Shas, like Hamas, can be considered a product of contemporary globalization; but can they be fruitfully compared? On the face of it, there would appear to be very little in common between them. The disparity in power between the two movements is impossible to ignore: one represents the occupier and takes advantage of its disproportionate political power in a functioning ethno-democratic society to secure public goods, and respect, for its constituents; the other represents an occupied people, is on the front lines of a bloody independence struggle, and at the time of writing was in charge of a government that had been completely isolated by the world community. Moreover, while Hamas uses violence and terrorism among its most important instruments, most Shas members avoid military service and rely on the power of the party to ensure the provision of a level of public services that Palestinians can only dream of.

But beyond the use of violence and the fact that the two movements stand against each other in the Israeli–Palestinian conflict, there are strong similarities in the dynamics that led to the foundation and evolution of the two movements. Indeed, Israeli officials have in the past specifically likened Shas to Hamas, while secular Israelis often compare Shas to fundamentalist Islamic movements, including Hamas.[61]

Shas's rise to power involves two specific elements, both related to the fact that the movement's founders were disappointed Sephardi members of the Ashkenazi-dominated ultra-Orthodox Agudat Yisrael party. The first is based on the theological motivations of the movement's religious leader, Rabbi Ovadia Yosef, for whom the movement was an instrument for 'returning the crown to its former glory' – that is, increasing religious observance among Israeli and particularly Sephardic/Mizrahi Jews and returning Sephardic religious customs to their historical pre-eminence over the Ashkenazi tradition inside the Land of Israel. What motivated most MENA Jews to gravitate towards Shas, however, was decades of political, economic and cultural discrimination and second-class treatment at the hands of the Ashkenazi establishment, which provided the fuel for Mizrahi anger towards the country's political establishment.

Indeed, in this context the rise of Shas is mirrored by the rise of the Islamic movement inside Israel, which during the last generation has grown from a politically marginal force to perhaps the pre-eminent political and cultural force among Israel's Palestinian citizenry. It has done so precisely by bending the boundaries between territoriality and national identities; using religion as a platform for political and cultural critiques that can't be easily reduced to what from Israel's perspective are far more dangerous 'nationalist' considerations, yet which equally challenge the basic narrative and interests of Israel's dominant Zionist-Jewish identity.

And globalization has everything to do with this trend. As the head of one of the two main branches of Israel's Islamist movement, Sheikh Abdullah Nimr Darwish, explains, globalization is like one wing of a jet plane, with democracy and development the other. 'Even the Concorde can't fly with only one wing,' he argues, meaning that the project of globalization in Israel is doomed in the long run internally if Israeli society and government cannot deal justly with Palestinians on both sides of the Green Line, while more broadly, if the United States does not act wisely, Middle Eastern leaders could well 'get off the American globalization Concorde' – taking their oil with them – and instead board an equivalent made by an inevitably resurgent China.[62]

In this context, while the Likud rode to power in good measure because of the defection of a large share of the MENA Jewish vote from the Labor Party, its economic policies exacerbated the problems faced by MENA Jews, as the faltering economy put Mizrahim into direct competition with Palestinians. Regardless of which party was in power, for MENA Jews of low socio-economic status, liberal-ization meant not only economic decline but also a reduction of social services and of the relative privileges associated with being Israeli Jews. A state that traditionally treated them as second-class citizens became much more important to them because it was their only protection against the ravaging effects of economic liberaliza-tion, and an affirmation of their privileged status as Jews in the society.

This has contributed to the clinging of Shas's constituency to the ethno-national and religious components of the Israeli discourse of citizenship, in a manner that parallels in some form the Islamiza-tion of Palestinian identity. Since many Shas members correctly identified the peace process as the capstone of liberalization, they came to view it with increasing hostility, at the same moment that Hamas's discourse was exhibiting similar sentiments.

Making such an identity more complex, as we'll discuss below, is the fact that culturally the Mizrahi core of Shas's identity has always been culturally closer to Palestinian Arab identity than to the dominant European Jewish one; in the context of a century in which the latter derided North African and Middle Eastern Jews as not sufficiently Zionist (or modern, for that matter) because of their Arab-Muslim cultural heritage, displacing that component of their identity with a universalist Jewish identity (which one scholar situates midway between 'Mizrahiut and Harediut') that both sep-arates them from the 'Arabs' while claiming theological primacy over Ashkenazim, was a natural response to the situation in which most Mizrahim find themselves.

Yet unlike that of both the settler movement and Hamas, Shas's priority has never been securing sovereignty or control over all the territory of Palestine/Israel. Indeed, in some ways it exists outside the framework of the nation-state that defines the settlement movement, precisely because its ideology is ultimately not territorially grounded. Instead, the goal of Yosef and the leadership has ultimately been to redefine Jewish identity in Israel,[63] and to do so in a manner not derived from any specific part of territory controlled by the state. But instead of removing the Mizrahim from the Zionist camp, it defined them as the central camp – 'the real Zionism.' Instead of being defined by the semi-pejorative term (in practice if not theologic-ally) '*edot*' (ethnic groups), which marked MENA Jews as culturally and politically marginal to the central, European Zionist narrative, Mizrahi identity and Shas in particular sought to conquer the center of legitimacy of Israeliness.

The problem, of course, is that Israeli identity has since 1967 been increasingly defined by two trends: settlement and the maximalist nationalist project it entails, and consumerist individualist liberal-ism, neither of which are very accommodating to Shas's tendency towards either political moderation or religious purification. Like so many Israelis, when forced to choose between religious, nationalist and cultural ideals, Shas's members have tended to fudge the former and fuse the latter into an identity that exists well within the main-stream of the Zionist right, and therefore outside of any discourse that could work towards generating a workable compromise with Palestinian nationalism.

Conclusion

Hamas, the Israeli settlement movement and Shas are all pro-ducts of the unique ethnocratic system that evolved within the space of Israel/Palestine during the last century. The key to dominating the system is the ability to maintain control through the exclusion, marginalization or assimilation of minority groups, depending on their relationship with the dominant group. Not all minorities are treated equally in this scenario; some are 'internal'; others need to be assimilated, coopted and exploited; others are marked as 'external' and are thus dealt with far more harshly. In this framework it is not surprising that Palestinians, as the weaker side by far, have ultimately been unable to negotiate the contradictions of their internal identities without resort to force, while Israel, as a wealthy nation-state, possesses a constitutional and legislative architecture that has served, for the most part, quite well in deflecting internal conflicts that might challenge national unity.

In this context, Hamas and Palestinians more broadly were from the start stripped of any identification with the territory of Palestine by the more powerful Jewish/Zionist ideology and practices.[64] As we'll see in the next chapter, as long as this dynamic of exclusion and hierarchization, both of which are at the roots of the larger modern project and its discourses of capitalism, colonialism and nationalism, continues to define the larger story of Palestine and Israel's troubled relationship, Oslo will remain an elusive and even dangerous dream.

6 | Violence, chaos, and the history of the future

Violence has always been at the heart of the Israeli–Palestinian conflict – shaping the territorial, economic, political and even cognitive-psychological map of Israel/Palestine for well over a century. Indeed, in the decades before the arrival of Zionism in Palestine – before either nationalism had been imagined – the local population violently resisted the transfer of land to Europeans based on the threat it represented to their land and livelihoods. Before that, the indigenous population violently resisted the attempt by Egyptian ruler Muhammad Ali's son, Ibrahim Pasha, to rule the country, and before that Napoleon's, both of which, though relatively short lived, were achieved and maintained only through a significant amount of violence.

The role of violence in the unfolding of Zionist colonization in Palestine has a similarly long history – from Ahad Ha Am's 1891 description of early Zionist–Palestinian conflict, through the formation of the first Jewish-only 'guarding societies' Bar Giora and Hashomrim in 1907 and 1909,[1] and subsequently the creation of Hagana in 1920, its right-wing/revisionist counterparts, the Irgun and the Stern Gang, in the following two decades, and culminating in the establishment of the Israel Defense Forces with Israel's Declaration of Independence on May 15, 1948.

The violence of globalization and foundations of chaos

More than just a name change occurred when the Hagana became the IDF. The former was an 'underground' militia wielded by a nationalist movement in search of a state; the latter was the military arm of a newly existing state. As such, the State of Israel's deployment of violence had a far greater degree of international legitimacy than did its precursor's – not to mention the violence deployed by its primary adversary, the Palestinians.

The modern understanding of the intimate relationship between violence and politics goes back to the writings of Machiavelli, Hobbes and Locke, and was perhaps most succinctly stated by Leon Trotsky when he argued that 'every state is founded on force.' But it was Max Weber who made the strongest argument for the intimate relationship between modern states and violence.

As Weber describes it, 'Ultimately one can define the modern state sociologically only in terms of ... the use of political force ... If no social institutions existed which knew the use of violence, the concept of "state" would be eliminated, and a condition would emerge that could be designated as "anarchy" in the specific sense of this word.' Moreover, Weber explained, 'Today the relation between the state and violence is an especially intimate one ... because [the modern] state is a human community that (successfully) claims the monopoly of the legitimate use of physical force within a given territory.'[2]

Today the majority of scholars might agree more with the view of power put forward by one of Weber's intellectual heirs, Michel Foucault, whose vision of power is less focused on power as a 'thing' or 'quality' that can be possessed and deployed by an all-powerful state, and more on power as a quality that takes shape through the agency of all the actors involved in its experience – however unequal their positioning with a particular field of power.[3] Such a view has the advantage of enlarging the field of play in which power operates, and in so doing revealing a greater degree of agency than is often attributed to subaltern actors within given political contests. This would include actors, like Palestinians, involved in independence struggles).

But in the case of Israel/Palestine, Weber's focus on the 'monopoly' of the legitimate use of force within a territory – in his terminology, 'violence-monopoly' or *Gewaltmonopol* – reminds us that for the vast majority of Israelis, and for most Americans and a large proportion of Western publics, the *State* of Israel does in fact enjoy a monopoly on the legitimate use of force in the territory of Mandate Palestine. Palestinians have, at best, the *authority* (as recognized in the name of their para-state, the Palestinian Authority) to deploy violence solely against their own people, and then only in order to prevent them from using violence against Israel and its citizens.

Frantz Fanon's theory of violence as embedded in politics is also relevant in the case of Israel/Palestine. Fanon sees a tripartite division of politics into the 'domination' of the colonizer, through the mechanisms of capitalist and colonial exploitation and oppression, over the colonized people; the 'corrupt party politics' of nationalist elites whose power rests on their willingness to ignore continued colonial violence and suppress the violent reactions to it by their people;[4] and finally, the 'virtuous,' 'ethical' and instrumental use of violence by the people themselves in pursuance of freedom.[5] This analysis comes fairly close to depicting, in the first two cases, the reality on the ground in Israel/Palestine, and in the third the justification of their actions by Palestinians involved in the ongoing violence of the al-Aqsa intifada.

Yet as Hannah Arendt points out in her critique of Fanon, there is a certain amount of wishful thinking, if not naivety, in his belief that any group, including the colonized, can use violence instrumentally and with a high degree of ethical grounding. Indeed, this self-perception has long been claimed by the Zionist movement and then the State of Israel in defending their use of violence against Arabs (that is, it is always defined as based on 'self-defense' and governed by a code of 'purity of arms' and 'restraint' – *havlaga* in Hebrew, one of the mottoes of the Hagana).[6]

Although accepting that violence can be justified as a response to 'extreme injustice,' or if it can 'open the space to politics,' Arendt argues that violence is very difficult to instrumentalize because it is so unpredictable; like the medieval golem it can easily turn on those whom its deployment was meant to protect, regardless of the (perceived) justice of the claims behind its use.[7] This is in line with Weber's belief that without a monopoly on the legitimate use of force states devolve into 'anarchy.'

In fact, anarchy is a good description of the situation in the Occupied Territories during the al-Aqsa intifada, when precisely a combination of a greatly weakened Palestinian para-state and a powerful Israeli state bent on removing the vestiges of its independent authority combined to produce an unprecedented breakdown in political authority and social cohesion. So dangerous did the situation become that Palestinians coined a new Arabic word, *intifawda*, to describe it, which combines the word intifada with the Arabic word for 'chaos,' *fawda*.

My own experience, observing the Occupied Territories sink deeper into chaos in the last half-decade, coupled with my observation of a similar situation at work in Iraq in the years after the US invasion and occupation, led me to describe the situation in both countries as one of 'managed' or 'sponsored' chaos, in which ongoing territorial-nationalist conflict is combined with the negative impact of neoliberal policies to produce a dangerous mixture of political despair and social disintegration. Indeed, such was the continued and striking imbalance of power between Israel and Palestinians that during the early 2008 Israeli siege of Gaza, when NGOs in Gaza tried to stage a peaceful mass march to the Erez border crossing to continue the momentum they had gained when Hamas soldiers blew down part of the border fence between Gaza and Egypt, a line of armed Hamas policemen stopped the 5,000-strong marchers a half-mile south of the crossing to prevent a confrontation with Israel.[8] An organization – and now a government – that bases its legitimacy in good measure on its use of violence against the occupier was, in this instance, reduced to playing the same role as the PLO by acting to stop Palestinians from engaging in activities that truly threatened the Occupation. (Later that afternoon, Hamas launched its regular rocket assault on Sderot, injuring a small Israeli girl.)

The roots of the violence in Israel/Palestine don't just lie in the territorial conflict between Jews and Palestinians, however; the conflict has become instrumental to the proper functioning of the larger world system, and in particular the global economy. Simply put, the functioning of a major part of the world system as presently configured depends on the continuance of the Israeli–Palestinian conflict, and through it the larger Israeli–Arab conflict and the broader War on Terror it helps fuel.

It is well known that the Middle Eastern countries devote a disproportionate share of their national budgets and GDP to weapons and other military expenditures. Even during the so-called peace years of the 1990s, military spending in the region was well above the world average of about 4.2 percent of GDP (a number that itself was skewed upwards because of the huge defense budgets of the

United States and leading NATO allies). Israel and the major Arab states spend between 8 and 13 percent of GDP, well over twice the world average – in fact, arms spending is trending downwards in most countries. This dynamic constitutes an important reason why it has been so hard for non-oil-rich Middle East countries to attain adequate levels of economic, social and human development.

What makes this process much more powerful is its relationship to the most important strategic commodity produced in the region, petroleum. What Israeli economists Jonathan Nitzan and Shimshon Bichler term the 'weapondollar-petrodollar complex' has ensured a recycling of oil profits (which accrue also to the major Western companies who pump and sell the oil) back to the USA, the UK, France, and, increasingly, Russia, China and Israel, in the form of massive and long-term arms purchases, which in turn give the petroleum and defense sectors of these countries' economies disproportionate political and economic power in their larger political economies.

In their *Global Political Economy of Israel*, Nitzan and Bichler provide a level of analysis and insight that until now has been sorely missed in the study of globalization in the Middle East. They demonstrate that 'during the 1970s there was a growing convergence of interests between the world's leading petroleum and armament corporations ... The ... *politicization* of oil, together with the parallel *commercialization* of arms exports, helped shape the uneasy weapondollar-petrodollar coalition between these companies, making their differential profitability increasingly dependent on Middle East energy conflicts.'

What is most important here is that in this process, and viewed from within the larger context of neoliberal globalization, 'the lines separating state from capital, foreign policy from corporate strategy, and territorial conquest from differential profit, no longer seem very solid.' Crucially, the lines separate at the same time that these processes 'deepen' the wealth and power of a certain cluster of companies (especially oil, defense and heavy engineering companies), while often undermining the broader health of the economy (leisure, civilian high-tech, and other sectors that did so well during the 1990s 'peace dividend').

These dynamics have political and economic synergy with what I term the Wal-Martization of the economy, a signal transformation associated with contemporary post-Fordist globalization compared with the previous era of Fordist-Keynesian principles, in which the social compact between labor, business and government that defined the welfare state in the post-war era and provided decent wages for the Western working class breaks down as the new technologies and economic models of neoliberalism enable a corporate-sponsored transformation of the economy towards both low-priced consumer goods and even lower wages and fewer benefits for workers (both in the name of free market principles).[9]

When you enlarge the weapondollar-petrodollar complex into the 'Wal-Mart-weapons-petrodollar complex,' it becomes clear how an unparalleled concentration of wealth and power is reshaping – often brutally – the world in its image. It is not coincidental that as the US economy is said to be entering a stagflationary economic period in early 2008, three of the only sectors that are reporting strong profits are the defense and oil industries, and Wal-Mart.[10]

More specifically, in the era of neoliberal globalization, the profits of the oil and defense companies ride on top of the myriad conflicts along the 'arc of instability' that stretches from Central Africa through the Middle East and to Central Asia. Viewed from this perspective, it is no surprise that the Middle East spends by far the most money as a percentage of GDP on arms of any region in the world. Israel's defense budget rose to as high as 9 percent of GDP (at least 2 percent of which includes the massive US weapons aid programs) and 25 percent of the overall budget by 2005, a number that has remained fairly constant since the beginning of Oslo.

If Israel's spending on defense equals the combined total of the states with whom it shares borders, its arms sales have become equally important. Israel has become the eleventh-largest arms exporter in the world, with over 10 percent of the world's arms sales.[11] This while remaining the beneficiary of the largest military aid program in the world, courtesy of the United States.

In Chapter 3 I explained the relationship between the militarization and neoliberalization of the Israeli economy during the last thirty years. As Israel moved into the 1990s, however, the economic dynamics changed as the 'warfare state' began to come under pressure from an emerging globalized financial and corporate class whose interests lay in diversifying the economy and opening it to foreign ownership while opening foreign markets to Israeli capital.[12] For a significant sector of the country's economic elite, opening new factories was more important than building new settlements – which is precisely why the government tried to put both in the same space.

In some ways, the old order was restored with the al-Aqsa intifada and the September 11 attacks. But as Nitzan and Bichler demonstrate, 'The new conflicts of the twenty-first century – the "infinite wars," the "clashes of civilization," the "new crusades" – are fundamentally different from the "mass wars" and military conflicts between states that characterized capitalism from the nineteenth century until the end of the Cold War.'[13]

The main difference was not so much in the military nature of the conflicts, as in the broader role that war plays in capitalism. On the one hand, the continuation of violence and the breakdown of Oslo were most definitely not in the interests of what could be termed Israel's 'New Economy Coalition,' which had expanded the scope of the Israeli economy and developed a growing export market tied more to the emerging high-tech industries than to the military economy. But while the New Economy Coalition was 'interested' in peace, it was 'unable and unwilling to bring it about,' which left room for an even more powerful force to remilitarize the political economy of a now globalized Israel: the weapondollar-petrodollar coalition of the United States.[14]

Because of this dynamic, the al-Aqsa intifada developed under very different conditions and constraints than the first one, which occurred within the framework of the cold war that was then just ending. 'Capitalism itself has changed,' Nitzan and Bichler explain, and with it so would the modes of domination. The defense and particularly petroleum sectors were able to re-establish their political dominance within American and Israeli societies without having to force a return to the unsustainable levels of military spending (for the USA, upwards of 14 percent, for Israel 25 percent, of GDP) that occurred during the height of their cold war conflicts.

The problem for Israeli society, besides the continuation of a conflict many thought was on the verge of being solved, is that this process left a political space that was filled 'by fifth-rate politicians, many with criminal connections and neo-Nazi worldviews. The bellicosity of these politicians is harmful to the interests of Glob[al]-Israeli dominant capital, but it is highly serviceable to the Weapondollar-Petrodollar Coalition and the current U.S. Administration that seek to keep the regional turmoil going.'[15]

This point is crucial for two reasons: first, because it points to a level of corruption inside Israeli society that few outsiders are aware of: 75 percent of Israelis believe there is a great deal of official corruption in the country; politicians as senior as the head of the Tax Authority and even the president of the state have been indicted for corruption; Israel is in the bottom third of advanced countries in its levels of corruption and dropped five places between 2005 and 2006 alone; and this corruption is intimately tied to the Occupation. As former Labor Party Speaker of the Knesset Avraham Burg explained, 'The Israeli nation today rests on a scaffolding of corruption, and on foundations of oppression and injustice.'[16]

As important, this argument directly contradicts the accepted wisdom, articulated most recently and famously in the book *The Israel Lobby and US Foreign Policy* by John Mearsheimer and Stephen Walt, that Israel is forcing the USA to accede to its continued occupation of the West Bank because of undue political power. In fact, the reality is that it is the dog wagging the tail, not the other way around, much to the detriment of most Israelis and Palestinians.

Indeed, as I finish this chapter the USA has just announced a $20 billion ten-year series of deals with Saudi Arabia, which won the approval of Israel after the USA promised to sell and give Israel $30 billion during the same period in order to ensure its continued technological superiority. Egypt will likely get around $10 billion based on the long-standing ratio of US aid and arms sales to the two countries. That's at least $60 billion in profits for US and Israeli defense companies, all because of the larger conflicts in the region, whose continuation rests at least partly on the Israeli–Palestinian conflict, which in turn ensures the continued centrality and power of the military class in Israeli society and politics.[17]

It is hard to see what chance Palestinians could ever have had against such an array of interests and money, no matter what the texts of the agreements and intentions of their authors were – especially once the sponsored chaos I discussed in the Introduction began to have its intended effect during the withering violence of the first two years of the al-Aqsa intifada.

It is clear that there are serious structural impediments that have blocked the creation of a viable culture and framework for peace within Israeli society. Their impact has been even heavier on Palestinian society, as the combined negative power of the US and Israeli 'war' coalitions have created a situation in which Palestinians who try to resist the ongoing occupation have felt it almost impossible to do so without resorting to mass violence. But violence reinforces the very power of the Israeli occupation it seeks to weaken.

As one Hamas analysis explained, during Oslo 'Israeli military power [went] hand in hand with economic power under US direction,' bringing 'disorder and chaos and economic collapse,' along with a 'retreat of Arab power' in their wake. Moreover, the reality of Israeli power, not just over Palestine, but over the whole Middle East, makes it impossible to achieve national goals against it.[18] In the same vein, Palestinian political scientist Bassem Ezbidi explains that the lack of power, and, as important, the perception of a lack of power, made it incredibly hard to develop a democratic political culture in the Occupied Territories, in good measure because it makes it so hard to generate the correct level of political trust between citizens and their leaders.[19]

Today, the structural violence of the Occupation and of Palestinian resistance to it have combined with the structural violence of the global system, especially after 9/11, to produce a situation that is inimical to achieving the 'just and lasting peace' that was supposed to be the end result of the Oslo process. Instead, as we've seen, the situation on the ground deteriorated until its inevitable end in a renewed intifada, which split if not destroyed the PA, leaving political, economic and social chaos in its wake. And when Hamas finally stepped into the political ring, the best it could achieve was a kind of 'order without law' that stood little chance against the 'instrumentalized disorder' that was the goal of Israeli policies to quell the resistance.[20]

The failure of the Palestinian Authority, and of Oslo

Given the balance of forces – local, regional and international – shaping the Oslo process it is little wonder that it created a 'politics of dependence, coercion and resignation' in which older dynamics such as factionalism and class distortions, economic underdevelopment, and a re-emphasis on patriarchal relations in society combined to undermine whatever positive achievements were brought by the peace process.[21]

These dynamics impacted another problematic relationship – that between the PA and the PLO. According to the PA's own rendering of the relationship, because Israel would not allow it to be endowed with such an important trapping of sovereignty it remained subordinate to the PLO, which is 'superior to the PA and its terms of reference' and continued to execute tasks for formulating Palestinian 'foreign policy.'[22] Indeed, the lack of a clear border between the two institutions 'vitiat[ed] institutional mechanisms of accountability,' while encouraging pressure on reformers by the powerful 'PLO institutional culture' that was at odds with the democratic practice that was supposed to define the PA.[23]

The internal structure of the PA also played a problematic role in Palestinian political life. Its three branches – executive, legislative and judicial – were from the start marred by problems of corruption, inadequate financing, politicization and impotence in the face of continued occupation and an Oslo process that severely circumscribed the power of the PA to enact and enforced democratic legislation. As Oslo wore on and real sovereignty was not approaching, the various ministries of the executive (security, local government, justice, finance, trade, labor, information, telecommunications, health, housing, education, sports, religion) came to be identified, politically and economically, with the ministers controlling them, while the security forces became factionalized.

The Palestinian Legislative Council (PLC) had perhaps the most potential of any of the three branches to lay the foundations for a democratic government, but precisely for that reason Arafat, in cooperation with the Israelis and the United States (specifically through regular meetings with security officials from all three parties), worked to undermine the Council and stymie its efforts to curb corruption and demand more equitable terms during the negotiations. Similarly, the Palestinian judiciary remained marginalized from the rest of Palestinian economic life during Oslo, suffering from problems of underfunding, and lack of a clear structure and independence.

These structural deficiencies meant that the PA could not stem violent opposition to the Occupation which emerged in good measure because it had too little power to move Palestinians towards independence. As Rema Hammami and Salim Tamari argue, 'The Authority has shown that it was incapable of basic governance and, at the same time, was unable to operate as a national liberation movement.'[24] In such a situation it was inevitable that in order to maintain power internally the PA would have to pursue repressive policies against its own people which would erode the democratic foundation of Palestinian politics, which would in turn break down trust between citizens and the government, thus creating conditions for corruption that reinforces the repression.

The staunch opposition to the Oslo process by Hamas and other militant groups and Hamas's willingness to use violence and terrorism to resist the Occupation made it the primary political alternative to the PA for a large proportion of non-elite Palestinians during the Oslo process. Its actions naturally led to strong Israeli responses, which in turn weakened a PA that was increasingly seen as a handmaiden to the Occupation, and whose leaders benefited economically from their position while most Palestinians suffered. Hence the graffiti once scrawled on current PA head Mahmoud Abbas's house: 'This is your reward for selling Palestine.'

Corruption and the roots of chaos

From the time of its inception in 1994, the structure of the Palestinian Authority promoted the centralization of decision-making and resources, starving other, more local and accountable sources (such as municipalities) of the resources they needed to provide for their citizens and for local development. This phenomenon was in marked contrast to the situation during the intifada and the larger pre-Oslo era, during which time Palestinian civil organizations of necessity had learned to organize their own affairs.

Indeed, in a sense the Oslo process was initiated precisely to bypass Palestinian civil society on the ground in the Occupied Territories. Because of this, it was to be expected that corruption would become a significant problem almost from the start of the PA. As Fanon would have predicted, Israel certainly had an interest in creating a weak and corrupt 'national' institution whose leadership would be beholden to it for power and funds, and quickly set up secret accounts for Arafat that totaled hundreds of millions of dollars when they were exposed in the late 1990s.[25] But there were internal reasons for the level of corruption that quickly became endemic to the PA, first among them being a structure that placed inordinate power in the hands of the executive branch compared with the judicial and legislative branches according to the terms of the Oslo agreements.[26]

It should be noted that the corruption within the PA was not geared primarily to personal aggrandizement, although Palestinian leaders did benefit from their political and ministerial positions. Rather, in the main the corruption helped generate and sustain a number of slush funds for keeping members of the ruling Fatah party in paying jobs. Indeed, more than half of the Palestinian security services were paid through money generated from the monopolies – upwards of twenty-seven of them – that were the linchpin of the PA's political economy and a source of some of the most signficant corruption.[27]

Yet the result was equally deleterious; as detailed most comprehensively in a 1999 report by the Council on Foreign Relations (known as the Rocard Report), the corruption associated with the PA made it impossible for an independent Palestinian economy to develop, particularly when such a task involved directly challenging Israeli economic and political interests. As the Rocard Report showed, however, dealing with corruption would necessitate addressing core issues such as just what kind of polity and politics Palestine would have, and how far the PA should go in reflecting the increasing anger by Palestinians towards the lack of negotiating progress, the worsening economy, and ongoing occupation.[28]

As one leading Palestinian businessman explained, 'Every revolution has its fighters, thinkers and profiteers. Our fighters have been killed, our thinkers assassinated, and all we have left are the profiteers

... They are just transients here, as they were in Tunis, and, as with any regime whose end is near, they think only of profiting from it while they can.'[29] This is an important insight, for it demonstrates how many Palestinians viewed the PLO-turned-PA leadership as unrooted in the territories and the concerns and interests of most Palestinians. Indeed, when Palestinian intellectuals and activists came together in November 1999 to demand change in a petition entitled 'A cry from the homeland,' Arafat ordered PA security forces to arrest, beat or otherwise abuse numerous intellectuals and even Legislative Council members who were involved with or sympathetic to the effort.[30]

The dashed hopes of civil society

At the same time as the Oslo process was taking shape a revolution was taking place – not on the ground in the Middle East as much as in the way social scientists were studying the region. Recognizing the role played by civil society organizations in the 'velvet revolutions' that toppled communism in eastern Europe, scholars began to search for similar phenomena in the Middle East. Perhaps civil society would bring about a transition from the authoritarian past and present towards a more democratic, pluralistic and tolerant future. Palestine was a natural place to look because it had already been home to many foreign NGOs, and it was accepted wisdom that one of the main successes of the first intifada was precisely in nurturing grassroots independent civil society organizations that served the interests of the local population.

By the mid-1990s upwards of 1,400 locally based NGOs were providing the Palestinian population with social, industrial, agricultural, medical, housing and public services; they were joined by innumerable American and European foundations, NGOs and donor organizations, which were spending tens of millions of dollars a year in the Occupied Territories in direct aid to the people, and in training and logistical support for the local organizations (the Islamic charity networks had their own, equally rich source of funds).

Together they performed many of the essential functions of building infrastructure and providing crucial public services – more than 50 percent of health services, and a large share of preschool and agricultural programs as well – that the PA was unable to provide, both because of a lack of competence and also because in the neo-liberal 1990s governments across the globe were downsizing their provision of such services.[31] (Making matters worse was the fact that so much of the PA's budget had to be spent on security in order to satisfy Israeli and Western governments of its bona fides in fighting terror and to preserve its dominance vis-à-vis other groups, most notably Hamas, that might want to challenge it.)

Despite many obstacles, the NGO system continued to function throughout the negotiating process, but it was unable to help bring about a structural change in the dynamics of Palestinian resistance. This was not for lack of trying. Yet if the political obstacles faced by Palestinian civil society were grave, they were not all that dissimilar to those encountered by civil society movements across the developing world during the 1990s, particularly in the authoritarian states of the MENA.

The exacerbating problem, however, was that Palestinian civil society had to contend with an ongoing occupation along with the other challenges it faced. In this confusing landscape, members of the burgeoning NGO sector were constantly forced to choose between working at the grassroots level, and thus by definition in opposition to the government and the mainstream donor community, or being coopted, either by the PA or various political parties, or by the international donor community with its neoliberal agenda, for which civil societies and the NGO sectors at their lead had unwittingly become agents across the global South, often against the wishes or interests of their peoples.[32]

As A. R. Norton famously described it, 'If democracy has a home ... it is in civil society, where a melange of associations, guilds, syndicates, federations, unions, parties and groups come together to provide a buffer to the state.'[33] In this regard, there is a question of whether we can speak of a functioning civil society in the Occupied Territories, as both before and during Oslo there was never a sovereign state or government against which civil society could be counterposed. In both periods what existed was a constellation of civil organizations engaged simultaneously in various forms of resistance, relief and later development work, against the ongoing occupation.

A strong civil society is based on deep and organic connections between intellectuals and their environments. Palestine has more than its share of first-rate scholars and NGO activists, but the structure of the Occupation and corruption of the PA made it very difficult for them to play such a leading role in society at large; particularly those who were involved in creative ways of resisting the Occupation, such as the well-known non-violent activist Mubarak Awad, who was, not surprisingly, exiled by Israel for his activities only months after the outbreak of the intifada, in April 1988. Because of this, Palestinian society failed to organize a fully independent civil society of NGOs (or, as they are more often referred to in the Palestinian Arabic literature, 'civil society organizations' – *munaththamat al-mujtama' al-madani*), effective opposition parties, a viable public sphere and other trappings of democracy.[34]

In the end, a combination of mismanagement, patronage and unequal privileges between elite Palestinians and the remainder of the society all contributed to the growing sense of Palestinian weakness and Israeli dominance. Making matters worse, however, was that the NGO or civil society community in Palestine became 'professionalized,' and as a consequence increasingly beholden to Western donors, at precisely the moment (the early 1990s) when their independence and critical stance towards either Israeli or Palestinian 'authority' were most needed. Indeed, NGOs came to be seen by many Palestinians as an employment sector for the economically privileged. Like political parties, the NGO community was believed to have lost its popular legitimacy.[35]

Attendant upon the professionalization of NGOs was the 'developmentalization' of NGO discourses. Oslo radically changed the dynamic of mass organizations geared to either supporting the intifada or ameliorating the impact of Israeli measures taken to crush it. A whole new set of organizations, and their attendant knowledges and networks, emerged which were no longer geared to resistance but instead to 'development.' It was in this context – one where historically development had meant development of Palestinians off their land (that is, using the rhetoric, languages and discourses of development to help gain control over the country's territory) – that the contemporary NGO sector emerged and began its struggle for democracy, freedom and development.

The struggles between the PA and the NGO sector were related to the struggles for power between the PA and the PLC, which resulted in the marginalization of the PLC by the PA. This was made easier by the factionalism and lack of professionalism among many members of the legislature. With the NGO sector the PA adopted an attitude of antagonism mixed with attempts to coopt it – antagonism because the movement constituted a legitimate rival to an already weak PA; cooptation because harnessing its social power and access to funds would strengthen its weak grip on society

Throughout the mid-1990s one would hear complaints from NGO activists of attempts by the PA to interfere in their activities or coopt them. But for the most part the 250-member-strong NGO network maintained a fair degree of political independence, even if on the ground the developmentalist policies pursued by many were in line with the World Bank/IMF prescriptions favored by the Oslo political and economic elite.

A major victory for the movement came with the passage in 1998 of the NGO Law, which was far more liberal than the originally proposed 1995 law modeled on the restrictive Egyptian law. This victory was threatened, however, by the increasing transfer of donor funds from the NGOs to the PA, despite worries over efficiency and corruption. At the same time, the PA balked at implementing the law's far-reaching recommendations, meant to ensure the NGO sector's continued independence, and in 1999 actually launched an all-out attack on the sector, accusing it of being corrupt and an instrument of foreign domination because of the tens of millions of dollars it was receiving from abroad.[36] The outcome of the struggle was never decided, however, as the eruption of the intifada a year later superseded the internal conflicts.[37]

Development in the context of a weak para-state and a weakened society

The PA successfully weakened the Legislative Council and to a certain extent civil society, although here it must be remembered that the occupation exerted the determinative influence on these sectors. Yet the Palestinian executive also remained weak, producing a sociologically distinctive situation of a weak state *and* a weak society that has slowly been drained of its ability to maintain the functioning of its civil, social and political institutions.[38] In this situation violent organizations such as the Tanzim and Hamas filled the gap, challenging the PA and Arafat's 'monopoly over the use of force,' as well as their larger legitimacy with the so-called Palestinian 'street.'

This dynamic, in the context of the al-Aqsa intifada, led to the *fawda*, or chaos and anarchy, I described above. While generated primarily by Israel through the mechanics of the ongoing occupation and large-scale violence against Palestinians during the intifada, the weak state/weak society dynamic ultimately led the intifada to feed on itself rather than build the effective grassroots structures that, at least for a time, supported Palestinian society during the first intifada.[39]

Because the PA controlled so little territory, it was almost impossible for it to engage in a realizable development program. The leadership had to be more concerned about controlling its population than territory, since most of that remained under Israeli control. As Rema Hammami explains, 'The space opened up for development by Oslo was not a geographical one but a political one.'[40] And in this political space Palestinian civil society ultimately had to confront not just the Israeli occupation but its own increasingly corrupt and authoritarian leadership.

As if this wasn't enough to contend with, the very framework of development, so closely tied to the neoliberal policies imposed on Palestinians by the World Bank, the IMF, the United States, and Israel, tore at the loyalties of the emerging NGO sector, which was portrayed as the savior of society (based on the perception of civil society's role in bringing down the eastern European communist states) when it had neither the tools nor the power to serve such a function.

If before Oslo development was seen as part of a larger process of resisting the occupation, with Oslo the occupation was written out of the development process. This is clear even from the way reports by the World Bank defined the occupation, which by 1996 was described as merely a historical episode that was no longer relevant, even though it had then become more entrenched than ever.[41] Indeed, as international agencies entered Palestine's political and social space, they changed the nature of the NGO community from supporting resistance – *summud* – to supporting development policies that often conflicted with their original grassroots goals.

The most important dynamic facilitating the depoliticization of many NGOs (but by no means most of the sector) and civil society more broadly was how the activities of these organizations were divorced from the continued reality of the occupation: 'The occupation was beyond the imaginary' of the NGO system, even if as individuals almost every civil society worker knew full well that the occupation was continuing.

And so 'Medical NGOs campaigned and lobbied for the formation of a universal health insurance scheme; women's organizations undertook a campaign for the reform of existing family law, NGOs working with the disabled campaigned for legislation that would guarantee ... social services.' All worked toward the 'empowerment' of their constituency against the state. The problem, of course, was that the state was never empowered against Israel, leaving goals such as introducing rural women to the 'concept of full citizenship' practically inconsequential.[42]

The one exception to the dynamics I have just described was the NGO sector of the Islamic movements within the West Bank and Gaza Strip, and Hamas in particular. Because of their strident opposition to Oslo and unwillingness during the period to participate in the emerging machinery of (quasi-) governance, Hamas's charitable institutions and other Islamic NGOs operated in a 'counter-world' to the more mainstream NGOs (which for their part often shunned Islamist NGOs).

In fact, Islamist charities constituted between 10 and 40 percent of all social institutions in the West Bank and Gaza Strip in the years leading up to Oslo. By 1993 they had constructed a large social service infrastructure of hospitals, clinics, educational institutions from the kindergarden through college level, social welfare services and sports clubs. In the transitional period they also founded two human rights organizations.

These institutions, in which women play a prominent role, constituted between 10 and 15 percent of the NGOs in the Occupied Territories during Oslo, and featured highly educated and trained professional staffs, many with Western educations, superior services and delivery compared with non-Islamic NGOs and the PA, and fulfilled crucial needs not addressed by the PA.[43] Despite the level of professionalization – or at least in part because of it – the militant and sometimes violent opposition to the negotiating process by Hamas led to the demonization of the Islamist NGO sector by the Israeli, American and even Palestinian leaderships.

What is most important about the Islamist NGO system is that in terms of funding and the very ideology and production of knowledge through which it operated, Hamas's NGO/social service system remained outside of the neoliberal globalizing discourse of development that structured Oslo. Instead, it has been part of another globalized network, financially, politically and, as important, epistemologically – that of the Saudi and Gulf Islam more broadly and the Gulf religious charities specifically, which have poured untold millions of dollars into charities run by Hamas, the Muslim Brotherhood, and Hezbollah (for Shia donors and Iran).[44]

The impetus for such a social focus wasn't just ideological, however. As the Oslo process proceeded and armed resistance lost a lot of its legitimacy, gaining a foothold in civil society and building deeper roots in the community were understood as keys to Hamas's long-term survival. Most important, and crucial to the overall social position of Hamas despite the failure of its military/terrorist activities, the methods and knowledge involved in establishing and administering such groups and the types of relationship they brought into practice differed fundamentally from the workings and perceptual frame of the secular NGOs; not just because of their focus on commitment to the most victimized of the occupation: widows, orphans, the poor, the handicapped and the destitute.

Where the secular/international NGOs rely on 'traditional' methods of statistical analysis and polling – the kind of data collection favored by the World Bank and similar agencies – to capture snapshots of need within a neoliberal framework of provision of services and solutions, the work of Hamas charities has long been based primarily on the experiences of workers as members of the community. People's needs were and continue to be uncovered through dense social networks that rely on the spirit of voluntarism to function. Deep local knowledge of, and engagement with, the immediate community has been both a main source of funds and a means to identify to whom they should be distributed.

This knowledge base has helped Hamas and other Islamist charities maintain their operations despite the increasingly tough sanctions imposed by Israel and the West. Indeed, one commentator described how Islamist charities were 'living in a golden age' during the second intifada precisely because they were the only groups in society that had access to foreign funds, and were both free to pursue their larger goals and to remain viewed as one of the few forces of social conscience in an otherwise disintegrating Palestinian society.[45]

Women and the search for freedom

As we've seen, one of the negative consequences of the interaction between the PA, the international donor community, and the local NGOs in Palestine was the erosion of mass-based political activism during Oslo. This created an elite leadership in the West Bank and Gaza that was never responsible to specific constituencies and made it harder for women and men alike to forget any kind of civil resistance to the state. Indeed, women's rights are inseparable from the larger struggles faced by Palestinians, yet the nationalist narrative has tended to obscure women's roles, or place them uncritically as an adjunct to or merely supporter of men's struggles.[46]

At the same time, women were active in both intifadas in a variety of roles: from breaking up rocks, throwing stones, shielding young children and running relief committees during the first intifada, to directing joint protests with Israelis or, in extreme cases, becoming suicide bombers after the collapse of Oslo in 2000. Behind the range of activities that have defined women's participation in the struggle for independence, from civil society to the front lines of violent confrontation, has been a powerful but 'unstable mix of gender and politics in Palestine' that arose following the first intifada, and became even more acute once women became more directly involved in politics as legislators, government officials, and NGO workers during Oslo.[47]

By the late 1980s, women and men, especially young people in the universities, understood the necessity of reimagining their political lives, and thereby their interactions with each other. In universities such as Birzeit, Hamas men and bare-headed women eyed each other warily across the cultural-religious and gender divides, and even began working together through the emerging nationalist framework.[48]

During the intifada women made important strides in convincing society at large to grant them greater personal freedom. In the service of working for resistance and liberation, women were able to move more freely, and work and interact with the opposite sex in a manner that would previously have been hard to do. But at the same time, the intifada era produced adverse effects for many women, particularly in rural areas, where it led to a lowering of the age of marriage to 'protect' women's honor.

With the start of Oslo women activists operated in the context of four important developments: the decline of PLO political parties; the influx of foreign donor support for NGOs; the rise of Hamas and other Islamic movements and their attendant charity networks (where women played a primary role); and the establishment of the PA ministries geared to women's issues. The movement was both pulled together and apart in this new political landscape, changing the nature of women's politics and solidarity in the face of the clearly patriarchal nature of the PLO leadership returning from exile, and the continuing occupation.

It is clear that the ongoing occupation helped maintain the patriarchal basis of Palestinian society because it hindered the development of a constitution or progressive laws. Moreover, by making land, Jerusalem and refugees the primary issues of contention, the Occupation pushed women's issues off the table. Meanwhile the increased violence of the al-Aqsa intifada has been borne by women, both as direct victims of political violence and because of the increased violence within the home such a stressful situation creates.[49]

Indeed, at the most upbeat moment of Oslo, women activists felt 'diminished hopes and anxiety over the future [as] political fundamentalism, sanctioned by conservative nationalist forces, was imposing new repressive conditions on women.'[50] Yet if this was the feeling of many women working for the mainstream, large-donor-funded NGO sector, for religious women and those involved in smaller NGOs funded by more progressive groups such as Grass-roots International, the NGO process and the international funding it brought in opened up new spaces, not just for individual and gender-based advancement, but for shaping the emerging Palestinian public sphere. One could observe this at first hand by visiting not just schools and health clinics, but, as important, the television or radio production studios in the West Bank and Gaza, funded by myriad smaller international donors with precisely the goal of giving women greater access to and control of media technologies.[51]

But outside the space of the enlarging public sphere, in the years leading up to Oslo women were forced to take on new burdens because of the intifada. Yet their contribution was largely invisible, even to Palestinian men, and this was made worse by the difficulties faced by civil society in continuing to function adequately during the intifada. A problem related to increased gender repression was that the new struggles of the Oslo era were overlaid by a split within the women's movement, as in the civil society/NGO movement more broadly, between women activists who stayed at the grassroots level, and those who gradually moved into quasi-governmental positions. Activists were unsure whether to allow the already scarce funds allotted to women's issues to flow through the PA (which they instinctively distrusted) or to fight to retain control over donor money and government funds for 'women's issues.'

A key decision faced by women activists was whether to oppose or work through an Oslo process that was set up to 'demobilize' all non-state social and political actors, and which most activists knew was likely to fail to deliver on its political or social promises. Since so few women were part of the Palestinian power structure established by Oslo, few had any incentive to participate in it. What women instinctively understood, however, was that women's rights and democratic rights were inextricably linked, and thus any program of development designed by or geared towards women would have to fight for both simultaneously.

This realization proved little help, however, once the younger brothers of the boys that led the first intifada took matters into their hands in the fall of 2000. The drive by women to obtain crucial rights (of movement, education, etc.) was rendered moot by the forcible Israeli denial of all these rights to the Palestinian population at large. As in so many other conflicts, women, who had so much to offer in building a viable political culture of resistance to the occupation, wound up among the chief victims of the Oslo process, and then the al-Aqsa intifada that it produced.

Conclusion: Oslo and the burdens of history

Despite the often heroic actions of Palestinian and Israeli activists, scholars, journalists, and a few politicians to salvage something from Oslo, the very terms of the accords made it impossible to escape from the century-long history of colonization and conflict, asymmetric power relations, violence and corruption they reflected. In fact, the 'peace process' ultimately preserved and in many ways intensified these prevailing problems. Indeed, one of Oslo's singular achievements was a dissolution of political life and a decline of ideology and Palestinian nationalist consciousness that both allowed the Israeli occupation to continue, while making its continuation seem the result of Palestinian failures or intransigence – or, most ironically, its inability to move beyond its history of rejecting Israel's right to exist.

Moreover, a look at the red lines of even the most dovish members of the Israeli governments that negotiated Oslo reveals that the accords were doomed from the start, precisely because they reflected the unwillingness of the stronger party as much as the weaker one to compromise on its core goals.[1] The Palestinian Authority was crippled from the start, structurally prevented, by the terms of its mandate, from protecting or advancing the interests of the Palestinians it was charged with serving. When combined with the corruption of its leaders and their inability to offer a coherent plan to overcome the very system that made their return to Palestine possible, the inevitability of the 'tragedy of Oslo' – as so many Israelis and Palestinians alike describe it – becomes in equal measure impossible to ignore and vital to transcend. Neither the Palestinian nor Israeli leaderships as of early 2008 seem capable of leading their peoples in this direction.

This is not surprising. The roots of Oslo's failure are far deeper and more complex than the dynamics that set the process in motion. Over a century of conflict, in which the Jewish/Israeli side has become stronger with each passing decade, produced a situation on the eve of Oslo whereby Israel had very little incentive to make the hard sacrifices – withdrawal from most settlements, return of most land, equitable division of water and other resources, admitting a significant number of refugees – that would be required to enable a viable, and therefore peaceful, Palestinian state to come into being. Indeed, it would seem that leaders rightly calculated that a return to violence with Palestinians would be less dangerous than declaring war on the Israeli settler movement, which is what the creation of a contiguous Palestinian state would quite likely necessitate.

In 1996, on a bright and unseasonably warm January day, I walked into the 'Jerusalem Hall' in Abu Dis and watched Palestinians young and old wait in line for hours to vote for the first president and the Legislative Council of the Palestinian Authority. I felt that I was watching history unfold before my eyes as two young Palestinian policemen, in their clean and freshly pressed uniforms, carried an extremely old Palestinian man in traditional dress, his body too frail to walk, into the polling station to vote. That night I wrote a story about the elections entitled 'Birth of a nation, end of a dream?' in which I argued how the coming together of generations displaced in the moment I'd witnessed earlier that day presented a challenge to Zionism and its traditional dreams of full sovereignty over its ancient homeland which I wasn't sure Israel was ready to accept.

Yet it was undeniable that the joy – and it was joyful – of witnessing the freest elections in the history of the Middle East, and the sense that real peace and real independence were tantalizingly close for both Israelis and Palestinians, finally muffled the echoes of the shots that had killed Prime Minister Rabin only two months before, which were still ringing in the ears of everyone who was present in Israel and the Occupied Territories at the time. The weight of history seemed to be lightening. The conflict had certainly not come to an end, but perhaps there would be a new beginning for Israelis and Palestinians, if they could seize the moment and address the 'final' issues that were left open by the interim agreements.

I wasn't sure whether the two peoples, or their leaders, were prepared for the journey ahead – thus the question mark at the end of my title. But whatever the structural problems of Oslo, which were already clear to knowledgeable observers, no one could deny that peace and independence were closer than at any time in the century-long conflict.

But then Yahya Ayyash, the engineer of so much violence during the previous two years, was himself killed, and Hamas responded with a spate of suicide bombings that helped secure a victory for Benjamin Netanyahu – whose campaign featured photos of Rabin in the guise of Hitler or Arafat that many Israelis felt had helped create the atmosphere in which Rabin's assassin felt comfortable to act – over Oslo's principal architect, Shimon Peres. The New Middle East was once again trumped by the old one, and the long road to the *intifawda* and soul-numbing violence on both sides was opened.

If Oslo was supposed to symbolize the birth of the Palestinian nation, al-Aqsa signaled the end of the dream of Palestinian statehood. As for the Zionist dream, depending on one's point of view, it has either become a nightmare or is worth clinging to more strongly than ever. As Meron Benvenisti understood a generation ago, Israel and the West Bank are so interconnected that it's almost impossible any longer to consider dividing the land of Palestine between the two peoples.

If there is ever to be a just and lasting peace in the Holy Land, both Israelis and Palestinians will have to escape from the burdens of their shared yet conflicted histories and imagine new identities and new forms of citizenship that can provide a decent life, with dignity, security and hope for the future for both peoples. Until that happens, Oslo's legacy will be more blood and tears.

Notes

Introduction

1 Al-Jazeera, January 17, 2008.

2 I switch the order after 1948 because Israel becomes a *de jure* state, while Palestine has yet to achieve independence.

3 See 'UN court rules West Bank barrier illegal,' CNN.com, July 9, 2004.

4 Here I am borrowing Michel Foucault's understanding of the function of his research into the birth of modern public health systems vis-à-vis the way people experience the myriad issues surrounding their own health and public health more broadly in modern times (*The Birth of the Clinic*, p. 199; full citation p. 209).

5 Friedrich Nietzsche, *On the Uses and Disadvantages of History for Life*, Internet edition, p. 116.

6 The dominant paradigm of Zionist and Israeli historiography until the 1980s was the 'dual society' paradigm, which is exemplified by the writings of scholars such as S. N. Eisenstadt (particularly his widely cited *Israeli Society* (London: Weidenfeld & Nicolson, 1967), and the works of Dan Horowitz and Moshe Lissak and Palestinian scholars writing during this period, such as 'Abd al-Wahhab al-Kayyali and Muhammad Nakhla. Its hallmark is that it allows for little interaction between Jews and Palestinian Arabs except through violent conflict (see Lockman,

Comrade and Enemies, Introduction; full citation p. 209).

7 Ben-Gurion's remarks were made at the Fourth Conference of Ahdut ha-'Avoda, 1924 Report, p. 4, protocols of which are on file at the archives of the Labor Movement in Tel Aviv. Also quoted and discussed in Joseph Gorny, *Zionism and the Arabs, 1882–1948* (New York: Oxford University Press, 1987, p. 140).

8 I summarize these arguments in the first two chapters of my *Overthrowing Geography*.

9 During this period of great unrest and violence between the government and student and leftist groups, Foucault's advocacy for the activist students led to his being beaten by several men, in an attack that most people believe was ordered by the government (see David Macey, *The Lives of Michel Foucault*, New York: Pantheon Books, 1993. In this way both *The Birth of the Clinic* and subsequently *Discipline and Punish* were motivated by and written through a concern with our present structures (Michael Roth, 'Foucault's "history of the present,"' *History and Theory*, 20(1): 32–46; 43.)

10 Ibid., pp. 32–46; 44.

11 For a detailed analysis of Tel Aviv as a modern city, see my *Overthrowing Geography*.

12 That is, it is impossible to

imagine the spread of capitalism, the nation-state, or the ideology and processes of modernity without European imperialism and colonialism as their driving force. The notion of 'generative orders' of discourses and processes in the unfolding of nationalism was developed by Israeli geographer Juval Portugali in his book *Implicate Relations: Society and Space in the Israeli–Palestinian Conflict* (Dordrecht: Kluwer Academic Publishers, 1993), and developed by me in my *Overthrowing Geography*, throughout the book. For a detailed analysis of the term the 'four-fold matrix of modernity,' see *Overthrowing Geography*, Introduction and ch. 1, and *Why They Don't Hate Us*, Introduction through ch. 5.

13 Michel Foucault, *Politics, Philosophy, Culture*, p. 36 (full citation p. 209).

14 AHR Conversation: On Transnational History, with C. A. Bayly, Sven Beckert, Matthew Connelly, Isabel Hofmeyr, Wendy Kozol, and Patricia Seed, III(5), 2006, Internet version.

15 Amnesty International, Report 15/085/2003, 'Israel and the Occupied Territories: the issue of settlements must be addressed according to international law,' <http://web.amnesty.org/library/index/ENGMDE150852003>.

16 Ibid.

17 Sources for numbers of Israeli and Palestinian dead compiled from data drawn from the Israeli Foreign Ministry, the Zionist Organization, Human Rights Watch, the *Journal of Palestine Studies*, *News from Within*, and the *New York Times*.

18 For discussions of Palestine's development during this period, see *Overthrowing Geography*, Introduction through ch. 2; Beshara Doumani, *Rediscovering Palestine*; Khalidi, *Palestinian Identity*; and the work of Alexander Scholch.

19 Theodore Levitt, 'The globalization of markets,' *Harvard Business Review*, May 1983.

20 The (in)famous phrase 'Washington Consensus' was coined by economist John Williamson in 1990 to refer to the lowest common denominator of policy advice being addressed by the Washington-based institutions like the IMF to Latin American countries, including trade liberalization, fiscal austerity, deregulation, securing property rights, tax reform, competitive exchange rates, and a redirection of public expenditure toward primary health and education systems, at the same time focusing on high-income-generating activities.

21 For a more detailed argument and data set supporting this claim, see *Why They Don't Hate Us*, chs 3–4, 9.

22 For a detailed analysis of how the countries of the MENA fared in the 1980s through early 2000s period, see *Why They Don't Hate Us*, chs 3–4.

23 There were two important factors in this transformation. The first was that the economy was increasingly driven by trends and demands related to consumption as opposed to production, which was the driving force in the previous, 'Fordist' or 'Keynesian,' era. The second was a new cycle of rapid technological innovations in production and communication that has been labeled by scholars

'post-Fordist, flexible accumulation.'

24 *Overthrowing Geography*,
Introduction and ch. 1; and *Why
They Don't Hate Us*, chs 2–4.

25 David Harvey, 'The "new"
imperialism: on spatio-temporal
fixes and accumulation by dispossession,' available at <http://titanus.
roma1.infn.it/sito_pol/Global_emp/
Harvey.htm>. In fact, just as massive transnational corporations
have distorted Adam Smith's
original vision of free markets
comprised of individuals and small
firms operating in local contexts,
so today militarized capitalism
distorts the potential for increased
freedom, solidarity, and justice that
could be realized through a (very
different kind of) globalization of
the world's economies, cultures
and politics.

26 *The Global Political Economy
of Israel* (see Nitzan and Bichler
2003, p. 212).

27 *The Economist*, special issue
on globalization, September 23,
2000.

28 <www.dnb.com/UK/
communities/intlbusiness/
resource_center/middle_east/
sep_2002.asp>.

29 Here I am considering the
Israeli–Palestinian conflict as an
internal conflict, not an external
one.

30 For a critique of the idea of
the fading away of the state, see
Why They Don't Hate Us, chs 3–4.

31 Here I am referring to the
pioneering work done of Joel
Migdal, in his *Strong Societies and
Weak States: State–Society Relations
and State Capabilities in the Third
World* (Princeton, NJ: Princeton
University Press, 1988).

32 Shimon Peres, *The New Middle East* (New York: Holt, 1993).

33 Ibid., pp. 80–81.

34 Felix Frankfurter, 'The Palestine situation restated,' *Foreign
Affairs*, April 1931.

1 From modernity to the Messiah

1 Dan Rabinowitz and Khawla
Abu-Baker, *Coffins on Our Shoulders: The Experience of the Palestinian Citizens of Israel* (Berkeley:
University of California Press, 2005,
pp. 95–100).

2 For an example of the dual-
society paradigm, see the writings
of Horowitz, Lissak, Metzer, and
most other Israeli scholars writing
until the 1980s. For a critique, see
Zachary Lockman, *Comrades and
Enemies*; cf. Khalidi, *Palestinian
Identity*, p. 92.

3 Felix Frankfurter, 'The Palestine situation restated,' *Foreign
Affairs*, April 1931, p. 18.

4 See Yitzhak Elazari-Volkani,
'The transition from primitive to
modern agriculture in Palestine,'
Palestine Society Economic Bulletin,
June 2, 1925, pp. 3–9, for a direct
challenge to this view, written by
the father of Zionist agronomy.

5 I explore the ambivalent
reactions of Palestinians to Zionist
development discourses in 'The discourse of development in Mandate
Palestine,' *Arab Studies Quarterly*,
Winter/Spring, 1995, and in chs 2–7
of *Overthrowing Geography*.

6 See Tamari, *The Mountain
against the Sea*, p. 122.

7 This is in contrast to Barbar
Smith's argument that before
World War I the Zionist movement
had 'developed a unique form of
colonization ... the replacement

rather than the exploitation of the "natives"' (Barbara Smith, *The Roots of Separatism in Palestine: British Economic Policy, 1920–1929*, Syracuse, NY: Syracuse University Press, 1993, p. 11).

8 See 'The discourse of development in Mandate Palestine,' pp. 95–124, and chs 5–7 of *Overthrowing Geography*, for a discussion of the views of British officials in Palestine vis-à-vis Zionist development schemes.

9 See Samir Farsoun, *Palestine and the Palestinians* (Boulder, CO: Westview Press, 1998, pp. 34, 50). The most detailed analysis of the changing role of women is Iris Agmon's 1997 dissertation at Hebrew University, as well as the first three chapters of my *Overthrowing Geography*, and Mahmoud Yazbak's detailed review of the Islamic court records of Haifa and Jaffa in several books and articles on the late Ottoman history of the two cities.

10 Ironically, this perspective helps reveal the increasingly imperialist – as opposed to imperial – policies of the Ottoman state towards the Arab provinces, which meant Palestinians would gain little sympathy from the Porte for their complaints against the growing Zionist presence. Thus the state portrayed itself as a 'modern member of the civilized community of nations,' the 'committed advocate of reform in the Orient' (Selim Deringil, *The Well-Protected Domains: Ideology and the Legitimation of Power in the Ottoman Empire, 1876–1909*, London: I B.Tauris, 1998, pp. 136–7, 148, 154, quoting Ottoman official correspondence).

11 See Beshara Doumani's description of Nablus in the late Ottoman period in his *Rediscovering Palestine*. The most detailed analysis of the emergence of Palestinian identity during the late Ottoman and Mandate periods is Rashid Khalidi's *Palestinian Identity*.

12 In its opening clause Article 22 states that 'To those colonies and territories which as a consequence of the late war have ceased to be under the sovereignty of the States which formerly governed them and which are inhabited by peoples not yet able to stand by themselves under the strenuous conditions of the modern world, there should be applied the principle that the well-being and development of such peoples form a sacred trust of civilization and that securities for the performance of this trust should be embodied in this Covenant.' Africans were considered by and large unfit for independence in the near future. As for the MENA: 'Certain communities formerly belonging to the Turkish Empire have reached a stage of development where their existence as independent nations can be provisionally recognized subject to the rendering of administrative advice and assistance by a Mandatory until such time as they are able to stand alone. The wishes of these communities must be a principal consideration in the selection of the Mandatory.'

13 Excerpts from League of Nations *Official Journal* dated June 30, 1922, pp. 546–9.

14 Roger Owen and Sevket Pamuk, *A History of Middle East Economies in the Twentieth Century* (London: I. B. Tauris, 1998, p. 57).

15 Also, jobs in the all-important government sector (railways, post, telegraph) had to be distributed to both communities.

16 Baruch Kimmerling, *Zionism and Economy* (Cambridge: Schenkman Publishing, 1983, p. 20).

17 Owen and Pamuk, *A History of Middle East Economies*, pp. 57, 60.

18 He continued, 'We are used to thinking of the Arabs as primitive men of the desert, as a donkey-like nation that neither sees nor understands what is going around it. But this is a great error ...' (Quoted in Segev, *One Palestine*, p. 104; full citation p. 211).

19 Shafir, *Land, Labor and the Origins of the Israeli–Palestinian Conflict*, p. 89.

20 Ibid., pp. 81, 89.

21 These statistics are derived from *The Survey of Palestine*, 1947. A good summary of the various, and often widely divergent, estimates for the late Ottoman period is provided on Mideast West, at <www.mideastweb.org/palpop.htm>.

22 Ted Swedenburg, 'The role of the Palestinian peasantry in the Great Revolt (1936–9),' in Pappe, *The Israel/Palestine Question*, pp. 129–68; pp. 136–7. (Full citation p. 210.)

23 Swedenburg, 'The role'. The most detailed discussion of the conflicted nature of Palestinian politics during the Mandate period is Weldon Matthews, *Confronting an Empire, Constructing a Nation: Arab Nationalists and Popular Politics in Mandate Palestine* (London: I.B.Tauris, 2006), which focuses on how elite and popular politics interacted during this period, and how the British successfully manipulated Palestinian leaders,

particularly the Grand Mufti Husseini, into continued dependence upon them for their position in Palestinian society.

24 Labor Archives (LA), IV/219/239, 23/5/44 protocol of Arab Secretariat.

25 Salim Tamari, 'Factionalism and class formation in recent Palestinian history,' in Roger Owen (ed.), *Studies in the Economic and Social History of Palestine in the Nineteenth and Twentieth Centuries* (Oxford: St Antony's College, 1982), p. 147.

26 Rashid Khalidi, 'The Palestinians and 1948: the underlying causes of failure,' in Shlaim and Rogan, *The War for Palestine*, pp. 12–37; p. 30 (full citation p. 210).

27 Lockman, *Comrades and Enemies*. Cf. my *Overthrowing Geography*, chs 4–7.

28 *New York Times*, December 1, 1947.

29 Quoted in Tom Segev, *1949: The First Israelis* (New York: Free Press, 1986, p. 75). Cf. ISA, Protocol of the Meeting of the Provisional Government, June 16, 1948. For an analysis of the Right of Return of Palestinian refugees under international customary law, see Kathleen Lawand, 'The Right of Return of Palestinians in international law,' *International Journal of Refugee Law*, 8, 1996, pp. 532–68. For an Israel/Zionist perspective, see 'Right of Return of Palestinian refugees: international law and humanitarian considerations,' at <www.zionism-israel.com/issues/return_detail.html>. It should also be noted that this policy was in sharp contrast to British policy after they conquered Palestine – which nearly every adult Palestinian would have had in his or her mind during

the war – under which the government allowed most Palestinians and Jews who were displaced by the war to return to their homes. Ultimately, while international law as of 1948 did not yet mandate the permission for all refugees to return home after fighting, Israel was bound to do so when it accepted the terms of General Assembly Resolution 194, which did call for a return of refugees, as the price of its admission to the United Nations.

30 Sources for the population statistics include the *Survey of Palestine*, United Nations statistics, Government of Israel statistics, and US State Department statistics.

31 Benny Morris, from *The Birth of the Palestinian Refugee Problem*, p. 14; quoted in *Al-Ahram Weekly*, 14–20 December 2000.

32 Statement by Moshe Sharrett, June 16, 1948.

33 Morris, *Righteous Victims*, p. 268.

34 There were three main groups of immigrants from the Arab/Muslim world: Sephardim, technically Jews whose ancestors lived in Spain and Portugal, but today used to refer to most immigrants from countries along the Mediterranean basin; Mizrahim, Jews from the eastern Arab world and beyond, particularly Iran, Iraq, and Syria; and Teimanim, or the Jews of Yemen and the Arabian peninsula.

35 In the first days of the state, those Jewish immigrants, both from MENA and from the remnants of Europe's decimated Jewish community, who did not have relatives or friends in Israel or sufficient capital to find their own accom-

modation were housed either in the former residences of Palestinians, or, particularly for MENA Jews, in squalid tent cities (known as *ma'abarot*). Soon thereafter, most MENA Jews were 'coercively moved' into newly established 'development towns,' the majority of which were located along the frontiers between the Jewish and Palestinian Arab regions of the country, such as the Galilee and the Negev (Aziza Khazzoom, 'Did the Israeli state engineer segregation? On the placement of Jewish immigrants in development towns in the 1950s,' *Social Forces*, 2005, 84(1): 115–34). Once in the development towns immigrants faced cultural disorientation, discrimination and even humiliation at the hands of the state, followed by indoctrination into an Israeli identity that largely erased MENA Jews from the Zionist master narrative.

36 A good article which discusses this process in the Galilee, particularly in response to the outbreak of the al-Aqsa intifada, is Assaf Adiv, 'Israel's reponse to the October Uprising: "Judaize the Galilee",' *Challenge*, 67, May/June 2001.

37 For a classic analysis of the development towns and the larger issue of 'Oriental Jews,' see Shlomo Swirski, *Israel: The Oriental Majority* (London: Zed Books, 1989). For the most recent discussion of these issues in English, see Peled and Shafir, *Being Israeli*.

38 For the similar war goals, see the various contributions to Shlaim and Rogan's *The War for Palestine*.

39 See Peled and Shafir, *Being Israeli*, pt I. For economic data during this period, see David Levi-

Faur, Gabriel Sheffer, David Vogel (eds), *Israel: The Dynamics of Change and Continuity* (London: Routledge, 1999); Centre d'information d'Israel, *Réalités d'Israel* (Jerusalem, 1992, pp. 26–46, 196–203).

40 With GDP growing at less than half the 9.2 percent average of the previous period (4.2 percent) and 3.2 in the 1970s and 1980s.

41 Roger Owen and Sevket Pamuk, *A History of Middle East Economies in the Twentieth Century*, p. 194.

42 Cf. Pappe, *A History of Modern Palestine*, p. 167 (full citation p. 210).

43 Until the first intifada, Palestinian per capita income actually doubled compared to Israel's, although eventually it was reduced by half at the height of the Oslo period – once again demonstrating the negative power of the policies of neoliberalism pursued as part and parcel of the Oslo process (as we'll see in the next chapter). This also occurred at the same time that for political and security reasons most Palestinians were replaced by foreign guest workers.

44 Real per capita national income grew at an annual rate of close to 20 percent in 1969–72 and 5 percent in 1973–80.

45 Many of the early infiltrators were merely trying to return to their homes or farm their lands, but ultimately most consisted of military raids in which the attackers had little hope of returning alive.

46 The epitome of this dynamic was perhaps the massacre at the border village of Qibya in the West Bank in 1953, in which sixty Palestinians, almost all civilians, were killed by IDF troops in retaliation for the murder of an Israeli woman and two children days earlier in Tel Aviv.

47 One of the most comprehensive analyses of the Suez crisis is David Tal (ed.), *The 1956 War: Collusion and Rivalry in the Middle East* (London: Routledge, 2001).

48 See Pappe, *A History of Modern Palestine*, p. 167.

49 The most authoritative account of this assessment of a swift Israeli victory is provided by William B. Quandt, *Peace Process: American Diplomacy and the Arab–Israeli Conflict since 1967* (Washington, DC, and Berkeley, CA: Brookings Institution and University of California Press, 1993).

50 Once again, it is important to bear in mind that while in the first days of the war it appeared that Israel's very existence was at stake, neither Egyptian nor Syrian leaders had such a goal in mind when launching the invasion. Rather, for the Egyptians the goal was much more limited: to cross the Suez Canal and force Israel into a weakened position that would lead to negotiations for a return of the Sinai, which until then Israel had been unwilling to consider.

51 Greater Jerusalem, West Samaria, West Benjamin, the Jordan Valley and Judean Desert, the Reyhan-Dotan Bloc, the 'Einav-Sal'it Bloc, and the the Eshkolot-Shim'a Bloc.

52 While there were numerous conflicts between secular and religious Jews in the Mandate period, it was Prime Minister Ben-Gurion who granted orthodox Judaism sole authority over Jewish life in the new state, which meant that large sums of money were directed to yeshivas and other religious institutions

that helped lay the foundation for the 'religious revival' that occurred after 1967.

53 Milton-Edwards, *Islamic Politics in Palestine*, p. 96 (full citation p. 213).

54 The rise of the religious right in the United States is an example of this phenomenon, while the rise of so-called 'Islamic fundamentalism' across the Muslim world can also be attributed, in part, to the decreasing salience of secular nationalist identities in the wake of the defeat of 1967 and the rise of a global consumer culture, which has been a central focus of criticism by Islamist activists in the last generation (see *Why They Don't Hate Us*, ch. 5, for a detailed discussion of Muslim critiques of consumerism).

2 From handshake to security state

1 Arnon Raz-Krakotkin, 'A peace without Arabs: the discourse of peace and the limits of Israeli consciousness,' in Giacaman and Lonning, *After Oslo*, pp. 59–76; p. 67.

2 PLO Peace Talks Follow Up Committee, 'Statement on ninth round of Arab–Israeli peace talks,' Tunis, May 17, 1993, reprinted in *Journal of Palestinian Studies*, 23(1): 104–24.

3 A good summary of this style of criticism is the *New York Times* editorial 'A faltering Mideast peace,' January 15, 1998.

4 Speech delivered September 15, 2000.

5 Sara Roy, '"The seed of chaos, and of night": the Gaza Strip after the agreement,' *Journal of Palestine Studies*, 23(3): 85–98.

6 Ibid.

7 Text of Camp David Accords, September 17, 1978, Framework Section A.

8 In part the goal of the Likud was precisely to weaken the hold of the historically dominant Labor Party and its vast patronage-welfare network. But ideology was also important, as Likud policy-makers had close relationships with American economists such as Milton Friedman and other members of the 'Chicago School,' who shaped the policies of Thatcher, Reagan, and a host of developing countries (particularly in Latin America) during the 1970s and 1980s. We'll explore the details of this transformation in the chapter on the economics of Oslo.

9 It soon became clear that another motive for the invasion was to ensure the election of a friendly Christian president, Bashir Gemayel, who would then sign a peace treaty with Israel.

10 Despite the violence and steady number of Israeli soldiers being wounded or killed, and even unprecedented mass protests against the ongoing war (upwards of 400,000 people marched in Tel Aviv demanding 'Peace Now' in September 1982), the occupation became normalized. After fifteen years of occupying the West Bank, Gaza and the Golan Heights, Israelis were able to add another major occupation without seriously impacting other aspects of national life.

11 This well-known quote was reported by John Kifner in the *New York Times*, January 20, 1988, and by Gene Frankel in the *Washington Post* the next day.

12 Helena Lindhom Schulz, *The Reconstruction of Palestinian*

Nationalism (Manchester: Manchester University Press, 2000), especially ch. 3.

13 'The intifada,' *Middle East Report*, undated, available at <www.merip.org/palestine-israel_primer/intifada-87-pal-isr-primer.html>.

14 Yossi Sarid, 'Let them look for me,' *Ha'aretz*, August 17, 1990.

15 The best official Israeli accounts from this period are Savir, *The Process*, and Makovsky, *Making Peace with the PLO*.

16 Ahmed Qurei', *al-riwayah al-filastiniyah al-kamilah lil-mufawadat – min Oslo ila kharijat al-tariq: 1-mufawadat Oslo, 1993* [The Complete Palestinian Account of the Negotiations – from Oslo to the Road Map: 1 – Oslo Negotiations, 1993] (Beirut: Institute for Palestine Studies, 2006, pp. 211–24).

17 Edward Said, 'The morning after,' *London Review of Books*, October 21, 1993.

18 The first ever suicide attack by Hamas occurred in the previous year, when a Hamas operative detonated a car bomb at a rest stop at the Mehola Junction, but because he was parked between two trucks, only he and a Palestinian working at the junction were killed.

19 Helena Lindholm Schulz, *One Year into Self-Government: Perceptions of the Palestinian Political Elite* (Jerusalem: PASSIA, 1995).

20 Ze'ev Schiff, 'What did Rabin promise the Syrians,' *Ha'aretz*, August 29, 1997.

21 Bishara, *Palestine/Israel*, p. 66 (full citation p. 211).

22 Conversation with Professor Salim Tamari, July 2007. See also Jamil Halal, 'The effect of the Oslo Agreement on the Palestinian political system,' in Giacaman and

Lonning, *After Oslo*, pp. 121–45; p. 127.

23 Nils Butenschon, 'Tthe Oslo Agreements: from the White House to Jabl Abu Ghneim,' in Giacaman and Lonning, *After Oslo*, pp. 16–44; p. 16.

24 Fatah Central Committee member Muhammad Ghunaym, interviewed in *al-Sharq al-Awsat*, September 24, 1997. In the same issue, senior Hamas officials pronounced Olso 'dead.'

25 Rema Hammami and Jamil Hilal, 'An uprising at a crossroads,' *Middle East Report*, 219, Summer 2001; analysis of content of Palestinian television media made by author during fieldwork in the Occupied Territories during 1997 through 1999. For criticisms of the United States, see *al-Quds*, November 3 and 5, 1997. Also see Voice of Palestine, September 16, 1997.

26 Polling during this period indicated that about one-fifth of the population supported suicide bombings and other acts of terrorism, most of them, however, not for ideological reasons, but instead out of a feeling that nothing else would pressure Israel to fulfill its agreements.

27 Arafat, quoted in *al-Ayyam*, November 16, 1998; Mahmoud Abbas, quoted in *al-Sha'ab*, September 14, 1998; Ahmed Qurei', quoted in *al-Ayyam*, September 13, 1998. Also see *al-Quds*, October 20, 1999.

28 Foundation for Middle East Peace, 'Extraordinary increase in settlement construction as diplomacy falters,' *Settlement Report*, 8(2), March/April 1998.

29 UNESCO, 'Program for cooperation for the West Bank

and Gaza Strip, 1998–1999,' Gaza, September 1997, reprinted in the *Journal of Palestine Studies*, 27(2): 137–64; 142.

30 Human Rights Watch, 'Palestinian self-rule areas under the PA,' New York, September 1997.

31 *Ha'aretz* poll, published August 21, 1998, Hebrew edition.

32 *Jordan Times*, June 23, 1999; *Jerusalem Times*, June 25, 1999.

33 Robert Malley and Hussein Agha, 'Camp David: the tragedy of errors,' *New York Review of Books*, 48(13), August 9, 2001.

34 Benny Morris, 'Camp David and after: an exchange (1. An interview with Ehud Barak),' *New York Review of Books*, June 13, 2002.

35 Yigal Carmon and Aluma Solnik, 'Camp David and the prospects for a final settlement, part I: Israeli, Palestinian, and American positions,' MEMRI Inquiry and Analysis, 35, August 4, 2000.

36 The administration by and large shared Arafat's views, and according to Malley and Agha, Clinton told Barak in June that 'I want to do this, but not under circumstances that will kill Oslo,' and also urged Barak to put himself in Arafat's shoes and make substantive gestures to start the negotiations.

37 Swisher, *The Truth about Camp David*, p. 262.

38 Beilin, *Touching Peace*, p. 187.

39 Ben-Ami, *Scars of War*, pp. 206, 226, 254; Beilin, *Touching Peace*, p. 55.

40 Qurei', *al-riwayah al-filastiniyah*; chs 16–18 discuss the dynamics that produced the lopsided 'mutual recognition' from a Palestinian point of view.

41 Ibid., pp. 211–24; p. 346.

42 Munir Shafiq, *Oslo 1 wa 2, al-masar wa al-mal* (London: 1997).

43 Azmi Shu'aybi, Khalil Shikaki, 'A window on the workings of the PA: an inside view,' *Journal of Palestine Studies*, 30(1): 88–97; 88–9, 91, 95.

44 Malley and Agha, 'Camp David: the tragedy of errors.' Also see their 'The Palestinian–Israeli Camp David negotiations and beyond,' *Journal of Palestine Studies*, 31(1): 62–85.

45 In a Washington meeting the PA negotiating team asked Dennis Ross to urge Barak not to allow the visit (*Washington Post*, September 28, reported in 'Peace monitor,' *Journal of Palestine Studies*, 30(2): 191–217.

46 *al-Ayyam*, November 25 and 28, 2000.

47 Press release from Barak's media advisor, Israeli Ministry of Foreign Affairs, February 8, 2001.

48 See interviews with Ahmed Qurei', Nabil Shaath and other senior negotiators in *al-Ayyam* and *al-Quds*, January 28–30, 2001.

49 *Palestine in Review – This was 2001* (Jerusalem: PASSIA, 2003).

50 'Chronology: 16 February–15 May 2001,' *Journal of Palestine Studies*, 30(4): 172–93.

51 'Documents and source material,' *Journal of Palestine Studies*, 30(4): 143–71; B'tselem, statistics on deaths during the intifada, updated regularly at <www.btselem.org/English/Statistics/Casualties.asp>.

52 Hammami and Hilal, 'An uprising at a crossroads'; Helena Lindholm Schulz, 'The "al-Aqsa Intifada" as a result of politics of transition,' *Arab Studies Quarterly*, September 2002.

53 Human Rights Watch's report is available at <http://hrw.org/reports/2002/israel3/israel0502-01.htm#P49_1774>.

54 Edward Cody, 'Unnoticed Nablus may have taken West Bank's worst hit,' *Washington Post*, May 21, 2002.

55 'President Bush commends Israeli prime minister Sharon's plan,' Text of press conference with President Bush and Ariel Sharon, April 14, 2004, <www.whitehouse.gov/news/releases/2004/04/20040414-4.html>.

3 No land, no peace

1 Baruch Kimmerling, *Zionist and Territory: The Socio-Territorial Dimension of Zionist Politics* (Berkeley: University of California Press, 1983).

2 It is worth noting, however, that in the immediate aftermath of the 'miracle' of 1967, the Labor government of Prime Minister Levi Eshkol was willing to hand back most of the conquered territories to Jordan and Egypt in return for peace and official recognition (the Syrian Golan Heights were annexed along with Jerusalem to Israel and were outside the negotiating framework until the Oslo period). Nasser's infamous 'three noes' – no negotiations, no recognition and no peace – made such willingness moot.

3 Dror Etkes, Hagit Ofran Peace Now Settlement Watch Team, 'Breaking the law in the West Bank,' October 2006, p. 15. The 1979 'Elon More Case' saw the Israeli Supreme Court prohibit the state from using seizure of land for 'military purposes' as a basis for confiscating Palestinian-owned land for Jewish settlements.

4 Resolution 242 called for 'the establishment of a just and lasting peace in the Middle East,' to be achieved by 'the application of both the following principles: Withdrawal of Israeli armed forces from territories occupied in the recent conflict … [and] Termination of all claims or states of belligerency and respect for the right of every state in the area to live in peace within secure and recognized boundaries.'

5 Graham Fuller, 'Is Shamir irrelevant? Both sides know that land for peace is inevitable,' *Washington Post*, October 27, 1991.

6 Ze'ev Schiff, 'Oslo may be dead, but occupation is not the solution,' *Ha'aretz* online English edition, November 24, 2000.

7 Geoffrey Aronson, 'Settlement monitor,' *Journal of Palestine Studies*, 29(2): 135–42.

8 It was Ben-Gurion who first envisioned the idea of achieving sovereignty over any part of Palestine, and then using it as a 'decisive stage along a great path of Zionist implementation' for the large-scale settlement enterprise that commenced once the Likud achieved power in 1977 (quoted in Ben-Ami, *Scars of War*, p. 24).

9 Jonathan Rynhold, 'Reconceptualizing Israeli approaches to "Land for Peace" and the Palestinian question since 1967,' *Israel Studies*, 6(2): 33–52.

10 Unlike most Israeli leaders of this era, Allon was born in Palestine, and his understanding of the country's geography was unsurpassed.

11 See executive summary for *Land Grab*, available at <www.btselem.org/English/Publications/Summaries/200205_Land_Grab.asp>.

12 See diagrams 1 and 2 in B'tselem, *Land Grab*, p. 19.

13 Jackson Diehl, 'Jewish settlements grow in Occupied Territories; Israel allows communities to expand,' *Washington Post*, June 23, 1990, p. A19.

14 In fact, Benvenisti understood this almost a decade earlier, in 1979, when he argued that the settlements had already 'assumed a quasi-permanent nature ... the process set in motion after 1967 appears so strong that integration has passed the point of no return.' See Benvenisti, *The West Bank Data Base Project*, p. 67.

15 Ibid.

16 Jackson Diehl, 'West Bank's hidden housing boom; government smoke screen obscures vast Jewish settlement program,' *Washington Post*, January 29, 1992, p. A1. Only a few astute members of the press had already concluded that the settlement process had already doomed the two peoples to permanent conflict. See Deborah Horan, 'The promised land grab: Israel's West Bank,' *Washington Monthly*, May 1993.

17 Fatah Higher Organizational Committee summary of meeting, on Voice of Palestine, September 27, 1995.

18 Geoff Aronson, 'Israeli government adopts policy of accommodating settlers,' *Settlement Report*, 6(1), January 1996.

19 Max Singer and Michael Eichenwald, 'Making Oslo Work,' *Mideast Security and Policy Studies*, 30, February 1997.

20 Roni Shaqed and Oron Me'iri, 'PPSS denies connection with land dealers' murder,' *Yediot Aharonot*, May 22, 1997; 'PA

security officials arrest three more land-sellers,' AFP, May 24, 1997; *al-Ayyam*, December 8, 1997.

21 'Israeli land confiscations reportedly continue,' *al-Quds*, November 11, 1997.

22 Ibid.

23 Clyde Haberman, 'Israel orders tough measures against militant settlers; Arafat dismisses Rabin's moves as "hollow,"' *New York Times*, February 28, 1994, p. A1.

24 Information in the last three paragraphs drawn from the following sources: Voice of Palestine, March 25, 1997; Sa'eb Erakat, interviewed on *Kol Yisra'el* radio news, April 2, 1997; Voice of the Arabs radio program, June 22, 1997; *al-Quds*, August 11, 1997 and September 23, 1997; Voice of Palestine, September 25, 1997; Kol Yisrael Radio, January 19, 1998; Abbas Zaki, interviewed in *al-Sharq al-Awsat*, February 5, 1998, p. 3; *al-Ayyam*, February 5, 1998; *al-Quds*, April 30, 1998 (regarding resistance to the expansion of the Efrata settlement south of Bethlehem); Faisal Husseini, quoted on Jordan Television Network, June 22, 1998; Palestinian cabinet secretary General Ahmad 'Abd-al-Rahman, quoted on *Voice of Palestine Radio News*, Voice of Palestine, June 2, 1998, and on MENA News, Cairo, June 16, 1998.

25 The phrase was uttered to settlers on November 16, 1998, and reported by Geoffrey Aronson in *Settlement Report*, 9(1), January/February 1999.

26 This included 2 percent of the West Bank in Area C, which then became part of Area B, and 7.1 percent in Area B, which was transferred to Area A.

27 Quoted in Aronson, 'Settlement monitor,' pp. 128–38. The acceleration of settlement activity was documented in a special report by Orient House (the unofficial seat of Palestinian governance in East Jerusalem), which revealed twelve new Israeli settlements, eight settlements in industrial zones, and six new settler bypass roads, which, as we'll see below, were crucial to cementing Israeli control over these regions (see the yearly report by the Jerusalem Media and Communications Center, JMCC, on settlements, at <www.jmcc.org/media/report/98/Jan/2b.htm>, for details of the settlement expansion during this period).

28 According to the Israeli Bureau of Statistics the percentage of increase in population in the settlements from 1995 to the end of 1998 was 24.8 as compared to 6.6 in Israel.

29 Aronson, 'Settlement Monitor,' pp. 135–42; p. 138.

30 'Settlement timeline,' *Settlement Report*, 9(6), November/December 1999.

31 'Optical illusion at Havat Ma'on,' *Ha'aretz*, November 11, 1999.

32 A dunam is approximately one quarter of an acre.

33 See B'tselem, *Land Grab*, p. 116.

34 Baruch Kra, 'Only the left can build Har Homa – and it is,' *Ha'aretz*, February 6, 2000.

35 'Barak's record of settlement expansion,' *Settlement Report*, 10(2), March/April 2000.

36 Meron Rapoport, 'Har Homa neighborhood slated for "absentee" Palestinian land,' *Ha'aretz*, January 6, 2008.

37 Salim Tamari, 'June 6: Jerusalem's future: sovereignty, administration, and property claims,' *Information Brief*, 35, June 6, 2000.

38 Ibrahim Matar, 'Israeli policy in Jerusalem: a chronology of dispossession,' *Palestine-Israel Journal*, 7(3/4), 2000.

39 'US believes Jerusalem plan to "blur" Green Line borders,' *Ha'aretz*, June 22, 1998.

40 Jeff Halper, 'The end of a viable Palestinian state,' *Catholic New Times*, April 24, 2005.

41 'Sharon's West Bank policy leaves little role for the PA,' *Settlement Report*, 15(6), November/December 2005.

42 Human Rights Watch, 'Israel: expanding settlements in the occupied Palestinian territories,' December 27, 2005; Peace Now, 'Summary – Peace Now settlement/outpost report 2006,' February 21, 2007; Tovah Lazaroff, 'Peace now: Israel is building 3,000 new homes in West Bank,' *Jerusalem Post*, February 22, 2007.

43 'Settlers force desertion of Yanun village,' *Settlement Report*, 12(6), November/December 2002.

44 Geoffrey Aronson, 'Sharon government's separation plan defines Palestine's provisional borders,' *Journal of Palestine Studies*, 33(1): 139–47.

45 Fatah Central Committee member Sakhr Habash, interviewed in *al-Sharq al-Awsat*, October 22, 1995.

46 Jeff Halper, 'The matrix of control,' Mediamonitors.net, January 29, 2001.

47 Ahmed Qurei', interviewed in *al-Quds al-Arabi*, May 9, 1998, p. 6.

48 Jeff Halper, 'The 94 percent

solution: a matrix of control,' *MER*, 216, Fall 2000.

49 Eyal Weizman, 'The art of war: Deleuze, Guattari, Debord and the Israeli Defense Force,' *Frieze*, 99, May 2006.

50 A good summary of these strategies is provided by Jeff Halper, 'The key to peace: dismantling the matrix of control,' ICAHD website, <http://icahd.org/eng/articles.asp?menu=6&submenu=3>, 2007.

51 For Sharon's early use of the term canton, see Uzi Benziman, *Sharon, an Israeli Caesar* (New York: Adama Books, 1985), p. 131. Cf. *Al-Ayyam*, March 26, 1998.

52 See discussion on the bypass roads in *al-Muntaqar al faqri al-arabi/Arab Thought Forum*, October 12, 2006.

53 The bypass road network, joined by the settlements and the wall, also helps protect Israeli control over Palestinian water resources in the West Bank (Jad Isaac, 'Water and Palestinian–Israeli peace negotiations,' *Policy Brief*, 4, August 19, 1999).

54 Geoffrey Aronson, 'Mapping the future of Palestine,' *Journal of Palestine Studies*, 30(1): 136–43; see map on p. 138.

55 Jeff Halper, 'The key to peace: dismantling the matrix of control,' Israeli Committee Against Home Demolitions, undated, available at <www.icahd.org/Eng/articles.asp?menu=6&submenu=3>.

56 See Peter Lagerquist, 'Tasiij al-sma' al-akhira: al-Taqtib 'an falastin ba'd 'jedar al-fasl' al-isra'ili' [Fencing the last sky: excavating Palestine after Israel's 'Separation Wall'], *Hawliyyat al-Quds*, Spring 2005.

57 International Court of Justice, 'Legal consequences of the construction of a wall in the occupied Palestinian territory,' July 9, 2004, available at <www.icj-cij.org/docket/files/131/1671.pdf>.

58 PASSIA, 'Settlements and the wall: preempting the two-state solution,' Internet version, Jerusalem, 2004, available at <www.passia.org/publications/bulletins/Settlements2004/>.

59 Salim Tamari, interviewed by Elisabeth Farnsworth, *The News Hour with Jim Lehrer*, February 2004.

60 PASSIA, 'Settlements and the wall.'

61 The situation in Abu Dis is similar to that in most of Jerusalem's satellite villages, and reflects East Jerusalem's relationship with the remainder of the West Bank, as described by Amr Karmi, 'Judran al-fasl fi al-quds al-'arabiyya: manfan thalatha lil-sha'ab al-falastini' [The Separation Wall in Arab Jerusalem: the third exile for the Palestinian people], *Hawaliyyat al-Quds*, Spring 2006.

62 Qurei', *al-Riwayah al-filastinihah, al-Kamila*, Vol. 2, p. 358.

63 Benvenisti, *The West Bank Data Base Project*, p. 70.

64 Ibid., pp. 70–71.

65 Pierre van den Berghe, *Race and Racism* (New York: John Wiley & Sons, 1967), p. 29.

66 Kenneth P. Vickery, '"Herren-volk" Democracy and egalitarianism in South Africa and the US South,' *Comparative Studies in Society and History*, 16(3): 309–28.

67 As important because the segregation of Palestinians is at root based on territorial and nationalist considerations rather than racial prejudice; the notion

of avoiding any physical contact or mixing is not a relevant considera-tion.

68 Indeed, Israel is a unique case of apartheid in that it follows one of the core principles of South Africa in stripping Palestinians of citizenship and forcing them to live in cantons surrounded by white-controlled territory, yet the segregation is specifically based on territorial nationalism rather than racial identities, which was the basis for South African apartheid and many of its most infamous laws and ideologies.

69 Oren Yiftachel, 'Neither two states nor one: the disengagement and "creeping Apartheid" in Israel/Palestine,' *Arab World Geographer/Le Géographe du monde arabe*, l 8(3): 126.

70 Ibid., pp. 125–9.

71 Ibid., pp. 125–9; p. 125.

72 Yiftachel, *Ethnocracy*.

4 The economics of failure

1 Shimon Peres, interviewed on al-Jazeera, August 24, 2007, by Walid al-Umari. About a year be-fore, in a *Jerusalem Post* interview, Peres was asked whether he would have to talk to Hamas about his economic plan. His answer was simple and succinct: 'No.' Clearly there are some voices Peres felt that still didn't need to be heeded (*Jerusalem Post* interview, May 6, 2006).

2 Indeed, a year earlier, the Peres Peace Center put out a report explaining that 'despite intifada and all out war,' business people on both sides still believed there was lots of room to work together, with 'great potential for economic co-operation and for widening of trade relations' (Peres Center for Peace,

press release, dated December 31, 2006).

3 Upwards of 75 percent of all Palestinian imports to and 95 percent of all exports from the West Bank and Gaza involve Israel, while the Palestinians still have no meaningful autonomous trade relations with any other country.

4 Bishara, *Palestine/Israel*, p. 118.

5 See Adel Samara, 'al-Iqtisad al-falastini wa al-amaliyya al-salam al-tawsiya' [The Palestinian economy and the peace process], *Kana'an*, 1999, 96: 39–67.

6 'Female bomber, 68, wounds 3 IDF troops,' *Jerusalem Post*, Nov-ember 23, 2006.

7 Central Zionist Archives (CZA), S25/5936, minutes of May 16, 1940 meeting of representatives of Jaffa's Jewish neighborhoods with officials from the Tel Aviv municipality and Zionist officials. Memo is entitled 'Jewish neighbor-hoods within the borders of Tel Aviv,' but that is clearly a mistake as the subject is clearly Jaffa's Jewish neighborhoods and their relation-ship to Tel Aviv.

8 This according to Assaf Razin, an economist who briefly served as chief economic adviser to the government of Israel under Ehrlich in 1979, as described in an online 'biographical note' on Cornell University's website from Novem-ber 2006.

9 Israel quickly 'became an extreme case of an extremely overburdened state incapable of stemming stagnation and spiraling inflation' (Michael Shalev, 'The contradictions of economic reform in Israel,' *Middle East Report*, Sum-mer 1998, pp. 30–33, 41).

10 Stanley Fischer, 'The Israeli stabilization program, 1985–86,' *American Economic Review*, 77(2): 275–8.

11 Michael W. Klein, 'Studying texts: a Gemara of the Israeli economy,' NBER, May 6, 2005, pp. 25–35.

12 Ibid.

13 Jonathan Nitzan, 'From war profits to peace dividends: the new political economy of Israel,' *Capital and Class*, Autumn 1996.

14 Jonathan Nitzan and Shimshom Bichler, 'Israel's roaring economy,' Unpublished paper, June 2007.

15 Roni ben Efrat, 'The first post-Zionist war,' *Challenge*, 99, September/October 2006.

16 Bishara, *Palestine/Israel*.

17 Sara Roy succinctly describes the process of de-development as the deliberate, systematic deconstruction of an indigenous economy by a dominant power. It is distinguished from underdevelopment, the situation prevailing in much of the Third World, by both the intentions of the occupying power and the consequences of its policies. Roy, *The Gaza Strip*.

18 Official of the Tel Aviv Labor Exchange, quoted in Aushalom Kaveh, 'The Histadrut and discrimination,' *Journal of Palestine Studies*, 12(4): 185–7.

19 UN Office for the Coordination of Humanitarian Affairs, 'ISRAEL-OPT: House demolitions cause Palestinians to leave village,' February 21, 2008; Samara, 'The Palestinian economy,' pp. 39–56.

20 World Bank, 'Long term policy options for the Palestinian economy' (Washington, DC: World Bank, 2002), p. 72. The difficult business environment with respect to uncertainty, property rights, financing, and transparency further dissuaded investment in growth-generating activities.

21 Pappe, *A History of Modern Palestine*, pp. 232–4.

22 Adel Samara, 'Globalization, the Palestinian economy and the peace process,' *Journal of Palestine Studies*, 114: 20–39; 22.

23 Quoted in Guy Ben-Porat, 'Between power and hegemony: business communities in peace processes,' *Review of International Studies*, 2005 (31): 325–48.

24 Beilin, *Touching Peace*, p. 128.

25 Bishara, *Palestine/Israel*.

26 Shimon Peres, *The New Middle East* (New York: Holt, 1993), pp. 44–50.

27 Shimon Peres, Speech before the United Nations, Sepetmber 29, 1994.

28 Yet when the military devised the Sadan Plan to manage local Palestinian development, it was opposed by the Israeli business community, which was wary of losing its captive market.

29 Salim Tamari, 'Who rules Palestine?', *Journal of Palestine Studies*, 31(4): 102–13; 104.

30 Beilin, *Touching Peace*, p. 166.

31 As the newspaper *Ha'aretz* reported, the intelligence services understood that employment in Israel was a prime component of the Palestinian economy.

32 Samara, 'Globalization,' pp. 20–39; p. 21.

33 Ibid.

34 World Bank, 'Developing the Occupied Territories: an investment in peace' (Washington, DC: World Bank, 1993); see, *inter alia*, pp. 7, 58.

35 Jennifer Olmstead, 'Thwarting Palestinian development,' *Middle East Report*, 201: 11–13, 18.

36 Brynen, *A Very Political Economy*.

37 Diwan and Shaban, *Development under Adversity*.

38 Steven Barnett et al., 'The economy of the West Bank and Gaza Strip: recent experience, prospects, and challenges to private sector development' (Washington, DC: IMF, 1998).

39 Salem Ajluni, 'Palestinian economy and the Second Intifada,' *Journal of Palestine Studies*, 32(3): 64–73.

40 Among the most detailed examinations of childhood malnutrition in the West Bank and Gaza Strip in the first years of the al-Aqsa intifada is that undertaken by CARE International and the Johns Hopkins University, in conjunction with al-Quds University, entitled 'Nutritional assessment of the West Bank and Gaza Strip.' It was published in September 2002 and is available at <www.reliefweb.int/rw/rwb.nsf/AllDocsByUNID/6a58b2b41de887e2c1256ca8003800do>.

41 Karen Pfeifer, 'The mercurial economics of the phantom Palestinian state,' *Dollars and Sense* magazine, January/February 2002.

42 Adel Samara, 'Globalization,' p. 20.

43 Jamil Hilal, 'The Palestinian elite,' *La Rivista del Manifesto*, 28, May 2002.

44 Robinson, *Building a Palestinian State*.

45 Jamil Hilal, 'Problematizing democracy in Palestine,' *Comparative Studies of South Asia, Africa and the Middle East*, 23(1/2): 163–72.

46 Minister of Finance Muhammad al-Nashashibi, quoted in *al-Ayyam*, April 17, 1998; 'PA formulating plan to reduce dependence on Israel,' *Jordan Times*, August 19, 1997; *al-Sharq al-Awsat*, June 2, 1997, p. 13.

47 Rex Brynen, 'The dynamics of Palestinian elite formation,' *Journal of Palestine Studies*, 24(3): 31–43.

48 Hawartani, interviewed on Kol Yisrael Radio, June 22, 1995; Qurei', interviewed in *La Vanguardia* (Barcelona), November 13, 1996; Nabil Sha'ath, interviewed on Voice of Palestine, June 16, 1998.

49 Sai'b Bamiyah, director of the Palestinian Economic Ministry, interviewed in *al-Sharq al-Awsat*, June 2, 1997, p. 13.

50 *al-Ayyam*, May 12, 1998; Peres, quoted in *Ha'aretz*, April 3, 1996; *al-Hayah al-Jadidah*, August 23, 1997.

51 World Bank, 'Long term policy options for the Palestinian economy,' July 2002.

52 World Bank, 'Disengagement, the Palestinian economy, and the settlements' (Washington, DC: World Bank, June 2004, p. ii).

53 World Bank, 'Two years of *Intifada*, closures and Palestinian economic crisis,' Report, March 5, 2003.

54 World Bank, 'Investing in Palestinian economic reform and development,' Report for the Pledging Conference, Paris, December 17, 2007; World Bank, 'Disengagement, the Palestinian economy, and the settlements,' pp. 4–9.

55 Along the detour routes many students as young as seven were forced to take to school, there was routine harassment and even

physical attacks by soldiers and masked assailants, leading also to the injury of international observers (United Nations, Office for the Coordination of Humanitarian Affairs [OCHA], 'Humanitarian update', November 2004).

56 World Bank, 'Long term policy options for the Palestinian economy,' pp. xiii–xiv.

57 As the first PA meeting in Tunis on September 30, 1994 described it.

58 Usher, *Palestine in Crisis*, p. 36.

59 World Bank, 'Long term policy options for the Palestinian economy,' p. xii.

60 Sébastien Dessus, 'A Palestinian growth history, 1968–2000,' Unpublished research paper, World Bank, pp. 3, 5–6.

61 Samir Huleileh, 'Restructuring Palestinian–Israeli relations: an interview,' *Palestine–Israel Journal of Politics, Economics and Culture*, VI(3), 1999.

62 Interviewed in *al-Sharq al-Awsat*, June 2, 1997, p. 13.

63 Ibid.

64 Burhan Dajani, 'The September 1993 Israeli–PLO documents: a textual analysis,' *Journal of Palestine Studies*, 23(3): 5–23; 11–12.

65 Olmstead, 'Thwarting Palestinian development,' p. 13, also points to this article's importance.

66 Sara Roy, 'De-development revisited: Palestinian economy and society since Oslo,' *Journal of Palestine Studies*, 28(3): 64–82.

67 An English version of the platform is available at <www.israelipalestinianprocon.org/Treaties/hamas2006platform.html>.

68 UNRWA produced a study in late 2006 that reported that the number of 'deep poor' increased by over 64 percent just in the first half of 2006 (UNRWA, 'Prolonged crisis in the occupied Palestinian territory: recent socio-economic impacts,' November 24, 2006).

69 Sara Roy, 'De-development revisited,' pp. 64–82; p. 69.

70 UN Office for the Coordination of Humanitarian Affairs, 'ISRAEL-OPT: Israeli experts propose radical changes to West Bank closure regime,' February 14, 2008.

71 UN News Centre, 'UN humanitarian chief assesses impact of closures on West Bank residents,' February 16, 2008.

72 Akiva Eldar, 'UN: despite Israel's promises, West Bank barriers have increased,' *Ha'aretz*, January 22, 2008.

73 Leila Farsakh, 'Palestinian labor flows to the Israeli economy: a finished story?', *Journal of Palestine Studies*, 32(1): 13–27; 19.

74 World Bank, 'Two years after London: restarting Palestinian economic recovery,' Economic Monitoring Report to the Ad Hoc Liaison Committee, September 24, 2007. Also see E. Ben-Ari and Y. Bilu (eds), *Grasping Land: Space and Place in Contemporary Israeli Discourse and Experience* (Stony Brook, NY: SUNY Press, 1997).

75 Amir Peretz, interviewed on Israel Television Channel 1 News, November 10, 1996.

76 Leila Farsakh, 'Economic viability of a Palestinian state in the West Bank and Gaza Strip: is it possible without territorial integrity and sovereignty?', *MIT Electronic Journal of Middle East Studies*, 1, May 2001.

77 Ibid., p. 15.

78 A free trade agreement (FTA)

is an agreement between two or more countries to allow uninterrupted trade in commodities produced in each country.

79 Peres used the term 'common market' in *The New Middle East* (p. 99).

80 World Bank, 'Stagnation or revival: Israeli disengagement and Palestinian economic prospects,' December 2004.

81 A detailed analysis of the QIZ and related MEFTA-type programs is provided by Bessma Momani, 'A Middle East Free Trade Area: economic interdependence and peace considered,' *The World Economy*, unindexed online version of forthcoming article, July 2007.

82 Peter Lagerquist, 'Privatizing the occupation: the political economy of an Oslo development project,' *Journal of Palestine Studies*, 32(2): 5–20.

83 Paltrade and Peres Center, 'The untapped potential: Palestinian–Israeli economic relations: policy options and recommendations,' p. 22.

84 Yusuf Mansur, 'Lessons from the QIZs in Jordan,' *Bitter Lemons*, 20(5), May 24, 2007.

85 For the increase in Israeli poverty as of 2008, see Shay Niv, 'Higher old age pensions fail to halt poverty: a larger number of wage-earners has fallen below the poverty line,' *Globes*, February 14, 2008. For the plight of Palestinian citizens of Israel, see Sharon Roffe-Ofir, 'Report: most Arabs below poverty line,' *Yediot Aharonot*, February 16, 2008.

86 Adel Samara, 'Globalization, the Palestinian economy, and the "peace process,"' *Journal of Palestine Studies*, 114, Winter 2000.

87 Ibid.

88 Adel Samara, 'The "Palestinian" economy and the "TAWSIYA" peace process,' *Kan'an*, 96: 39–67; 40.

89 Khalil Nakhleh, *Astura al-Tanmiyya fi falastin: al-da'am al-siyasi wa al-murawagha al-mustadayima* [The myth of Palestinian development: political aid and sustainable deceit] (Ramallah: Muwatan, 2004).

90 Sara Roy succinctly describes the process of de-development as the deliberate, systematic deconstruction of an indigenous economy by a dominant power. It is distinguished from underdevelopment, the situation prevailing in much of the Third World, by both the intentions of the occupying power and the consequences of its policies. Roy, *The Gaza Strip*.

5 Religion, culture and territory

1 Two of the most important works exploring the role of Islam and the emerging Muslim public spheres in shaping nationalist movements beginning in the late nineteenth century are Armando Salvatore's *Islam and the Political Discourse of Modernity* (London: Ithaca Press, 1998), and Michael Gasper, 'Abdallah Nadim, Islamic reform, and "ignorant" peasants: state-building in Egypt? Muslim traditions and modern techniques of power,' in Armando Salvatore (ed.), *Yearbook of the Sociology of Islam*, vol. 3 (Hamburg/New York: Lit Verlag and Transaction Books, 2001).

2 The first 'genuine' Palestinian Muslim Brotherhood organization was formed in 1943 in Jerusalem (Hroub, *Hamas*, p. 14). Al-Qassem

was in fact Syrian; his taking up of the Palestinian cause marked the first of a recurring theme of non-Palestinian Arabs and Muslims championing the Palestinian cause.

3 Hroub, *Hamas*, p. 27.

4 Ibrahim Maqadima, *Ma'alim fil-tariq ila tahrir filastin* (Gaza: Aleem Institute, 1994), pp. 254–5; cf. Hroub, *Hamas*, p. 28.

5 Mishal and Shela, *The Palestinian Hamas*, ch. 2.

6 Ibid., ch. 2.

7 For a discussion of Israel's support of the Islamic movement in the 1970s and 1980s, see Robert Dreyfuss, *Devil's Game: How the United States Helped Unleash Fundamentalist Islam* (New York: Metropolitan Books, 2005), pp. 195–200.

8 Milton-Edwards, *Islamic Politics in Palestine*, p. 104.

9 Ibid., p. 134; Shaykh Awwad of the Mujamma', quoted in ibid., p. 109.

10 We can interpret this as effectively proclaiming the PLO's charter null and void, asserting its replacement by 'a true covenant that was uncompromisingly faithful to both Palestinian national principles and Islamic beliefs and values.'

11 'HAMAS – the Islamic Resistance Movement,' IDF spokesman briefing, January 1993; available at <www.fas.org/irp/world/para/docs/930100.htm>.

12 Associated Press, 'Hamas's secretive military branch reveals its structure: details attacks in bid to get credit for Gaza pullout,' September 4, 2005.

13 Hamas's Gaza head, Mahmoud Zahar, is considered very extreme, while its West Bank head, Hassan Yousef, former head of the Zakat, or charity wing, of al-Quds University in Jerusalem, has spoken openly of a truce with Israel.

14 Bradley Burston, 'Background/Hamas vs. Abbas: the lethal wild card, a profile,' *Ha'aretz.com*, undated.

15 Council on Foreign Relations, 'Hamas,' June 8, 2007.

16 Although, when I used to visit Gaza before Sheikh Yassin's assassination in 2004, one of the 'highlights' of such tours was passing by his home, surrounded by rubble-strewn buildings from various attempts to assassinate him, where a Star of David was painted on the street to provide drivers with the symbolic victory of running it over.

17 Hamas leaflet, undated, catalog number HMS01, in Jean-François Legrain, *Les Voix du soulèvement palestinien, 1987–1988* (Cairo: CEDEJ, 1991), p. 12.

18 Lindholm Schulz, *The Reconstruction of Palestinian Nationalism*, p. 151; cf. Milton-Edwards, *Islamic Politics in Palestine*, *inter alia* pp. 185, 207.

19 Ahmad, *Hamas*, p. 11 (full citation p. 213).

20 Musa K. Budeiri, 'The nationalist dimension of Islamic movements in Palestinian politics,' *Journal of Palestine Studies*, Review essay, Spring 1995, 24(3): 93.

21 Hamas Covenant, Clauses 6, 9 and 12. Cf. Meir Litvak, 'The Islamization of Palestinian identity: the case of Hamas,' Moshe Dayan Center, <www.dyan.org/d&a-hamas-litvak.htm>.

22 Catarina Kinnvall, 'Globalization and religious nationalism: self, identity, and the search for ontological security,' *Political Psychology*, 25(5): 741–67.

23 Mishal and Shela, *The Palestinian Hamas*, Preface.

24 Islamic Jihad pamphlet, quoted in Milton-Edwards, *Islamic Politics in Palestine*, p. 118.

25 Hamas leader, quoted by Hatina, *Islam and Salvation in Palestine*, p. 19.

26 Hamas leaflet, undated, catalog number HMS18, in Legrain, *Les Voix du soulèvement palestinien*, p. 159. Also, see the Hamas Charter, Article 28.

27 Sheikh Hamad Bitawi, interviewed by Ahmad, *Hamas*, p. 109.

28 Hamas leaflet dated 23 February, 1988, entitled 'Full strike against the new American plot' (*Idrab Shamil fi wajha al-u'amara al-Amarikiyyah al-jadida*).

29 Former head of the Hamas Political Bureau Musa Abu Marzouq, interviewed by Hroub, *Hamas*, pp. 44–5.

30 Sheikh Hamad Bitawi, interviewed by Ahmad, *Hamas*, p. 109.

31 For a detailed discussion of the experience of penetration as a seminal part of the experience of European colonialism, see LeVine, *Overthrowing Geography*, ch. 2; Timothy Mitchell, *Colonising Egypt* (Berkeley: University of California Press, 1991), p. 126.

32 Hamas leaflet number 82, dated 18 August 1988.

33 Hamas, Introductory memorandum, contained as Appendix, doc. 3, in Hroub, *Hamas* (full citation p. 213).

34 Ibid.

35 Sheikh Ahmad Yassin, quoted in Hroub, *Hamas*, p. 62.

36 Hamas, Introductory memorandum, undated, in Hroub, *Hamas*, p. 292.

37 If one searches the Internet for coverage of almost any suicide bombing in Israel, the story will feature the same terms – justified and legitimate – used by Hamas in its announcement of responsibility for its actions.

38 For a good discussion of the psychological roots of suicide bombers associated with Hamas, see Eyad El Sarraj and Linda Butler, 'Suicide bombers: dignity, despair, and the need for hope,' *Journal of Palestine Studies*, 2002, 31(4): 71–6.

39 Senior Hamas political operative, interviewed in Gaza City by author, September 2003.

40 Khaled Meshal, interviewed by Alex Van Buren, *La Repubblica*, April 27, 2006.

41 Ghazi Abed, then editor of *al-Risalah* newspaper, interviewed by author, September 2003, in his office in Gaza.

42 Abu Omar Al-Baghdadi, commander of the al-Qaeda-founded organization Islamic State of Iraq (ISI), February 14, 2008; video posted on the al-Hesbah website, as referenced at <www.memri.org/bin/articles.cgi?Page=archives&Area=sd&ID=SP184508>.

43 On the internecine violence during the al-Aqsa intifada, see Avi Issacharoff, 'The battle within,' *Ha'aretz*, January 18, 2007.

44 Quoted in Mohammed Daraghmeh, Associated Press report on the clashes, June 21, 2007.

45 'Hamas and Fatah trade fire in power struggle,' Guardian.co.uk, December 15, 2006.

46 Mahmoud Abbas, quoted in *al-Hayat*, November 26, 2002.

47 Ehud Sprinzak, *Gush Emunim: The Politics of Zionist Fundamentalism in Israel* (Washington, DC:

The American Jewish Committee, 1986). Also see Robert Friedman, *Zealots for Zion* (New York: Random House, 1992).

48 Samuel C. Heilman, 'The vision from the madrasa and Bes Medrash: some parallels between Islam and Judaism,' *Bulletin of the American Academy of Arts and Sciences*, 49(4): 6–37.

49 Ian Lustick, *For the Land and the Lord: Jewish Fundamentalism in Israel* (New York: Council on Foreign Relations, 1988), Introduction. A good early analysis of Gush Emunim is Kevin A. Avruch, 'Traditionalizing Israeli nationalism: the development of Gush Emunim,' *Political Psychology*, 1(1): 47–57. For the basic writings of Cook, see A. Y. Cook, *Orot* [Lights] (Jerusalem: NP, 1950).

50 Ehud Sprinzak, 'Gush Emunim: the tip of the iceberg,' *Jerusalem Quarterly*, 21, Fall 1981, web archive.

51 A good summary of the party's platform and history is at <www.mafdal.org.il/default.asp>.

52 A detailed description of Moledet's platform is available, in English as well as Hebrew, at <www.moledet.org.il/english/>.

53 Israel Shahak and Norton Mezvinsky, *Jewish Fundamentalism in Israel* (London: Pluto Press, 1999), ch. 5, online version without pagination.

54 The best English-language analysis of the religious discourses surrounding Rabin's murder is Michael Karpin and Ina Friedman's *Murder in the Name of God: The Plot to Kill Yitzhak Rabin* (New York: Metropolitan Books, 1998).

55 For a discussion of 'settler Judaism,' see Michael Lerner, *Jewish Renewal: Path to Healing and Transformation* (NY: HarperCollins, 1995).

56 Yoav Peled (ed.), *Shas: Etgar hayisra'eliyut* [Shas: The Challenge of Israeliness] (Tel Aviv: Yediot Ahronot Publishing, 2001), editor's introduction, p. 11.

57 Yoav Peled, 'The continuing electoral success of Shas: a cultural division of labor analysis,' in Michael Shamir and Alan Arian (eds), *The Elections in Israel, 1999* (Albany, NY: SUNY Press, 2002).

58 Sara Helman and Andre Levy, 'On the cultural assumptions of the public sphere: Shas' representation in the Israeli press,' UCI, October 2002.

59 The class position of Ashkenazim and Mizrachim, combined with the contemporary surge of identity politics in Israeli Jewish society, are two of the most important factors determining the course of Israeli politics today (Michael Shalev et al., 'The political impact of inequality: social cleavages and voting in the 1999 elections,' Discussion Paper 2-00, Pinhas Sapir Center for Development, Tel Aviv University, January 2000).

60 There Barak begged forgiveness of the Sephardi immigrants on behalf of the Labor movement and promised to do all he could to improve their disadvantaged status in Israeli society.

61 Thus, Itzchak Levy, former minister of education, in defending his decision to allot Shas's youth organization public funds, was quoted as saying: 'Budgets will be granted even to the Hamas if it commits itself to promote democratic values' (*Ha'aretz*, September 18, 1998).

62 Sheikh Abdullah Nimr Darwish, interview with author in Kafr Qassem, December 2000.

63 Peled, *Shas*.

64 Oren Yiftachel, '"Ethnocracy" and its discontents: minorities, protest and the Israeli polity,' *Critical Inquiry*, 26: 725–6.

6 Violence, chaos, and the history of the future

1 Before then, most guards of Jewish settlements were from the local non-Jewish Arab population.

2 Quotations taken from Max Weber, *Politics as Vocation*, Internet edition.

3 Foucault's understanding of power emerged in a clear form first in *Discipline and Punish* and continued to be developed in various directions until his last book, Volume 3 of the *History of Sexuality*. I owe this particularly succinct description of Foucault's discussion of power to Steven L. Winter, 'The "power" thing,' *Virginia Law Review*, 82(5): 721–835; 728.

4 PA president Abbas would accuse Hamas of facilitating and nurturing the rise of al-Qaeda in Gaza; NGOs accuse him of creating a military dictatorship. Prime Minister Fayyad called for 'intense and active cooperation' with Israel, criminalizes the resistance and dubs it 'catastrophic,' and argued that Hamas rather than Israel had 'destroyed our national project completely' (Bashir Abu-Manneh, 'Symptoms of decay in occupied Palestine,' Znet.org, July 16, 2007).

5 Frantz Fanon, *The Wretched of the Earth*, trans. Constance Farrington (New York: Penguin Books, 2001).

6 Israeli critics of this ideology have dubbed the supposed righteousness of Israeli soldiers when they shoot Palestinian civilians or children throwing stones as 'shooting and crying.'

7 Hannah Arendt, *On Violence* (New York: Harcourt Brace, 1969), which is in good measure written in response to Fanon's *Wretched of the Earth*. The best analysis of the two thinkers' views on violence is Elizabeth Frazera and Kimberly Hutchings, 'On politics and violence: Arendt contra Fanon,' *Contemporary Political Theory*, 7: 90–108.

8 Isabel Kershner and Taghreed al-Khodary, 'Gazans protest at border fence,' *New York Times*, February 26, 2008.

9 That is, where Henry Ford paid his workers high enough wages so they could afford to buy his cars, Wal-Mart pays its workers so little they can't afford to shop anywhere else besides Wal-Mart and other discount stores.

10 'Wal-Mart Stores reports higher profit,' Associated Press, February 19, 2008.

11 Zvi Lavi, 'Defense Ministry: Israeli defense exports 10–12% of global total,' *Globes*, July 6, 2004.

12 Shimshon Bichler and Jonathan Nitzan, 'Israel's roaring economy,' June 2007, posted on their website, bnarchives.york.ca.

13 Shimshon Bichler and Jonathan Nitzan, 'Cheap war,' Alternative Information Center, November 2006.

14 Shimshon Bichler and Jonathan Nitzan, 'Israel's global capitalism,' June 2004, posted on their website, bnarchives.york.ca.

15 Ibid.

16 Avraham Burg, 'A failed Israeli society is collapsing,'

International Herald Tribune, September 6, 2002.

17 It should be pointed out that Saudi military expenditures decreased in the mid-1990s because of the fall in oil revenues, but had picked up and stabilized by the latter half of the decade at between 13 and 15 percent of per capita GDP and between US$17 and 20 billion per year (see Anthony Cordesman, 'Saudi Arabia: the broader factors driving the need for foreign investment and economic diversity,' Center for Strategic and International Studies paper, April 2002, <www.csis.org/burke/saudi21/saudi_broaderneed.pdf>).

18 Munir Shafiq, *Oslo 1 wa 2: al-nasar wa al-mal* (London: Falastin al-Muslima, 1997), pp. 18–23.

19 Ibid.

20 Moussa Abu Marzook, 'Hamas is ready to talk,' *Guardian*, August 16, 2007.

21 See Parker, *Resignation or Revolt*, p. 9.

22 For the structure of the PA, see the chart at: <www.PA.gov.ps/Government/image/plo_PA.jpg>.

23 Nathan Brown, article in the USIP's journal *Peaceworks*, December 2002.

24 Rema Hammami and Salim Tamari, 'Anatomy of another rebellion,' *Middle East Report*, Winter 2000, p. 14.

25 Specifically, Israel allowed Arafat to establish secret bank accounts in Tel Aviv that left tens if not hundreds of millions of dollars owed to the PA for taxes and other duties collected by Israel at his discretion (as allowed by the Interim Agreement), with no oversight or accountability. Indeed, within two years of the 1996 elections the Legislative Council was unable to use its mandated investigative and oversight authority to act on a scathing report from the PA's General Control Institution detailing irregularities in accounting in most of its ministries and agencies (Nathan Brown, *Palestinian Politics after the Oslo Accords: Resuming Arab Palestine*, Berkeley: University of California Press, 2003, p. 108).

26 The president could veto legislature, issue laws by decree, make appointments to the civil service and the police, establish or dissolve public institutions and, crucially vis-à-vis corruption, could disburse public funds. Along with his control of numerous security services, and a manipulation of his cabinet and other senior posts that stimulated inter-clan or other factional rivalries (particularly between 'Tunisians' and local activists), this allowed Arafat to establish the kind of neo-patriarchal or patrimonial regime that resembled in many ways those of neighboring Arab states, clearly against the wishes of the majority of Palestinians, who hoped for a real democratic transformation as part of the road to independence (Helena Lindholm Schulz, 'The "al-Aqsa Intifada" as a result of politics of transition,' *Arab Studies Quarterly*, Fall 2002).

27 The extent of the PA's corruption was revealed to the outside world in an April 1997 exposé by the Israeli newspaper *Ha'aretz*, which put the amount of funds deposited in Arafat's Israeli bank account(s) at upwards of $500 million per year. But beyond this '*al-sandooq al-thani*,' or second account, the PA and Arafat personally established well over two dozen monopolies

that controlled most every aspect of the Palestinian economy, rewarding his family and leading supporters (not the main beneficiaries – see note above) while remaining tied to the economic interests of Israel.

28 Nathan Brown, *Palestinian Politics after the Oslo Accords* (Berkeley: University of California Press, 2003). See Michel Rocard, 'Strengthening Palestinian public institutions,' Council on Foreign Relations, June 1999.

29 Quoted in Connell, *Rethinking Revolution*, p. 286.

30 'Urgent appeal to stop suicide bombings,' *al-Quds*, July 19, 2002.

31 World Bank, 'The Palestinian NGO project,' Public Discussion Paper, July 1997.

32 For a good analysis of the situation of MENA NGOs on the eve of the al-Aqsa intifada, see Sheila Carapico, 'NGOs, INGOs, GO-NGOS, and DO-NGOS: making sense of non-governmental organizations,' *Middle East Report*, 214, Spring 2000.

33 Norton, *Civil Society in the Middle East*, vol. 1, p. 7.

34 George Giacaman, 'In the throes of Oslo: Palestinian society, civil society and the future,' in Giacaman and Lonning, *After Oslo*, pp. 1–15.

35 Rema Hammami, 'Palestinian NGOs since Oslo: from NGO politics to grass roots movement,' *Middle East Report*, 214, Spring 2000.

36 Hadani Ditmars, 'Critiquing NGOs: assessing the last decade,' *Middle East Report*, 214: 18–19.

37 Denis J. Sullivan, 'NGOs in Palestine: agents of development and foundation of civil society,' *Journal of Palestine Studies*, 25(3): 93–100.

38 I provide a detailed analysis of the phenomena of weak states/weak societies as they have emerged in Iraq and Palestine in my article 'Chaos, globalization, and the public sphere: political struggle in Iraq and Palestine,' *Middle East Journal*, LX(3): 467–92.

39 Indeed, by the end of the intifada's third year the harsh anti-insurgency strategy pursued by Israel – which focused as much on rooting out, arresting and even deporting effective leaders of non-violent protests such as Mubarak Award as on stopping violence against soldiers and civilians – had effectively crushed the mass-based civilian uprising, leaving an increasingly violent cadre of young men to engage in violence, largely against suspected collaborators.

40 Rema Hammami, 'Palestinian NGOs, the Oslo transition and the space of development,' Birzeit University, February 2002.

41 Ibid.

42 Ibid.

43 Sara Roy, 'The transformation of Islamic NGOs in Palestine,' *Middle East Report*, 214, Spring 2000.

44 The two NGO worlds did not often intersect, and such was the separation and even hostility between them that Hamas and Islamist NGOs did not support the NGO sector when the PA began its campaign to crack down on the sector, despite the shared opposition of many in the NGO sector to the appeasement policies of the PA, and despite support offered by the official Hamas newspapers for the secular NGOs then under attack.

45 Joshua Mitnick, 'Palestinian charities help Hamas endure,'

Christian Science Monitor, October 16, 2006.

46 Penny Johnson and Eileen Kuttab, 'Where have all the women (and men) gone? Reflections on gender and the second Palestinian intifada,' *Feminist Review*, 69(1): 21–43.

47 Rita Giacaman and Penny Johnson, 'Searching for strategies: the Palestinian women's movement in the new era,' in Suad Joseph and Susan Slyomovics (eds), *Women and Power in the Middle East* (Philadelphia: University of Pennsylvania Press, 2000), pp. 150–58.

48 Ibid.

49 Hanadi Loubani and Jennifer Plyler, 'Occupation, patriarchy, and the Palestinian women's movement,' Znet.org, November 2003. Also see Nadera Shalhoub-Kevorkian, 'House demolition: a Palestinian feminist perspective,' *Markaz al-Quds lil-nisa'*, March 30, 2006. A good resource on continuing activities related to women's issues involving both Palestinian and Israeli women is <www.batshalom.org/>.

50 Giacaman and Johnson, 'Searching for strategies', p. 151.

51 This was clear from a tour of women's NGOs funded by the US-based charity Grassroots International in the West Bank and Gaza in which I participated in 1997, which visited television studios the group funded that were run by religious women.

Conclusion

1 And thus the idea put forth by Israeli peacemakers that the proper solution was one where 'each side concedes part of its dream' was in fact one where 'no partition of Jerusalem' was possible (as Beilin argued, 'Israel can't accept their demand for a united city comprising two capitals'), no refugees would be allowed to return to 1967 Israel ('We cannot countenance entitlement of refugees to choose between compensation and return to Jaffa, Haifa or any other place under our sovereignty,' he continued) and only some settlements would be removed, at Israel's discretion ('The Palestinians cannot countenance an arrangement whereby all Jewish settlements remain under Israeli jurisdiction,' he explained. How many would be left he never says) (Beilin, *Touching Peace*, pp. 186–8).

Suggestions for further reading

Introduction

Foucault, Michel (1973) *The Birth of the Clinic: An Archaeology of Medical Perception*, trans. A. M. Sheridan Smith, New York: Vintage.

— (1988) *Politics, Philosophy, Culture*, trans. Alan Sheridan, London: Routledge.

— (1995) *Discipline and Punish*, New York: Vintage.

Frank, Andre Gunder (1998) *Re-Orient: Global Economy in the Asian Age*, Berkeley: University of California Press.

Harvey, David (1989) *The Condition of Postmodernity: An Enquiry into the Origins of Cultural Change*, London: Blackwell.

LeVine, Mark (2005) *Why They Don't Hate Us: Lifting the Veil on the Axis of Evil*, Oxford: Oneworld Publications.

Nietzsche, Friedrich Wilhelm (n.d.) *On the Uses and Disadvantages of History for Life*, Internet edition.

— (1990) *Twilight of the Idols: Or, How to Philosophize with a Hammer*, New York: Penguin.

Nitzan, Jonathan and Shimshon Bichler (2003) *The Global Political Economy of Israel*, London: Pluto Press.

— <http://bnarchives.yorku.ca/>. Website, regularly updated, with latest articles from authors. A must read.

Pomeranz, Kenneth (2000) *The Great Divergence: China, Europe and the Making of the Modern World Economy*, Princeton, NJ: Princeton University Press.

Sassen, Saskia (1998) *Globalization and Its Discontents*, New York: New Press.

Chapter 1

For the late Ottoman and Mandate periods, see:

Agmon, Iris (2006) *Family and Court: Legal Culture and Modernity in Late Ottoman Palestine*, Syracuse, NY: Syracuse University Press.

Doumani, Beshara (1995) *Rediscovering Palestine: Merchants and Peasants in Jabal Nablus, 1700–1900*, Berkeley: University of California Press.

Khalidi, Rashid (1998) *Palestinian Identity: The Construction of Modern National Consciousness*, New York: Columbia University Press.

LeVine, Mark (2005) *Overthrowing Geography: Jaffa, Tel Aviv, and the Struggle for Palestine, 1880–1948*, Berkeley: University of California Press.

Lockman, Zachary (1996) *Comrades and Enemies: Arabs and Jewish Workers in Palestine, 1906–1948*, Berkeley: University of California Press.

Shafir, Gershon (1989) *Land, Labor, and the Origins of the Israeli–Palestinian Conflict*, Berkeley: University of California Press.

Slyomovics, Susan (1998) *The Object of Memory: Arab and Jew Narrate the Palestinian Village*, Philadelphia: University of Pennsylvania Press.

Swedenburg, Ted (2003) *Memories of Revolt: The 1936–1939 Rebellion and the Palestinian National Past*, Little Rock: University of Arkansas Press.

Tamari, Salim (2008) *Mountain against the Sea. Essays on Palestinian Society and Culture*, Berkeley: University of California Press.

For the 1948 war:

Khalidi, Walid (1992) *All That Remains: The Palestinian Villages Occupied and Depopulated by Israel in 1948*, Washington, DC: Institute for Palestine Studies, 1992.

Masalha, Nur (1992) *The Expulsion of the Palestinians: The Concept of 'Transfer' in Zionist Political Thought, 1882–1948*, Washington, DC: Institute of Palestine Studies.

Morris, Benny (2004) *The Birth of the Palestinian Refugee Problem Revisited*, Cambridge: Cambridge University Press.

Muslih, Muhammad (1989) *The Origins of Palestinian Nationalism*, New York: Columbia University Press.

Shlaim, Avia and Eugene Rogan (eds) (2001) *The War for Palestine: Rewriting the History of 1948*, Cambridge: Cambridge University Press.

For the post-1948 period:

Abu El Haj, Nadia (2001) *Facts on the Ground: Archaeological Practice and Territorial Self-Fashioning in Israeli Society*, Chicago, IL: University of Chicago Press.

Benvenisti, Meron (1984) *The West Bank Data Base Project: A Survey of Israel's Policies*, Washington, DC: American Enterprise Institute.

— (1987) *The West Bank Data Base Project, 1987 Report*, Boulder, CO: Westview Press.

Kemp, Adriana, David Newman, Uri Ram and Oren Yiftachel (2008) 'Israelis in conflict: hegemonies, identities, and challenges', *Israel Studies*, 13(1).

Khalidi, Walid (1947) *Palestine and the Arab–Israeli Conflict: An Annotated Bibliography*, Washington, DC: Institute for Palestine Studies.

Morris, Benny (1993) *Israel's Border Wars 1949–1956: Arab Infiltration, Israeli Retaliation, and the Countdown to the Suez War*, Oxford: Clarendon Press.

— (1994) *1948 and After; Israel and the Palestinians*, Oxford: Clarendon Press.

Newman, David (ed.) (1985) *The Impact of Gush Emunim: Politics and Settlement in the West Bank*, London: Croom Helm.

Pappe, Ilan (ed.) (1999) *Israel/Palestine Question (Rewriting Histories)*, London: Routledge.

— (2004) *A History of Modern Palestine: One Land, Two Peoples*, Cambridge: Cambridge University Press.

Peled, Yoav and Gershon Shafir (2002) *Being Israeli: The Dynamics of Multiple Citizenship*, Cambridge: Cambridge University Press.

Rabinowitz, Dan (1997) *Overlooking Nazareth: The Ethnography of*

Exclusion in a Mixed Town in Galilee, Cambridge: Cambridge University Press.

Sandler, Shmuel and Hillan Frisch (1984) *Israel, the Palestinians, and the West Bank*, Lexington, MA: Lexington Books.

Schiff, Zeev and Ehud Yaari (1984) *Israel's Lebanon War*, New York: Simon and Schuster.

Segev, Tom (2000) *One Palestine, Complete*, New York: Metropolitan Books.

Smith, Charles D. (2005) *Palestine and the Arab–Israeli Conflict*, London: Palgrave.

Swedenburg, Ted and Rebecca Stein (2005) *Palestine, Israel, and the Politics of Popular Culture*, Raleigh-Durham, NC: Duke University Press.

Yiftachel, Oren (2006) *Ethnocracy: Land and Identity Politics in Israel/Palestine*, Philadelphia: University of Pennyslvania Press.

Chapter 2

The most comprehensive source for the chronology of events during the peace process is the *Journal of Palestine Studies*, whose 'Chronology' section in every issue reports on every significant event related to the peace process and the larger conflict. Also useful in this regard are the *Palestine-Israel Journal*, <www.pij.org/index.php>, and various chronologies provided by the British newspaper the *Guardian*, <www.guardian.co.uk>, and *Ha'aretz* (<www.haaretz.com>). For the issue of settlements during the Oslo years, see the 'Settlement Watch' section of the Foundation for Middle East Peace website, at <www.fmep.org>.

Aburish, Said K. (1998) *Arafat: From Defender to Dictator*, New York: Bloomsbury Publishing.

Beilin, Yossi (1999) *Touching Peace: From the Oslo Accord to a Final Agreement*, London: Weidenfeld & Nicolson.

Ben-Ami, Shlomo (2007) *Scars of War, Wounds of Peace: The Israeli–Arab Tragedy*, Oxford: Oxford University Press.

Bishara, Marwan (2001) *Palestine/Israel: Peace or Apartheid. Occupation, Terrorism and the Future*, London: Zed Books.

Cobban, Helena (1984) *The Palestine Liberation Organisation: People, Power and Politics*, Cambridge: Cambridge University Press.

Gelvin, James (2007) *The Israel–Palestine Conflict: One Hundred Years of War*, Cambridge: Cambridge University Press.

Giacaman, George and Dag Jorund Lonning (1998) *After Oslo: New Realities, Old Problems*, London: Pluto Press.

Gowers, Andrew and Tony Walker (2005) *Arafat: The Biography*, New York: Virgin Books.

Hilal, Jamil (1998) *The Palestinian Political System after Oslo*, Washington, DC: Institute for Palestine Studies.

Lindhom Schulz, Helena (1999) *The Reconstruction of Palestinian Nationalism: Between Revolution and Statehood*, Manchester: Manchester University Press.

Makovsky, David (1996) *Making Peace with the PLO: The Rabin Government's Road to the Oslo Accord*, Boulder, CO: Westview Press.

PASSIA (1994) *The Palestinian Economy: A Bibliography*, Jerusalem: PASSIA.

Said, Edward (1996) *Peace and Its Discontents*, New York: Vintage.

— (2001) *The End of the Peace Process: Oslo and After*, New York: Vintage.

Savir, Uri (1999) *The Process: 1,100 Days that Changed the Middle East*, New York: Vintage.

Swisher, Clayton (2004) *The Truth about Camp David: The Untold Story about the Collapse of the Middle East Peace Process*, New York: Nation Books.

Usher, Graham (2005) *Palestine in Crisis: The Struggle for Peace and Political Independence after Oslo*, London: Pluto Press.

Chapter 3

The two most comprehensive sources for analysis of the last years and subsequent disintegration of the peace process are the *Journal of Palestine Studies* and *Middle East Report*.

Baltzer, Anna (2007) *Witness in Palestine: A Jewish American Woman in the Occupied Territories*, Boulder, CO: Paradigm Publishers.

Beitler, Ruth Margolies (2004) *The Path to Mass Rebellion: An Analysis of Two Intifadas*, Lanham, MD: Lexington Books.

Bishara, Marwan (2001) *Palestine/Israel: Peace or Apartheid. Prospects for Resolving the Conflict*, London: Zed Books.

Carter, Jimmy (2006) *Palestine: Peace Not Apartheid*, New York: Simon and Schuster.

Guyatt, Nicholas (1998) *The Absence of Peace: Understanding the Israeli–Palestinian Conflict*, London: Zed Books.

LeVine, Mark (2005) *Why They Don't Hate Us: Lifting the Veil on the Axis of Evil*, Oxford: Oneworld Publications.

Nitzan, Jonathan and Shimshon Bichler (2003) *The Global Political Economy of Israel*, London: Pluto Press.

Pappe, Ilan (2007) *The Ethnic Cleansing of Palestine*, Oxford: Oneworld Publications.

Parker, Christopher (1999) *Resignation or Revolt? Socio-Political Development and the Challenges of Peace in Palestine*, London: I.B.Tauris.

Parsons, Nigel (2005) *The Politics of the Palestinian Authority: From Oslo to Al-Aqsa*, London: Routledge.

Pearlman, Wendy (2003) *Occupied Voices: Stories of Everyday Life from the Second Intifada*, New York: Nation Books.

Robinson, Glenn E. (1997) *Building a Palestinian State: The Incomplete Revolution*, Bloomington: Indiana University Press.

Rothstein, Robert, Moshe Maoz Moshe and Khalil Shikaki (eds) (2004) *The Israeli–Palestinian Peace Process: Oslo and the Lessons of Failure: Perspectives, Predicaments and Prospects*, Sussex: Sussex Academic Press.

Yiftachel, Oren (2006) *Ethnocracy: Land and Identity Politics in Israel/Palestine*, Philadelphia: University of Pennsylvania Press.

Zertal, Idith and Akiva Eldar (2007) *Lords of the Land: The War for Israel's Settlements in the Occupied Territories, 1967–2007*, New York: Nation Books.

Chapter 4

Given the importance of economic issues to the peace process, there is a surprising lack of detailed scholarly research on this issue. The most important periodic analyses of the changing dynamics of the Palestinian and Israeli economies during the Oslo period can be found in *Middle East Report*. For the late 1990s and post al-Aqsa intifada periods, the Nitzan and Bichler archives are also a central source. Although often uncritically supportive of neoliberal policies, the numerous reports on the Palestinian economy by the World Bank and the IMF are among the most comprehensive data sources available to researchers.

Bishara, Marwan (2001) *Palestine/ Israel: Peace or Apartheid. Occupation, Terrorism and the Future*, London: Zed Books.

Brynen, Rex (2000) *A Very Political Economy: Peacebuilding and Foreign Aid in the West Bank and Gaza*, USIP.

Diwan, Ishaq and Radwan Shaban (eds) (1997) *Development under Adversity: The Palestinian Economy under Transition*, Washington, DC: World Bank and Palestine Economic Policy Research Institute.

Olmstead, Jennifer (1996) 'Thwarting Palestinian development,' *Middle East Report*, 201: 11–13.

Pfeifer, Karen (2002) 'The mercurial economics of the phantom Palestinian state,' *Dollars and Sense* magazine, January/ February.

Roy, Sara (1995) *The Gaza Strip: The Political Economy of Dedevelopment*, Washington, DC: Institute for Palestine Studies.

Samara, Adel (2000) 'Globalization, the Palestinian economy and the peace process,' *Journal of Palestine Studies*, 114: 20–39.

Chapter 5

There are very few analyses of Shas in English.

Abu-Amr, Ziad (1994) *Islamic Fundamentalism in the West Bank and Gaza*, Bloomington: Indiana University Press.

Ahmad, Hisham (1994) *Hamas: From Religious Salvation to Political Transformation: The Rise of Hamas in Palestinian Society*, Jerusalem.

Hatina, Meir (2001) *Islam and Salvation in Palestine: The Islamic Jihad Movement*, Tel Aviv: Dayan Center Papers, 127.

Hroub, Khaled (2000) *Hamas: Political Thought and Practice*, Washington, DC: Institute for Palestine Studies.

Jones, Clive (2001) *Israel: Challenges to Identity, Democracy and the State*, London: Routledge.

Milton-Edwards, Beverley (1996) *Islamic Politics in Palestine*, London: I.B.Tauris.

Mishal, Shaul and Avraham Sela (2000) *The Palestinian Hamas: Vision, Violence, and Coexistence*, New York: Columbia University Press.

Peled, Yoav and Gershon Shafir (2002) *Being Israeli: The Dynamics of Multiple Citizenship*, Cambridge: Cambridge University Press.

Tamimi, Azzam (2007) *Hamas: A History from Within*, Northampton: Olive Tree Press.

Yiftachel, Oren (2006) *Ethnocracy: Land and Identity Politics in Israel/Palestine*, Philadelphia: University of Pennsylvania Press.

Chapter 6

Abunimah, Ali (2006) *One Country: A Bold Proposal to End the Israeli–Palestinian Impasse*, New York: Metropolitan Books.

Connell, Dan (2001) *Rethinking Revolution: New Strategies for Democracy and Social Justice: The Experiences of Eritrea, South Africa, Palestine and Nicaragua*, Lawrenceville, NJ: Red Sea Press.

Habermas, Jurgen (1991) *The Structural Transformation of the Public Sphere: An Inquiry into a Category of Bourgeois Society*, Cambridge, MA: MIT Press.

Hammami, Rema (2000) 'Palestinian NGOs since Oslo: from NGO politics to grass roots movement,' *Middle East Report*, Spring.

Norton, A. R. (ed.) (1995/96) *Civil Society in the Middle East*, vols I and II, Leiden: Brill Publishers.

Salvatore, Armando and Mark LeVine (2005) *Religion, Social Practices and Contested Hegemonies: Reconstructing the Public Sphere in Muslim Majority Societies*, New York: Palgrave.

Willen, Sarah (ed.) (2007) *Transnational Migration to Israel in Global Comparative Context*, Boulder, CO: Lexington Books.

Index